# THE CENTURY SPEAKS

*voices of*

# NOTTINGHAMSHIRE

Stepping out at Northcote Terrace in The Meadows, 1951.

# THE CENTURY SPEAKS

# voices of
# NOTTINGHAMSHIRE

*Memories of Nottinghamshire people*
*compiled by Julie McGuinness from interviews by Jeremy Evans*
*for the* **BBC Radio Nottingham** *series*
**The Century Speaks**

TEMPUS

First published 1999
Copyright © BBC Radio Nottingham, 1999

Tempus Publishing Limited
The Mill, Brimscombe Port,
Stroud, Gloucestershire, GL5 2QG

ISBN 0 7524 1843 2

Typesetting and origination by
Tempus Publishing Limited
Printed in Great Britain by
Midway Clark Printing, Wiltshire

Wellow Village May Queen procession, c. 1950. (By permission of the Mansfield Chad)

# CONTENTS

# FOREWORD

As the twentieth century closes, the BBC has embarked upon the largest Oral History project ever undertaken in Europe. *The Century Speaks* forms one of the centrepieces of the BBC's Millennium celebrations, and BBC Radio Nottingham has joined forces with forty BBC stations across England, Wales and Northern Ireland to recreate the experience of the last 100 years in programmes made up of around 6,000 interviews. Every local and regional station has made a series of sixteen programmes and these, together with the vast archive of interviews, are being kept in the *Millennium Memory Bank* at the British Museum.

As producer of *The Century Speaks* programmes broadcast in Nottinghamshire, I spoke to nearly 180 people throughout the county. Often I'd leave interviews feeling warm inside, humbled that those who remembered the first years of the century were able to tell me about some of the things closest to their hearts. The fact that a complete stranger was willing to sit and listen to *their* memories and feelings seemed to make people feel that their thoughts counted – and they do. Some of these thoughts and memories are included in this book – a book that makes ordinary people's experiences matter.

Nottinghamshire is a county of many faces, with many differing people and a pride that runs deeply through all those living here. Due to its close links with communities across the county, BBC Radio Nottingham has been in an unrivalled position to tap a wealth of local anecdote and reflection. The result is an archive and a series of radio programmes that illustrate how different aspects of life have changed in our county over the last 100 years – a unique legacy for future generations.

Jeremy Evans
Millennium Oral History Producer
BBC Radio Nottingham

# INTRODUCTION

This book represents BBC Radio Nottingham's desire that some of the treasures of *The Century Speaks* programmes remain accessible for the folk of Nottinghamshire long after the broadcasts are over and the material sent to the national archive. Although not in at the start of *The Century Speaks*, I have quickly become personally involved and absorbed as I have listened to the interviews, and met the many contributors willing to help by loaning photographs included in this book.

So called 'ordinary people' often underestimate the interest and the value of their own story. Yet in a century of change, and in a county so rich in contrasts as Nottinghamshire, each person's unique story is as valuable as it is fascinating. History is so much more than facts, figures and dates: It's the unfolding story of ordinary people's experience, handed down from generation to generation. This book presents this experience in the people's own words, with minimal emendation only where absolutely necessary to the sense. The hours spent with my ear to the tape recorder and my hands on the word processor keys, simply writing what I heard, felt well rewarded when the son of one contributor, Arthur Plumb, read his words and exclaimed, 'Yes, that's it. I can hear my dad talking.'

This book is something of a patchwork: It's a colourful combination of different memories, yet I am aware I have only scratched the surface. The fact that Nottinghamshire is a mining county is an appropriate reminder that there is much hidden richness still to be discovered by those willing to listen. I hope these memories will inspire you to value your own story, as well as cherishing afresh the stories and lives of those around you.

Julie McGuinness

Nottinghamshire family day-trip to Skegness, in the 1950s.

# ACKNOWLEDGEMENTS

I would like to acknowledge my gratitude to those who have generously helped with the loan of personal photographs and memorabilia for this book. They are:

Norman Allcock, Paddy Bacon, Anne Benson, Dave Birkett, Wally Binch, Dorothy Bird, Diane Brown, Nigel Brown, Francesca Clayton, David Cope, Bill Cross, Gladys Dawson, Irene Dove, Geraldine Ellis, Roy and Pat Evans, Mitch Fenton, Derek Footit, John Laing, Tom and Margaret Leafe, Sheena Mabbott, The Macedon Trust, Keith Matthewman, Alan Merry, Geoffrey Oldfield, Rebecca Osborn, Roy Plumb, Florrie Radley, Bill Ragsdale, George Richardson, Joan Seager, Bill Simpson, Jim Taylor, Alan and Mary Trease, Walter Urban, Michaela White, Arthur Wybrew.

# CHAPTER 1

# Growing up

Pupils at the William Crane School in Aspley, 1950. A more informal school atmosphere prevailed than in the early 1900s.

## Inner Cleanliness

I went to a primary school in Nottingham called Clarendon Street. Now Clarendon Street was the other side of Waverley Street. I should think it must be three-quarters of a mile away. I was just under five, very nearly five years old, and I remember walking all along Peel Street on my own, no-one to take me except when they first introduced me. And it is amazing how many friends I've had of my age who were at Clarendon Street, with that wonderful headmistress Mrs Gowthorpe.

Now Mrs Gowthorpe, she was marvellous. What I remember so well of her is that during my very first term there (so I was just round about five years old), the mistress there – her name was Miss Tregaskis (strange name) during one of the mornings she said, 'Kenneth, that's a lie, and we mustn't have lies. You go along to Mrs Gowthorpe and tell her that you've told a lie. Go along.' So I went across the hall and I knocked on the door of Mrs Gowthorpe, and she said, 'Come in! Oh, Kenneth, yes, what do you want?' I said, 'Mrs Gowthorpe, I've told a lie!' 'You've told a lie? Come along here, come,' and she seemed to be absolutely ready for me. She said, 'Come along to this washbowl,' and she had a shaving brush already filled with soap. She said, 'Now, put your head back. We must wash this right out of your mouth!' And I put my head back, and the shaving brush went right down to my tonsils, and she said, 'Now go and wash your mouth out, and never, never let another lie come into that mouth!' And by Jove, it was so appalling that I don't think one ever has.

What she did that day I think she'd have got the sack for if she'd done it today. But Mrs Gowthorpe is remembered by all these friends I have and she was really terrific.

*Ken Parr, born 1912*
*Cropwell Butler*

## Pen-nibs and Punctuality

I went to St Ann's church school on St Ann's Well Road. In the Junior School I learned to write the Creed and Scripture verses, and we learned a lot of the New and Old Testament stories – 'David and Goliath' and 'Moses and Aaron'. It was a good education. We used to go out and do physical drill in the schoolyard, and we would take our skipping ropes and we would play rounders. I loved it.

In those days we had slates with slate pencils, and also we had copybooks with pens and pen-nibs and inkwells. And there were long forms; we didn't have separate little desks. And there were different kinds of nibs, and it was always difficult to find the right one, so we would make blots on the nice, clean, white paper. And on what we called the board and the easel there was a scroll. And you might be chosen to be the monitor, and lift up one leaf over the other, and the teacher would have a pointer and point to it.

Discipline was stern. You had to sit with your backs firm, and we didn't like it. The teacher would come and give you a thump in the back if you didn't sit with your arms folded. And if you were late, you'd have to put your hand out and have a nasty ruler on it! I remember

Dorothy Bird as a teenager.

that happening to me. When the school bell went, we used to run as fast as we could to get in the line, hang our clothes up in the clothes room, and march one behind the other into the classroom. And when your names were called at the register, if you didn't immediately answer, 'present', you'd get a nasty hit.

Miss Farrar, she wore a mortarboard. I think she must have been degreed. And to me she was an enemy. But I liked Miss Shaw. She had a long trailing dress, with nice long sleeves puffed at the top, and she had a big plait round her head. And she used to treat me gently and I loved her. But Miss Farrar used to hit me with the ruler. I couldn't

always remember the Creed. It was all about 'God the Father, God the Son and God the Holy Ghost,' and it was a bit difficult because for a child it was long, and I couldn't always get to the end. And then she'd say, 'You'll stay after school and you'll write it.' And then I'd get in trouble when I got home, because I was late.

*Dorothy Bird, born 1900*
*Nottingham*

## School Uniform

Highbury School in Bulwell backed onto Highbury Hospital. And there, it was a workhouse.

The kids that went in the workhouse, they was called Union boys at the school. They were the same age as me, eight or nine year old, and they were all dressed in the same coloured blue pullover, grey trousers (always short trousers in those days), and shoes. They all wore exactly the same clothes, and they were all spotlessly clean, because they was workhouse lads. We called 'em Union boys. Now there was a special unit for those with a matron who looked after 'em. I suppose they'd got no parents. They was orphans.

They stuck out a mile at school, you see, because they were so well dressed and clean. Where us kids, you'll never believe, your shirt used to hang out the back of your britches because wi' slidin' and goin' about, you wore all the backside out. We were all like urchins in *Oliver Twist!* You see, in summer, you never wore shoes in the street for one reason. You saved your shoes for school, 'cos you'd got to have shoes on to go to

Eleven-year-old Arthur Wybrew at Chandos Street School in September 1938.

# CHANDOS STREET BOYS' COUNCIL SCHOOL, NETHERFIELD.

Term Ending......14th Feb 1936......

Name..........Arthur Wybrew..........        Standard....2. Cl.VI....

No. in Class......48..........        Position in Class......41 10......

| Subject | | Marks | |
|---|---|---|---|
| | | Possible | Obtained |
| English | Reading | 10 | 8 |
| ,, | Recitation | 10 | 8 |
| ,, | Language | 40 | 39 |
| ,, | Composition | 40 | 36 |
| ,, | Dictation | 15 | 5½ |
| ,, | Writing | 10 | 4 |
| Arithmetic | Mental | 20 | 13 |
| ,, | Written | 40 | 20 |
| Geography | | 20 | 17½ |
| History | | 20 | 16 |
| Drawing | | 20 | 19 |
| Nature Study | | – | – |
| | TOTALS | 245 | 191 |

ATTENDANCES        CONDUCT  Good.

No. possible......207..........

Absences..............10..........

REMARKS : Arthur is always very interested & interesting in oral lessons. His work has improved a great deal, but he must still keep trying.

Class Teacher......N. J. Johnson..........

Head Teacher......J. R. Wood..........

Arthur's school report from 1936.

school, so you played barefoot in the street.

*Bill Cross, born 1918*
*Bulwell*

## An Only Child

My father joined the police force in 1908. He was very badly injured in the Chilwell Explosion in 1918, and was no longer fit to do outside duty, so he was moved down to Nottingham to take charge of the headquarters, and was promoted to police sergeant. The headquarters was next door to the

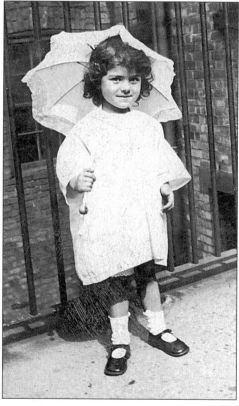

Anne Benson at home on the top floor of the county police station (now part of the Galleries of Justice Museum), 1924.

Galleries of Justice in the county police station.

We lived in a flat on the top floor of the building. We had half the floor, and the other half of the floor was police recruit accommodation. There were six 'cubicles,' I suppose you'd call them, where the recruits lived. From about 1927 they came in for three months' classroom training before they went onto the beat.

Living in this situation was perfectly normal for me, because I didn't know any other. There were no other children there. There was a little girl much younger than I who lived at the County Tavern, the pub more or less just opposite, and we played together a bit, but she was four years younger than I, so that didn't last for very long. I was always with adults and there were always loads of policemen there, including one man who was called Burton. He was very tall and I loved him dearly. I was about three or four, and I used to cling to his leg. He was called Big Burton, so he must have been six foot three or four, which was very tall in those days.

I was very, very short-sighted. It started because my parents knew I could read, and they would say to me when I was out, 'What does it say on that poster?' and I would say, 'What poster?' So they decided that something had better be done about this, and I've worn spectacles ever since I was seven. My eyes deteriorated very badly. So badly, that by the time I was twelve they were saying I might have to go into a dark room to give them complete rest. But that never happened.

I was the envy of my school pals, because I went all the way through

Anne Benson (on the right) and friend, with Anne's mother at home, 1924.

On a three-wheeled tandem in Querneby Road, Mapperley, 1940.

grammar school and never did any homework, because I wasn't allowed to. I also wasn't allowed to read from the time I was about seven and a half until I was fourteen, and my father read to me by the hour and I knew all the books, even though I hadn't read them. I was allowed to read in school, but not anywhere else. I wasn't allowed to sew, but was allowed to knit as long as I didn't look at it. My father made me something that used to be described as a punishment for Victorian children, which fitted round my neck so that I couldn't look down. I'd got to look up all the time.

I know my glasses must have been paid for privately, because they were nice little gold-rimmed ones and the ones that came through the school clinic were silver metal and oval ones. Mine were round because they had to be round.

*Anne Benson, born 1920*
*Mapperley Plains*

## Outdoor Pursuits

There was nothing to do in the house, because you couldn't read 'cos it were paraffin lamps. So at night or in daytime, off school, you used to play marbles. You used to find a hole in the street and throw these marbles at it, and them that got the most in would take the marbles. And then you'd have hopscotch: You'd draw great big squares on the road, and hop with one foot into different squares numbered. And then there was cigarette cards. Every packet of cigarettes sold had a cigarette card in. You used to line them up along the wall and flick the other cards to knock 'em down. If you knocked 'em down you got that card. And these are the sort of games you used to play, you see, because there were no other entertainment.

*Bill Cross, born 1918*
*Bulwell*

## Fun and Games

I enjoyed my childhood because in those days it was much more leisurely, not hurried. We used to play Ring-a-Ring o' Roses, Three Jolly Sailor Boys, A-Hunting we will Go. We skipped, we played lurky. Lurky's where you kick a tin and then hide, and somebody tries to find you. You'll perhaps be behind a door, or in the shop doorway. It was great. Life was innocent and it was fun, and we went to bed happy. I think children today want more care from nannies and from parents, because there are more dangers.

I used to love the corner shops that sold mixed sweets in big jars. I didn't have much money then, perhaps a half-penny a week, but that was everything, 'cos I looked forward to Saturday and wondered whether to buy an Everlasting Strip or a Yunky-Punky – that was all pink and white and yellow, and you could suck it for a long time. Or a Kayli Sucker. Oh, a Kayli Sucker was lovely. You put the Kayli in the palm of your hand and licked it with your tongue.

*Dorothy Bird, born 1900*
*Nottingham*

## Flying Lessons

Just near the bottom of Darky Lane in Wellow is the remains of the aeroplane tree. Every kid in Wellow for the last fifty years has played on the tree that is no longer there! The roots came out over the path and we used to sit in there and we was supposed to be driving an aeroplane. And my niece's generation did just the same thing.

*Bill Ragsdale, born 1918*
*Wellow*

## Village Play

There seemed to be a lot more children when I was younger. There's no village school in Epperstone now and they all tend to go off to private school, so they don't get together like we used to. There used to be a crowd of us. We used to meet at the corner and we used to do stupid things. I was desperate for a pony. Mum couldn't afford to buy me one. And we used to sit on the wall with a piece of string round a gatepost and make stirrups out of string, and sit on the wall.

They all tend to go off into town more now, ice-skating, bowls and things like this. They're not content like we were. I mean, I can remember there was probably eight or nine of us my age, and mum used to pack us picnics up for the day, and we used to go off down the field building dens and putting stones across the water and stepping stones. You can't do that now. I didn't let my girls do it, because you didn't know who was about. It was a lot safer when I was little. We used to just find our own enjoyment. As long as we sort of reported to one of the mums that everything was still all right, we used to go off again and just the spend the days in the summer holidays.

My girls weren't content to do what I did as a youngster. They started to go to town when they were probably eleven or twelve. I didn't dare go on a bus on my own at that age.

*Lesley Henshaw, born 1955*
*Epperstone*

## Making Mischief

We used to go spirit rappin'. There was a lot of trees in Arnold then, and we used to get up these trees, then run a cotton to a window, shove a bent pin into the window ledge, and then, a cotton down it and a button on the end, usually a lead button. And we used to sit in the tree, and it were swinging and banging on the window.

And there was one character, Jackie Brown, and we used to go and torment him, and we were doing wrong, but we did it, and he used to come running out with a carving knife. And I should think two or three times a night we used to tie a string across his gate – and he'd fall over it.

*Jim Turton, born 1909*
*Arnold*

## Birds and Bees – and Grapes!

I used to go to fetch my grandmother's medicine. Doctor Roach was our doctor. He'd brought me into the world. (His grandson is Bill Roach, who's in *Coronation Street*.) I was always pestering Doctor Roach to tell me where babies came from. I was fifteen, believe it or not, and he'd say, 'Oh, here's the nuisance again.' He always used to call me a nuisance.

One day I was sitting there in the conservatory – he used it as a waiting

Pupils at Epperstone Village School, 1930.

Children on the Whit Sunday Walk and Service in the Market Square, Sutton-in-Ashfield, 1934.

room, you see, and I was last there this particular day. So I says, 'Are you going to tell me where babies come from? And he says, 'Oh, for goodness' sake, come on.'

And he took me down the conservatory a little way, and he lifted a leaf up and there was a little grape. And he says, 'You see that? Well, when it gets bigger, and a lady wants a baby, I take it off and put it in a little bag for her.' So I says to my mother, 'I know where babies come from now,' and I told her. And she never said a word.

*Gladys Dawson, born 1903*
*Farnsfield*

## Pressures

There's a lot of pressure from other people, such as sex, drugs, alcohol, particularly when you're becoming more sixteen/seventeen age, perhaps, when, you know, you've got access to that sort of thing. So there can be a lot of pressure on people. So it's not easy by any means, but it depends what friendship groups you have – friendship circles. I've been lucky with the friends that I've had. Obviously you have the odd fall-out every now and again. But I've been one of the lucky ones.

*Jonathan Street, born 1980*
*Mansfield*

## An Impressive Welcome

I came from Iraq to do a degree in mechanical engineering in 1947. My first day as a student in Nottingham I was given some digs. The university had sent me a letter saying when you come, go to this address on Mansfield Road, that's where you're going to stay.

19

Goose Fair, 1950. (By permission of Nottingham City Council: Leisure and Community Services: County Library, Angel Row)

So I went and it was a large house, and there were about fifteen young men there. The landlady was fussing around, trying to make everybody comfortable, making sure that you had sheets on your bed and so on. Naturally, we were about four in a room. The first thing that struck me as being odd was that I was called down to have some tea. Now from what I knew about England, I thought that tea was at four o'clock, but this was at five o'clock. So I thought, well maybe we were late, because I came late. So I went down to tea, and of course a full meal came out. It was the Northerners' tea, which I ate, naturally, being young and hungry all the time, but it was a bit curious.

And then I decided to go out and have a look round, so I got out and went uphill and then I saw all these girls coming in the opposite direction with big hats with things like 'CUDDLE ME' on them. It was Goose Fair and I thought this was a fantastic city to come to. Look at all this, the lights and the girls and so on! It was the best impression anyone could have made on me in Nottingham; they laid on Goose Fair especially for me on the first day I arrived! It was a good start, and I've always loved the place.

*Nessim Haye, born 1927*
*Nottingham*

# CHAPTER 2
# *At home*

Wally Binch's brother Ken, in Northcote
Terrace. The lamp-post was the last thing to
remain standing when The Meadows was
demolished in the early 1970s.

## A Rarely-used Room

When I was eight we moved to Northcote Terrace in The Meadows. We lived at number 3. It was a small house. It had got a living room and a front room which nobody ever went into. It was just kept for visitors. We didn't live in there at all. As the years went on we had a gas fire in there. There was a settee and a gramophone, and that was it. But if somebody came in and you wanted to speak to them separately, you'd go into the front room, the parlour. There were two rooms downstairs, two rooms upstairs, and an attic.

That house got quite full, because I've got four brothers – Dennis, Ken, Tony,

St Cecilia Terrace in St Ann's, 1966.

Derek and myself, and not only this, but my mother also adopted a little boy – Charlie, so he became another brother to us. So it got quite crowded there at times.

*Wally Binch, born 1923*
*Bakersfield*

## Cold Convenience

We had an outside toilet. It was 'yellow ochre' – you touched the paint and it came off in your hands. We didn't have toilet rolls. There was a nail and square pieces of *News of the World* or the *Evening Post*, or the *Evening News* that we had then, and that was for toilet paper. We didn't have a bath either. There was no bathroom. If you wanted a bath you had to go to Portland Street Baths, which we went to once a week. You paid so much – I think it was about fourpence – and you could have a hot bath. As a small kid you'd have a bath at home in the tin bath that we kept in the shed, but as you grew up you wanted to be private, so you went to the public baths.

*Wally Binch, born 1923*
*Bakersfield*

## All Pulling Together

I was born in Nottingham in the St Ann's area, the youngest of eleven. My mother died when I was eighteen months old and father vanished, so I never knew him. My older sister brought me up to the age of about eighteen. She used to work. She went

Loco Terrace in the 1970s.

out to do domestic work or took washing in. I often think, looking back now, what a wonderful person she must have been.

We used to have to help with the housework. There were red and blue bricks and we used to have a pail and a floor-cloth and a scrubbing brush twice a week, and wash and scrub on a kneeling mat on Tuesday, because Monday was washday and always left a mess behind. On Saturday we had to get ready for Sunday, and I helped clean the knives and forks with emery paper, because they were steel, and we had a wooden table that had to be scrubbed clean. On Sundays we had a nice, big, red plush tablecloth with bobbles on it. Sunday was a special day. I used to like my Sunday dinner, because there was roast beef and Yorkshire pudding and vegetables, and we'd have a nice rice pudding with a brown covering on it that had been done in the fire oven.

Inside the house downstairs there was a little back kitchen with a stove and a big corner, where there was a copper where the clothes used to be boiled, and a sink where you washed your hands and your face. You see, there were no bathrooms then. And then you went into the big square kitchen with a dresser, a wooden table and the chairs round and a home-made hearth rug that we used to peg. We cut pieces out of old clothes. And then there was the front room. It's graduated since then into a parlour, a sitting room and a lounge! But then it was called the front room. And that led out to two steps straight into the street. There was no front garden.

There were wooden spiral stairs, no carpet, and then there was a little passageway and on one side there was a bedroom that my sister and I used to sleep in, in a double bed, with a big wooden chest where we kept our

Colwick Loco Yard. Loco Terrace is on the bottom right of the picture. Both terrace and yard are now part of the Victoria Retail Park.

clothes. There was no wardrobe. It was very sparsely furnished. On the other side of the passage was a bigger room where the older ones slept, and then there was another flight of stairs up to where the other brothers slept. They had a double bed with brass knobs, and at Christmas we hung our woollen stockings over the rail at the bottom. Sometimes my brother would come in and sleep in the middle between me and my sister. Life was very innocent in those days.

*Dorothy Bird, born 1900*
*Nottingham*

## Trains for Neighbours

We moved to 3 Loco Terrace, right embedded in Colwick Yard. It was handy for father at work on the railway. It was a house built by the railway in about the 1880s. The house isn't there any more. It was pulled down as soon as the railways closed. The Coal Board wanted to mine some coal underneath it. They'd been inhibited from doing so because of the railway works. But as soon as it was shut, they mined under there and that cracked all the mains and the fabric, and it was pulled down in the '70s.

It was a shame to see it go. Every memory I've got of my childhood days is associated with the railway. Every time we went out we had to walk past the front of Colwick Loco. At the back you could hear the wagons being shunted into the various roads going 'pink, pink, pink,' as they buffered up. The railway was just so close. If you went up the road, you went over the crossing into Netherfield Lane. You timed your day by the trains going by. There was a milk train in the morning and then something called 'the fish' went through from Grimsby. It was part of your life.

*Arthur Wybrew, born 1927*
*Tollerton*

## Wash Day

On wash day, grandad would get up early and light the fire. He would have filled the copper, just a basin-shaped thing, full of water. They would put some soap in it. Grandma would then get up and put all the clothes into it, shake it about with a stick, and then wait till it had boiled. They practically boiled the clothes, tipped them out in the sink, and then they'd pummel them about and wring them dry. Then they would take them to the outhouse, next to the coal shed. There was a great big mangle in that, and they put the clothes through it. I remember it had a great cast-iron handle. I could just about reach up and touch the handle, but then to turn it I had to be lifted up and turned round – although everything looked huge in those days. Then the clothes were hung up on a line which went right over the road at the back, right down to the toilet on the other side.

*Arthur Wybrew, born 1927*
*Tollerton*

## A Big Family

I was born at Fir Cottage, Victoria Street in Mansfield. The house was pulled down some years ago now. It was a detached house, and there was some land nearby that people used as gardens. When mother and dad got a bit more money, they bought quite a decent patch of land there. We had pigsties there as well and fowls and that sort of thing. It was on the edge of Mansfield.

My mother had ten boys and five girls. Two of the girls died before I was born. Before I was born, the doctor told my mother she'd only got a week to live. But instead of that, she had about five or six more children after that, so the doctors didn't know it all then.

When we were younger, you used to sleep five in a bed. Three would be one way and two the other. Very often you

Wash day in the Meadows in the early 1970s, just before the area was redeveloped.

25

Martha Cousins, mother of thirteen children, peels potatoes at 44 Upper Eldon Street, Sneinton, 1935.

Stanesby Rise, part of the new Clifton Estate, in the 1950s.

would wake up in the morning and somebody's big toe would be poking up your nose.

*Joseph Boole, born 1907*
*Sutton-in-Ashfield*

## Brand New Home

When my husband was in the Forces we decided we were going to get married. We put our name down on the council waiting list, which you were allowed to before you were married if the chap was in the Forces. After the war there was a five year waiting list for a house, so when we got married we had to go into rooms. We had some quite nice rooms in Radford – a bedroom and a sitting room, but we had to share a kitchen, and it was one of the old type of houses, so we had to go down to my mother's for baths and that sort of thing. But after a short time we were notified that we had been allocated a council house at this very new estate of Clifton, in an area called Belwood Close.

We moved in on a very cold March day, and we had no roads at all, so we were tramping over mounds of earth and building debris the builders had left, but we didn't mind because at last we were going to have place of our own. We hadn't got everything, obviously – I think the youngsters who get married today have far more than we ever had. But we had been saving up. We had contacted a very nice furnishing house and we had been paying for a bedroom suite and a dining suite, so we had got those two very big things that we had

27

from the shop. They delivered them the day we moved in. We were thrilled to pieces. It was lovely being able to set up home together, and go to bed when we liked and get up when we liked – work permitting.

Everybody was very friendly. Most of the people moving in were young couples just starting out in life. Most of the men had been in the Forces. We were all pretty young and there was a great feeling of aliveness in the air. There was a sense that we'd all got to pull together to make the place worth living in.

Quite soon they started to lay the minor roads and put in the street lighting, which was a great boon, especially in the winter. Everywhere was still very muddy. I worked in an office in Nottingham at the time, and I remember going to work and I had to wear my wellingtons and then when I got into town, people would be looking in amazement at this person walking around in wellingtons! It was very difficult to get into town, because Clifton Bridge hadn't been built, and we had to go over Trent Bridge. And you can imagine the huge queues that used to build up, even in those days.

It was a great thrill when the very first bus came onto Clifton estate, because until then, everyone had come on a South Notts bus which went to Loughborough, came up the main road, and everyone coming onto the estate had to get off at the old oak tree. All the first residents of the estate remember that old oak tree with great affection, because when you saw that, you were coming home. And it was a wonderful feeling.

Then we saw the shops begin to come. At first there were no shops. My first shops were two travelling shops on wheels that used to come round. One was the Co-op, and one was a family grocer's, which ran a business in Nottingham itself, called Marsdens. They were like coaches converted into mobile shops, and they were a lifeline, particularly to young mums at home with children.

*Mavis Harrison, born 1928*
*Clifton*

## High-tech Home

Life's so different in the home now. You've got washing machines, everybody's got a telephone, videos, all that sort of thing. Now we've all got dishwashers, lovely sink units, cookers, microwaves, all that. I tell you straight, at ninety-one, I've never been so well-off in my life.

*Daisy Mee, born 1908*
*Mansfield*

## New-fangled Things

I never use the telephone. I can pick the phone up and answer it, but I've never phoned a person in my life. If I wanted to ring my nieces up, I should have to ask somebody else to ring them for me. I can remember telephones coming in, but I don't know anything about phoning. I'm not that way inclined. If I want to tell anyone anything I have to write to them. I don't know a lot about these new-fangled things that are going off.

*Ethel Fenton, born 1896*
*Chilwell*

CHAPTER 3

# Families and relationships

War-time wedding at St Giles' in
Ollerton, 1915. The groom was a
blacksmith for the Ollerton pit-
ponies.

## Love Match

I got married during the war. I met my husband at Ranby. There was the tennis courts there and we used to play tennis, and we met. We got on well and we always have done. And I suppose, if you click, you click! And I think you have to make a go of it anyway. I don't think your family would have thought much of you otherwise. It's not like it is today when they can get up and leave. You just had to stick and work it out, which we did. If you niggled a bit, you niggled a bit. You got over that, and here we are, married for nearly sixty years!

*Florrie Radley, born 1917*
*Epperstone*

## Happy Wedding and Saucy Cake!

I got married in 1952, just prior to the Coronation year. We'd known each other for many years but never crossed paths until suddenly we did and hey bingo! That was that. We only lived about three or four streets away from each other. One evening we were both on the bus going down into Carlton and we got chatting, and things just went from the chat getting off the bus, until I ended up getting in a wedding car outside a church!

It was 20 March, a Thursday. It was a lovely cold spring day. We got married at St Cyprian's church. It was a happy day and we had a lot of family and friends around us. We had the wedding reception in the Church Hall and of course there was the wedding cake. And when the photographs came out, we

didn't realise it till then, but somebody had stuck an HP sauce bottle in front of the wedding cake and that showed up on the picture of the wedding cake.

In the evening we went down to the old Nottingham Empire, and then the following day we went to London and we spent a few days there on honeymoon.

*Bert Stringer, born 1924*
*Sutton-in-Ashfield*

## First Encounter

There's a club in Newark called Caesar's Palace, and after a few jars with a couple of mates, I was down there propping the bar up – slaughtered, that's the word I'd use. And I was leaning on the bar and Rosie was dancing on the dance floor with about six blokes all dancing round her, and she was laughing and smiling. And I was looking at her. And she came off the dance floor and dragged me up, and I thought I was going to get filled in by these six blokes staring at me. But she was as drunk as I was. When she came into a pub I was working in – The Mail Coach – a few days later, she couldn't remember me.

Then I went another night to a club I don't normally go to, on Castlegate, and she was there, and I thought it was really weird. So we started dancing and messing around. And she ended up kissing me mate. But she didn't fancy him, so she gave me her phone number and said, 'Ring me', and that was it. She actually rang me the next day.

Rosie's six or seven years older than me, but she doesn't look it. I thought

War-time wedding at All Souls, Radford, 1940. The groom was an Army cook – and also a Scoutmaster!

she was the same age as me when I met her. It's all in your mind, age. That's what I think. I'm nearly thirty, but I've still got the mind of a teenager.

*Mitch Fenton, born 1970*
*Newark*

## Ups and Downs

Like everything in life, marriage has its ups and downs. Nobody can ever say their married life runs smoothly all the time. It never did and it never will. I suppose at the end of the day the happiest part about falling out is falling in! You've got to be very, very tolerant.

Today life is so completely different with young people. In our day and age you needed a marriage certificate to legally go to bed with somebody. That was really the bottom line of it.

*Bert Stringer, born 1924*
*Sutton-in-Ashfield*

## Expectant Bride

We got married in Halam, this beautiful little village in a valley near Kirklington, and it was Canon Keene that married us. Rosie was

An engagement party at Clipstone, 1966.

pregnant at the time. We'd been seeing each other for a couple of months and I'd been out with enough girls to know that I'd met the right one. So we decided whether we got married or not to have a child, but in fact we got married before the baby was born. Rosie was about four months pregnant walking down the aisle, so you could definitely see the bump. Well, I could. I don't know about Canon Keene.

We lived together for about a year before we got married. If you can't live together, then you shouldn't get married. If you do get married and then find out you can't live together, then it becomes a very expensive little mistake, but we lived together prior to marriage and it was all hunky-dory for us. We found we could put up with each other, despite our differences – I'm the most untidy man in the world and can live in a messy house, but Rosie can't.

The best thing about being married is knowing that you've got somebody there for you. You're not going to grow old and grey on your own.

*Mitch Fenton, born 1970*
*Newark*

## Precious Years

I got married in 1932. I married late, and I didn't keep him long. His family were not a long-lived family, and when I first entered his family I was told that they didn't make old bones. My husband was not quite a year older than me, and he died ten days after his fifty-ninth birthday in 1954, so I've been a long time on my own. We had a very happy twenty-two years together. But it didn't last long enough. The secret of a good marriage is pulling together. Marriage is what you make it, but I had a very happy home life and a very happy married life. I still miss him.

I'd no idea I was going to get married till three weeks before. It all came about that quick, 'cos we were waiting for a house. We couldn't afford to buy one. I'd been to his home for the Easter holiday, for a day or two. I was back home and we were having our dinner on the Thursday, my dad and me, and my dad happened to look up and he says, 'There's Benny here! What's he after now?' And he'd come to tell me that he'd got chance of a house.

And we went to Bingham church in the afternoon to put my banns in, and he called on his road back home to put his notices in, and it was all done and we were married three weeks later. That's how quick I got married.

*Ethel Fenton, born 1896*
*Chilwell*

## A New Companion

My first wife died seventeen years ago. I'd married her in 1947, and she was only fifty-nine when she died. She'd been a good wife and a good mother to my son and daughter. I didn't think about getting married again at first. You don't think of anything except about the wife that you've lost for quite a while. It takes a lot of getting out of it. But I always thought that life's got to go on and I was becoming a lonely man.

Bill for a wedding reception, 1940.

George and Doreen Richardson on holiday in Malta, mid-1990s.

After a time I was on the Club Committee at the Calverton Miners' Welfare and I met Doreen up there. We gradually got to know each other and found we liked to do the same sort of things. My son and daughter had their own families to bring up and look after and I thought, well, when I'm with Doreen she's a good partner at dances and social events, and so I asked her to marry me.

It's just part of life now for a couple to move in without getting married, but I didn't think that way. I thought if I wanted a wife, then I would marry her. And so Doreen sold her home and moved into my place after we got married.

*George Richardson, born 1919 Calverton*

## Unexpectedly Independent

I got married in 1958 in Selston. I was twenty years old. I got married because I fell in love. I thought he was very nice: We had a lot of things in common; we both liked dancing and we used to get along very well. It never occurred to me when I got married that it wouldn't be for life.

The man I married was in the RAF, so we moved away and went to different places before coming back to Eastwood. When we came back to England it was such a big change. We'd had a marvellous time abroad, and coming back to cold England was too much, I think. And I'd changed so much. I was very quiet, but Forces life changes you. I was a completely different person when I came back, able to cope with things better.

We were married ten years before we got divorced. He met a lady who lived down at the bottom of the road, and that's the one he eventually married, but he'd already asked two others to marry him as well before that. It was a long while before I knew what was going on. If I'd known earlier, I'd probably have got divorced earlier.

The first inkling I had about this other lady was when there was a snowstorm one morning and I couldn't get my normal bus. I went down to the bus station and they were both standing there, and you could almost feel the tension. We had to walk up to

Eastwood, and I could feel their unease and I thought, 'we're off again,' and I'd had enough.

Divorce was a very unusual thing to happen at that time. Everyone thought he'd come back. In fact, it was in the Nottingham papers because it was so unusual.

The main thing that worried me was would I be able to feed the children and keep things going. I was virtually penniless. I couldn't take the kids out in the rain because of the holes in their shoes. It was 1968 when I got divorced and I had to get a full-time job then. I've never married again. I've lived on my own ever since.

*Jean Brinsley, born 1937*
*Eastwood*

## Important Choices

As a Franciscan Friar, I have taken a vow of celibacy. It's a deliberate choice. It's not a matter of denying something good. It's not just negative. The vow of celibacy is a positive thing. It doesn't deny the goodness of sex, but we refrain from it to devote all our energies to loving God.

It's not an opting out. It's part of everybody's business to work out their personal relationships, and that's the most important thing of your life. So it's a matter of choosing how to develop these. Marriage also is a matter of choosing. Our understanding of marriage is that it's permanent. You marry once and then that's for life, and that's not because of any obligation from outside. It's the nature of a human being. There's only one me; I can only

give myself once. If I really want to have a deep, personal, loving relationship, then I have to put everything into this without holding anything back. So married people and ourselves are taking two different but parallel lines towards the business of total self-dedication.

*Quentin Jackson, born 1930*
*Nottingham*

## Single, but not Alone

I've never been married. I've had my young men, quite a few. One has

Family greeting postcard of the type popular in the 1920s.

35

Grandmother and daughter out at Nottingham Castle, 1924.

followed another, and they've all been different. And I've learned a lot from them. It's nice to feel that you've been 'sorted out' as it were, that you have been attractive at some time to a man. But I never felt somehow that I wanted to be married.

The first one was a student in the training college to be a minister but after two years he jilted me for another.

The second one was a mystery man in the digs where I was living. From Monday to Friday he was there. He would go away and do his work. He was a motor mower, and I used to sometimes go with him and sit while he demonstrated on the lovely lawns of the big houses. But he always disappeared on a Saturday till early Monday morning, so he was mystery man. So after two years I got no further with him.

The third one loved me devastatingly, but unfortunately, he had made a very early, wrong marriage, and because he was now married, that was rather impossible. It was a big trauma in my life, but the Lord saw me through it. He introduced me to his wife and family, I became friendly with them, and was very happy with them for many years. But he eventually died.

And then the next one was a widower, and he said to me, 'My circumstances are such that I don't want to marry again, because I have a divorced daughter living with me.' So I said, 'That's quite all right. I'm quite happy to be friendly. If you'd rather we finished, that's all right with me. You live in Lancashire and I live in Nottingham. It's only a question of corresponding, which won't get us very far.' So that was it, but it was a very happy ten-year friendship. And he's in heaven now. I keep sending them to heaven!

Just occasionally I've thought perhaps it would be nice to have a child, and have some flesh and blood of my own, a feeling that somebody belonged to me, but nevertheless I've weathered and come through. I don't regret not getting married, but very, very occasionally now I'm in my nineties, there are certain moments when I feel alone. But I'm so fortunate that I have this great faith in God to supply that need. God is with me – I've a great companion.

*Dorothy Bird, born 1900*
*Nottingham*

## The Wonder of New Life

My midwifery career spanned nearly thirty years, and I became Senior Midwifery Manager at the Queens Medical Centre. When you start midwifery, there's something very special about being present at deliveries when a baby's being born. A lot of midwives will describe it as a privilege to be there. There's just something that gets you about the moment of birth, the actual delivery of the baby. I think that's what hooks you. It's like a surge of excitement; it's like butterflies in the tummy as the baby's actually born and you think, here it is! A true midwife will never lose that surge of excitement throughout her career. I have never lost it and I think I will remember it for the rest of my life.

*Iris Cooper, born 1941*
*Woodthorpe*

Baby in a washing basket, Newton Street, Mansfield, 1958.

## Teenage Mums

We've always had teenage pregnancies. It's society that's changed and become more accepting. It tends to peak periodically throughout decades, but nobody is ever disapproving. Their main concern is for the mother and the health of the baby. The fact that the poor thing has had an early pregnancy in her early teens, well, she just needs support and encouragement and help. But at one time, of course, these mothers were all shut away in an institution. In Nottingham, Highbury was where women who had 'fallen' were put, and they were kept there for the rest of their life. When I first came to Nottingham in 1979, as part of my induction, I actually went into Highbury and I spoke to these women. They were still there! They had been there for thirty years or so, and they knew that they couldn't now go back into society because they'd been institutionalised all those years – and they were perfectly normal, sane people kept in that situation. I was so taken aback.

These days we try to set up parentcraft classes for the teenagers and it's sort of on-off. Some of them will come and you'll feel that you're really getting somewhere and getting some information into them and help, and then all of a sudden, your class has dwindled to two or three. I don't know quite why that is.

*Iris Cooper, born 1941*
*Woodthorpe*

## Expanding Family

I didn't plan to have any children. Children never entered my mind, even when I was in my twenties. I had my first child just before I was thirty.

38

But really literally up until I was pregnant I hadn't ever given children a minute's thought. I didn't feel particularly maternal, and I was too busy with day-to-day living. I got married and immediately got pregnant, which was lucky – the right way round. I had five children in five years – that was good going! We had the first one, and then we had twins very, very soon after. Jenny was only five months old when I was pregnant with twins and didn't realise it. I thought I was just eating a lot.

Then we had another one, and thought this was it, and then somehow we had another one after that. I wouldn't change anything now, but I was really embarrassed when I got pregnant again, having the fifth one. I got bigger and bigger and just pretended it wasn't happening to me. My husband had to tell everybody if anyone asked; otherwise I just waited till they found out. And this friend told me I was responsible for the population explosion, which didn't help.

But everything changes when they're born. And now that he's around, I really can't believe I ever thought I didn't want him.

*Anna Joyce, born 1958*
*Southwell*


## A Different Sort of Mother

I am not married. I have no children, but I am now a Reverend Mother and I have seven children – and also all the guests who come into our convent at Rempstone. Maternity comes out in a different way. The fact that I have no physical children, on one level is a deprivation, but on another level, I have hundreds of children.

When I became a nun, one of my friends was fairly acute. She said, 'I don't think it's so much sex that you'll miss, as gin and tonic!' What you miss is the companionship of a man, the being one person for another one person, the intimate communion you get between a husband and wife. And when you see a really happy marriage you look and say, 'Oh it is lovely, it is beautiful, and I have given it up.' But you do get something instead. You

Three-year-old Norman Allcock, photographed at Mansfield studios, in sky-blue suit and hat with black patent shoes, 1944.

39

Eighteen-year-old Gladys Dawson in the uniform of her hoped-for profession of nursing.

don't just renounce, you get given something which is equally and quite often even more wonderful.

God helps one over the initial stages. You're more likely to come up against a great feeling of, 'What am I doing in a convent?' after a few years, when the first fervour has worn off. That is a stage you have to get through. It would be the same in a marriage. You're carried along on the crest of a wave for the first few years and then that thrill goes out of it and you think, 'What have I married this man for?' And then you get over that and discover that you actually do love him. And it's the same in the religious life. You go through periods when you question what your vocation is about, and then you're led through into a deeper realisation of what it is about. And it's even better.

*Sister Mary Wise, born 1940*
*Rempstone*

## Parental Oversight

I tried to go in for nursing, but my father didn't believe in vaccination. And me and my brothers weren't vaccinated. There was a smallpox scare, and the matron said I'd have to be vaccinated or I couldn't stay. And she waited two months for me to get my father's consent. Well, in those days you couldn't do as you liked till you were twenty-one, not eighteen, and I was about eighteen. And my father wouldn't give his consent. A lot of them in those days didn't believe in vaccinations, and you used to have to get a signature from a JP to exempt you. And my father went to a JP that he knew and he signed for me. And as the matron didn't dare keep me on any longer because of the scare, I had to come home.

*Gladys Dawson, born 1903*
*Farnsfield*

## Family Values

When England declared war on Germany my mother was a bit upset, because my brother joined up. And in 1942, I joined up, because I knew I'd got to do something. So I joined the WAAF.

After the war I had an offer to stay on in the job I was doing, or I could have had a job at the Air Ministry, and I came home to Bilsthorpe to discuss it with my mother and father. My father had just retired. He always said he would wait at least until the war finished before he retired, and he was seventy-five. I came home and everywhere was in darkness. I thought, whatever's going off?

My father heard me going through the back door, and he came downstairs and he said, 'Your mother's had a stroke in the night.' And I says, 'Huh, that's ky-boshed it,' just like that. And he says, 'What do you mean?' I says, 'Well, I came to talk it over with you about the jobs I've been offered.' So he says, 'Which are you going to take or what are you going to do?' And I says, 'Well, you silly, I'm not going to leave you am I? I can't leave my mother like that.' She was in bed. She was only semi-conscious and my father was seventy-five. He was active, but I couldn't leave them.

It was 1946 when I came out and that was it. It was a long time before my mother was able to get up, but from then on I was twenty-nine years just washing and dressing her.

*Gladys Dawson, born 1903*
*Farnsfield*

## Search for Understanding

I suspected that my son might be gay, because he was in Greece and all the photographs he sent me were all of men and not of the ladies, and I was suspicious. And I steamed open an envelope, and it was just as if I'd been struck by lightning, because that was a confirmation of what my fears were. And I was shattered, because I didn't understand. I thought it was my fault. I thought it was because I had done something in his childhood which had made him like that, and I felt guilty and bereft, because I didn't know how to deal with a son who was different from his father and his brothers.

I went to a man in the village who I respected, a retired surgeon in the Navy, and I asked his advice because I thought he would understand about men. And I asked if he could be cured, and he laughed and said, 'Put it out of your head. It is impossible. You have to learn to accept it and understand. You cannot change a human being from

Father and daughter: Florrie Radley with her father, 1929. Florrie's father was butler at Epperstone Manor.

being what they are,' and I was absolutely shattered.

I knew nothing about homosexuality, so I went to the library and asked for a book, and all I was given was a book on biology. I felt very sad, because I thought my son would have to go through life with this burden of people saying, 'Ooh, he's queer,' and awful names, and that he wouldn't be able to hold a job down. I imagined all the worst scenarios. I couldn't possibly imagine that he would be a happy person in the future, and it was the guilt that I felt – what had I done wrong? What had his father done wrong? I looked back to his childhood to try to think had I been too strict or too soft, or what had I done different from the other two brothers. It was a very traumatic time.

I went to my local vicar who didn't understand, but he said, 'Just keep on loving.' Well, I never stopped loving because the sadness was overwhelmingly full of love as well. We're very very close my gay son and myself. He rings me every week. But the only way that I could educate myself was by corresponding with a lady who was at Cambridge University, who was interested in that subject, and who put in my mind that it was because his brain was underdeveloped on the masculine side. It was a theory she'd got, and I had quite an angry correspondence with her, and I had a long time searching for somewhere to educate myself. There was nothing in the libraries, nothing in the shops at all that could give any help. Nowadays you can go in any bookshop and there are shelves and shelves and novels and all sorts. And over this last thirty years – because this was in 1968

when I found out – it has been wonderful, the progress of understanding. People are trying to understand, but in those days it was very, very hard.

*Norah Gutteridge, born 1915*
*Ruddington*

# CHAPTER 4
# *Indoor work*

Working in Boots' Biochemical Research Lab, Island site, 1950s. (By kind permission of the Boots Company Archive)

Aerial view of Boots Island site, in the early 1950s. It was so called because it was bounded by canal water on three sides. (By kind permission of the Boots Company Archive)

## A Job for Life

I came down from Scotland in 1958, just after I graduated, to work for Boots, and I remained with Boots all my life. I started off as a research chemist and I remained in the research department until the end of my working life, and I finished up as head of medicinal chemistry with a staff of about seventy-five.

Boots was regarded as a very paternalistic company, still having much of the aura of the family Boot, and they very much looked after their employees. I was told I was very lucky to get a job there because they were much sought after.

The initial laboratories we were in were at the bottom of Island Street,

which now no longer exists as such. But right at the bottom was this old warehouse, into the top floor of which the research department had been put because the original research department had been struck by a bomb during the raid of May 1941. The building was very shaky, so shaky in fact, that every six months workmen used to come round and tap the concrete ceiling with hammers to find out the loose bits and then chip them away so they wouldn't fall on people, because a chunk of concrete did fall out and struck one of the chemists. The walls were thick old Victorian brick. The windows were high. You couldn't see out of them unless you stood on a box. There was no air-conditioning. Being right at the top and with hot summers at the beginning of the '60s, we got extremely hot. In fact, one summer they actually had to come with whitewash and paint the skylights white to stop the sun getting in and killing us all! They used to give us salt tablets, almost as though we were in the desert, to keep us going.

And then we went into the new building in '64, which we called R4 – the green one on Pennyfoot Street. That was like a palace. The place had actually been designed by a man who himself had been a chemist, and this made a great impression on me.

*Ken Nichol, born 1933*
*West Bridgford*

## Invented in Nottingham

Ibuprofen is an active constituent of Nurofen, and it was invented, of course, in Nottingham in the laboratories in Island Street, by John Nicholson. And I must underline this, because a lot of people think it was invented in America. It is a Nottingham drug of which we ought to be enormously proud.

*Ken Nichol, born 1933*
*West Bridgford*

## Perfect Packing

I worked at Jessops when it was on King Street. I was only about sixteen. It was a good shop to be getting into. I always remember being taught how to pack a parcel up – the right way to do it. The right way to fold clothes and put them into trays and that kind of thing, so they were ready to sell. I was quite good at making displays. I was quite artistic.

*Florrie Radley, born 1917*
*Epperstone*

## Reluctant Apprentice

I left school in July 1958. In actual fact I wanted to stay on for further education. I'd done pretty well at school, and the headmaster wrote to my father and said I ought to stay on at school and possibly go to university. My father had other ideas. At the age of fourteen, he said, he'd left school and it had done him no harm and I'd had an extra year, I were leaving at fifteen. And he'd got me what was in those days quite a good job – to be a future technician at the Raleigh. They took about two people on a year, and it was quite a prestigious job to get one of these apprenticeships. My dad worked at Raleigh – just round the corner from where we lived – and he'd managed to get me one, and that's where I was going to go, but I'd got other ideas. I'd been round the Raleigh and the smell of machine oil really got up my nose literally, and I couldn't stand the smell of it. So I really upset the old man and we didn't get on for years after as a result of this. But my mother was working part-time at Players at the time and she said, 'Well, come along to Players. You've got to get your dad happy. There's a lot of trouble in the home with you not getting a job.'

So I went along for an interview. I told them I either wanted to work in the offices or get an engineering

Player's factory, Nottingham, 1929. (By kind permission of Nottingham City Council: Leisure and Community Services: County Library, Angel Row)

apprenticeship. Anyway, they looked at my papers and said, 'You've done quite well at school, so we'll consider it,' but then they came back and said, ' Well no, sorry, at sixteen you can start an apprenticeship, but you'll have to go to night school and you need English, Maths, Science and Technical Drawing, and for the office as well you need a GCE level.

Anyway I said I'd go a year to night school and they offered me a 'waiting' job as a barrow-lad. It was a general labouring job in No. 1 Factory on Beckenham Road, barrowing boxes about on the loading docks and generally loading up the lorries while I attended night school for a year to get my GCEs. My father were most upset about this and he used to call the Players' blokes 'nancy boys'. There were

no reason to it. He considered that it was not a real man's job, working at Players. It was a woman's job. Quite a few people thought that, because ninety per cent of the workforce was female and for guys to want to work with females, doing the sort of work that they did, it was looked down on. But it didn't bother me because it was a clean place to work compared to the Raleigh, which was a very filthy, dirty place. At Players, although we'd got the smell of tobacco, once you'd been there a few weeks, you never smelt it.

*Christopher Blackamore, born 1943*
*Cotgrave*

46

Player's Angels, out to visit a sick friend on a Sunday morning in 1937.

Machinists at Hollins' clothing factory, Nottingham, *c.* 1914.

## Heavenly Handrollers

My mother was a Players Angel. She worked at Players from when she left school at the age of fourteen, up till 1938, when Players girls were expected to leave when they got married (though she later went back on a part-time basis in the '50s). They were all young, attractive girls, so they were Angels. As soon as they got married, they had to leave, so it was a constant changing of young people coming into the company. The name first appeared in 1898, and by 1900 we'd got 200 of them handrolling cigarettes, and a top girl could roll 2,000 cigarettes per day.

*Christopher Blackamore, born 1943*
*Cotgrave*

## Big Spending

Players was a wonderful firm to work for. It was in the days of Ashley Player. He used to come round with a carnation in his buttonhole and speak to various girls on his way. Not like it is now. It was very good money. You started on seventeen shillings and sixpence, and you had a bonus once a year. You see, the Players family were Quakers and they believed in sharing. Everybody went to the Bonus Dance, which was in September. It was in the Sherwood Rooms. All the shops in Nottingham used to wait for Players' bonus, because the girls spent then. And they went to the guinea-shop to buy new dresses.

*Vera Hatfield, born 1917*
*Hucknall*

## Shift Ending

When Players closed, it was absolute Bedlam. You'd got 8,000 people rushing out onto the streets at the same time – people on cycles, cycle bells ringing, people shouting, people fighting to get on the buses at the bus stops, but it was generally a very happy release. It were like coming out of Forest football ground after you'd won, and everybody was happy and going home.

Raleigh was the same, along Farraday Road. It were just one mass of teeming humanity at four-thirty in the afternoon when the Raleigh turned out – cycles, motorbikes, crowds of people all flocking to Derby Road to catch buses, flocking through to Illkeston Road to catch buses.

At seven in the morning there was all the hustle and bustle with everybody going to work at the Raleigh for half past seven. The whole place was alive. It's not alive no more. It's gone.

*Christopher Blackamore, born 1943*
*Cotgrave*

Inside the National Westminster Bank, Thurland Street, Nottingham, 1935.

## Cautious Customers

I joined Westminster Bank in January 1959. At that time you really had the choice of jobs. It wasn't the same situation as you have today.

The public had a lot of fear about banks in those days. People were almost apologetic that they were going in to draw money out. They didn't feel comfortable, and banks were only places to be used if you really had to, because there wasn't the use of current accounts and all the facilities that you get today. People had their deposit accounts where their wages, which were paid in cash anyway, were paid in, and then they would come to the bank probably once or twice a week to draw cash out, but very humbly, and really apologetic that they were actually drawing the money out of the bank. They held the banks in such high esteem in those days, and I think they felt privileged to have an account, and they didn't want to do anything to upset the bank that would spoil that.

I moved to my home branch of Sutton-in-Ashfield and that was where I was given the chance to work as a cashier. I'd only been there a few weeks when I was put on the counter. And that was nice, to be at the Sutton branch, because I'd lived in Sutton-in-Ashfield and Kirkby all my life and so I knew a lot of the people that were in business, and over the next few years I got to know the community very well.

Banks, to me, always had the smell of a museum. Whenever I walked in the branch in the morning, you got this fusty smell. Probably that was because there was a lot of wood in banks at that time: Wooden counter – no screens,

there was no need for screens in those days, and a lot of paper, obviously, and money, and cash. There were a lot of notes in those days, ten shilling notes and one pound notes and so on, and they have a smell, particularly when it was the local fish and chip shop paying in, they really did have an awful smell!

The introduction of the bullet-proof screens was sad really, because that was sort of a barrier to communication. You didn't have the same rapport with customers because you'd got this actual physical screen between you, but unfortunately it became necessary.

*Norman Allcock, born 1941*
*Sutton-in-Ashfield*

## Hard Work for All

I worked at Southwell Union Workhouse for about six years. There was the infirm ward, where people had to go that couldn't look after themselves and was poorly and the nurses were there. Then there was what they called the house part – one half was for the men and one for the women. There was chiefly women there that had had children and weren't married, and their parents couldn't afford to keep them. The men had to do the gardening, which was a huge garden, and the women had to do the cleaning and some scrubbing, keeping the bedrooms clean and the washing. They used to keep pigs there and there was a pig man, and they used to have loads and loads of wood and one old chap used to chop all the wood.

Then there was what they called the casual ward where the tramps could go.

Master and Matron Willatt at The Workhouse, Southwell, *c.* 1925. (From The Workhouse, Southwell, by kind permission of the National Trust)

It was just a long bare ward with concrete floors and iron bedsteads, and they'd have a part of the room where there'd be a table so they could have their food. They were given a meal when they arrived, and they had breakfast when they went. If they got there for six o'clock, they could go the next morning at eight and if they didn't get there until ten, they could leave at eleven, 'cos they had to do some work till eleven o'clock – they didn't have to sleep in cardboard boxes in those days. And they was always sent off in the morning with a slice of bread and cheese and a bottle of water or tea. But they would not go to Newark Workhouse, they would rather walk to Retford. They hated Newark.

First of all I worked on the infirm ward, and then I went down to the house part into the laundry and the linen room. And then I became assistant matron, and I used to go along with the matron everywhere.

*Ada Pointin, born 1908*
*Clifton*


## School Exercise Books

I worked in the printing trade for fifty years. Our original works were in an old textile factory in the heart of Nottingham in what was then Granby Street. When they decided to build Maid Marian Way, we were bought out and we moved to another part of the city. We were set up by a Mr Allsopp, who saw an opportunity for making school exercise books, at the turn of the century. That was a seasonal thing. So in-between times he set up as

bookbinder and finisher to the printing trade.

We used to work for quite a lot of printers clustered in and around the Lace Market in Nottingham. And I remember the smell of a print works and a paper warehouse, and the smell of paper – that has a special aroma. And of course one of the great things about paper is the feel of it. I don't think there are the variety of papers today that there were then. Really nice hand-made paper in those days was readily available.

When I started we had ruling machines putting the lines on paper for exercise books, a battery of four of those, and we also had a battery of four pen-ruling machines. Now these were for ruling the lines for account books. And if you ever see an old-fashioned account book, it has lots of columns all along: blue columns, red columns, even orange, pink columns if you wanted them. You ruled one way on the sheet, and then you turned it over and ruled the back of the sheet. Then you turned it round, set up a new design – this is all with little brass pens, with felt over the top, which would be inked with the appropriate colour – and then the other direction of lines would be put in. That machine was a lovely thing. It was called a bedstead because it looked a bit like a bedstead. It was a bit of wood, with a great big canvas, and each sheet passed under these pens, one at a time, fed by a little girl at the front end.

That was how it was when I went in, and then gradually we improved those machines. We did away with the pen-ruling machines, and the others ruled with discs and were much faster and would do both sides of the sheet at once, and they were fed automatically.

*Gerry Gisborne, born 1912*
*Epperstone*

## From Baker to Butcher

At sixteen and a half I joined my grandfather's business. He was a pork butcher – T.N. Parr on Mansfield Road, and he had a very good shop in the centre of Nottingham. And as I arrived the first morning, he called me into his office and said, 'Now, Kenneth, it's nice to have you here, and I want to tell you that nearly every young man who comes here, they want to handle a knife. Now I'm going to tell you that you are not going to handle a knife here until you are a qualified baker, because all bakers can be butchers, but very seldom can a butcher become a baker, and baking is the basis of this trade'.

So I started off in the bakery, and each Christmas the Melton Mowbray pork pie makers came to help out, two of them, and I think they were a bit surprised that such a young man could be so keen on what they were doing, and they spent an awful long time telling me everything they could about Melton Mowbray pork pies.

*Ken Parr, born 1912*
*Cropwell Butler*

## Business Owner

When the war ended I went back to my grandfather's firm, but then I left it. Without the war I think I'd have just grown up in the family business, but

Pen-ruling machine as described by Gerry Gisbourne, in the Wollaton Park Industrial Museum.

the war had given me the confidence to go on my own. So I found a little firm on Alfred Street South called Farnsworth's, and he wanted a thousand or two, and a couple of friends came by and made certain that I'd got it. There were two little shops, just about a hundred yards apart. The only thing was I didn't like the name Farnsworth, and I couldn't really set up as Parr because I would have upset the family firm.

There was a little shop on Pelham Street and its name was Pork Farms. The name attracted me and I understood that it belonged to the household furniture fellow next-door, J.V. Hutton. I heard that it wasn't doing very well, and that Mr Hutton had retired and was living in Bournemouth,

Pork Farms' display in their Chapel Bar shop, 1960s.

Looking into Pork Farms' Chapel Bar shop from the rear, 1964.

so I wrote to him asking if he would sell me that little shop, which he did.

Well, the quality we were already making in Alfred Street South was pretty good. We had a lot of cars coming from all over Nottingham, stopping in Alfred Street because they'd heard that what we were making was good. So we put that over onto Pork Farms, and it wasn't long before we were having queues there, and this was exciting in the extreme. The queues at the weekend went down Pelham Street, along the High Street and quite a way up Victoria Street. The shopkeepers were complaining because they had a queue in front of their shops. They even complained to the police! It wasn't long before Sainsbury's moved from their corner position on the Council House and we were able to take it and operate that as Pork Farms. That went well immediately, queues went down the main street. And the excitement was quite intense.

*Ken Parr, born 1912*
*Cropwell Butler*

## End of an Era

The Corporation said that they were going to build houses on the very land that Farnsworth's had been operating on and they gave me three years' notice to find somewhere else. In the end it was a disaster for Pork Farms. By then we had a dozen shops, and here was the factory turning it out, and when I enquired about finding another place to build, the amount they talked about was something which would just have bankrupted me and I couldn't do it. And so here I was with this wonderful name and business, and I had to sell out.

And I sold to Associated British Foods, and then they sold it on. And so the lovely beginning of it and the excitement was just quenched a bit.

*Ken Parr, born 1912*
*Cropwell Butler*

## Crowning Glory

I enjoy hairdressing. You're given a job to do. There's a beginning and an end. Within a few hours you can start something and you get an end result. You can be very proud of it, particularly when you get the feedback of a client who's happy with it. She says 'that's great', and you think 'I've done a good job there', because you've made somebody happy. And they're going to pay you – so that makes you happy! But I enjoy doing it and I like people.

Sheena Mabbott at work in her Edwinstowe salon, early 1970s.

Hairstyles used to be all 'bouffante' – heavy fringes, Mary Quant eye make-up and Mary Quant hairstyles as well, with the long sides underneath your jaw, cut right up in the back of your neck. Then we all went razor-happy, razor-cutting very short, very spiky. And then of course the rollers went into the dim and distant and we all blow-dried hair.

Hairdressing's changed an awful lot. You used to be on a lady's shopping list on a Friday – 'Hair'. That was the days when it was wonderful. But it's not like that now. Nowadays people manage their own hair a lot more. They see you every so many weeks for a 'cut and blow' or the highlights, the colours and the perms and things, but most of it's not quite like it used to be.

With sport and leisure becoming far more fashionable, everybody does

something to keep fit one way or another. So you've got to shower and shampoo your hair, and the hairdresser isn't there at nine o'clock at night, you've got to do it yourself. There'll always be room for us though, because there'll always be people making their own disasters – and hair doesn't stop growing!

*Sheena Mabbott, born 1947*
*Edwinstowe*

## Family Business

This business came into my family in 1897. I'm the fourth generation. Now I'm joined by Mary, my daughter, who is the fifth generation. My great-great-grandfather came from Loughborough and bought a pub – Weavers in those days was a pub and since then we've changed to being a wine merchant's.

The pub was one of the last men's bars in Nottingham, and of course that would be illegal now, with sex discrimination and whatever, but it was very popular with the local lace trade. The men used to go in there and drink out of the silver tankards and a lot of business was done there, particularly over lunchtime.

The main pub was closed and sold when we developed as a wine merchant's in the early '60s. In those days there were a dozen independent wine merchants in Nottingham and now there are only two.

*Alan Trease, born 1937*
*Edwalton*

Weavers' original shop, looking down Listergate, 1960.

56

## Father and Daughter

As a child I can remember at Christmases dad always coming home late because he was busy with the Christmas trade, and he had piles of paperwork back at home.

When I'd left university, one Christmas I was unemployed and they needed someone at the shop to help out, so I did, and I thought well, actually the old boy's business is quite interesting. I still went off and did conservation work, which is what I did my degree in – geography and environmental work, but about five years down the line I didn't really know where I was wanting to go. I didn't feel I wanted to be digging ditches when I was thirty! A vacancy came up full-time and so dad said to me, 'Are you still serious about joining the business?' so I did, and I haven't looked back since.

I think I'll be staying in Nottingham. The family business is here and a wine merchant's is a thoroughly enjoyable business to be in. Who else can spend an evening drinking wine and claiming it as work?

*Mary Trease, born 1969*
*Gamston*

## Confidence for the Future

I think it's important to keep the family business going. I would be very sad to close the door. Possibly financially I would be better off, but I don't feel Weavers is my business in a way. I was lucky enough to inherit it and develop it, so to just pack up would be very bad, and there are very few family businesses

Weavers Wine Merchant's current shop on Castlegate, 1999.

in the city of Nottingham. They're being driven away by high rents – the business is sold, it becomes part of a big chain and it's gone forever. We started in the last century, and we're pleased to be going into the next century. I think there's a good future for wine merchants to carry on, so we'll see if we can keep going for a bit longer.

*Alan Trease, born 1937*
*Edwalton*

## Confidently in Control

The first time I sat as a judge it was very strange. I knew what happened in court, but like anybody doing the thing the first time, you're a bit nervous, and your sense tends to leave you. So when I got up there, I stood there, all the barristers were standing up, and I thought, 'now why don't they sit down?' And then thought, 'oh, they can't until I bow and sit down myself'. And that was my first experience as a Deputy Circuit Judge in 1977.

In your court, you are God, and that's the way it's got to be. If the court's going to be run properly, then you've got to be utterly in charge of everything that's going on. I suppose most judges, if the truth be known, are pleasantly arrogant, but you don't do the job unless you think you're capable of doing it. You've got to be in charge.

You can't ever think you are in the wrong, because if you went home at night and cried in your pillow because you thought you'd made a mistake, you'd never do the job. You've got to move onto the next case. A worried judge is bad judge. It's not to say that other people don't think I make mistakes – no doubt they do – but there's always the Court of Appeal there if I go wrong on law.

You have to focus on the facts. If you have a rapist of young kids to deal with,

Keith Matthewman, circuit judge, in working robes for Nottingham Crown Court, 1999.

you can't keep that in mind all the time, you have to be someone who takes it as a job. You've got to divorce yourself from the emotion, and that's what people don't understand. You've got to simply look at the case as a case, otherwise you're lost. I've appeared in every type of case in crime – many murders, and many rapes, I've done it all, and I've not been upset. You don't go on the bench unless you're the sort of person who's not easily upset.

Unfortunately, it spills over into your personal life. I know sometimes people say you're arrogant, you're cold. I don't like to give that impression and I don't think I do, but if you're in a mix of people and they talk about the sort of things you're getting at and they talk on the basis of being emotionally involved, I'm afraid I tend not to be.

*Keith Matthewman, born 1936*
*Bramcote*

## Not a Race Apart

We're still regarded as people who say silly things. I don't think jurors who've actually been into court think that. It's just the press who tend to pounce on some judge who said, 'Who are the Beatles?' or something like that. The trouble is, when people read that they think, oh, these pompous toffee-noses who don't live in the real world, and nothing could be further from the truth. Obviously there are some who don't, but basically we're people who all do live in the real world, and know who the Beatles are! When people see things like that in the press, they ought to take it with a pinch of salt.

But people are beginning to realise that although judges have a lot of power, we are basically human beings. We're not pompous prats. Obviously, we do dress up in wig and gown and go to the cathedral at Southwell and things like that, but it's unfair to say we are not part of ordinary civilisation.

I think wearing gowns and wigs is still very appropriate. It gives the court an air of something important and serious happening, a more solemn feeling. A court shouldn't be so intimidating that people forget what they've got to say, but it has got to be a place where they know that serious work is done.

*Keith Matthewman, born 1936*
*Bramcote*

## Divi Day

I went to work for the Nottingham Co-operative Society in their accounts section on Parliament Street, really just working behind the scenes.

The Co-op divi was based on the amount you purchased from the Co-op, and the dividend was a return to the particular customers for their loyalty in spending their money at the Co-op. At one time if you spent £1, then after three months you got 2s 6d back for every £1 you spent, in a lump sum.

When you shopped at the Co-op, you used to get a little paper receipt, and it had your share number on. And that was duplicated by carbon paper. Then those duplicates would go to the main office in Lenton to be recorded on your account.

When I worked at the Co-op, the

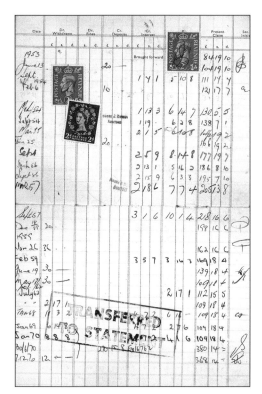

Nottingham Co-op Society Divi book, 1950s.

divi was paid in March and September. So if you didn't want to draw the actual money that day, you just ignored it, or you could pick up the slip which told you how much you were entitled to, take the book and the slip to the bank counter, and that would be entered into the book as an accumulative saving, or you could go to the cashiers and draw the money.

About a month before payment days, the signs used to go up, to say what payment dates there were. And because Nottingham was so big, you'd have to have certain share numbers on certain days. We used to do about 20,000 a day, and we had well over 100,000 members in Nottingham. So it took a good week to pay the divi out. And it really was something to see.

On opening day, the queue started on the Wollaton Street side of the Co-op, went down the stairs and right down the pavement almost to the theatre square, and everybody stood there with their book. They'd queue for a couple of hours.

They'd got to produce the book to get the slip, but some of them would probably bring the whole street's books in! And some of them would have every little slip, and at home they would add everything on, and if the slip they got from that day didn't match, they could tell you exactly what they'd spent. It must have took them hours to work out, and if it was as much as threepence out, they used to go and complain about it. The idea was, if you got your divi in September, you'd spend it on Christmas stuff, and if you got it in March, you'd spend it on holiday stuff. And it worked. Because the people that got the divi in the Co-op in Parliament Street used to spend it in the store, because the more they spent, the more divi they were getting next time. That's how it used to work.

We came across some real characters. There was one lady who lived in Lenton and she used to come every year, and she'd got this black hat, but obviously at some time or another it had fell near the fire and it had burned half of it, and it was all scorched on one side. We used to call her 'The Hat'.

*Dave Birkett, born 1938*
*Gedling*

60

# CHAPTER 5

# Outdoor and underground work

Dave Birkett starts out as a telegram boy, 1954.

## A Smart Turn-out

I used to be a telegram boy. They were eight-hour shifts and because of our ages – we were all fifteen to seventeen and a half – we weren't allowed to work before seven o'clock, and we weren't allowed to work after eight. So the first shift started at seven, and the last one at midday. We used to arrive at Norfolk Place, behind the big Queen Street post office, usually a few minutes before shift started, and we had to parade in front of the inspectors to make sure that we looked smart and clean going out onto the streets. The pushbike side wasn't too bad. But when we graduated to motorbikes when we were sixteen, we had to parade first, and then go down to Huntingdon Street to pick up our motorbikes, and then the shift started. To keep your boots nice and clean and shiny with oily motorbikes was pretty difficult, especially in the winter time. But once the inspector had had a look, then you were okay to go. If you weren't presentable, you went back into the Mess Room to tidy yourself up, and paraded again, and that's when your shift started.

*Dave Birkett, born 1938*
*Gedling*

## Standing out in the Crowd

I joined the Nottinghamshire Constabulary in 1974 and I've worked at Clifton since then. My role is as a community officer dealing with all sort of community problems. Anything that's thrown out at us I go and sort out; domestic disputes, neighbourly disputes, talking to schools, pensioner groups, anything that assists the community and breaks down the barriers that build up between the police and the community. When I started the first thing was the culture shock of having to have my hair

| PERSONAL | ADVICE OF PAY | | | | | P205D |
|---|---|---|---|---|---|---|
| | | | | | | (Rev'd. 63835/52) |
| | | | | PAY DAY | 1 9 MAR 1954 | |

| Gross Pay 12 | Income Tax | | DEDUCTIONS Inc. Nat. Ins. 15 | NET PAY 16 | NAME (Block Capitals) 17 |
|---|---|---|---|---|---|
| | Deduct 13 | Refund 14 | | | |
| £ s. d. | £ s. d. | £ s. d. | £ s. d. | £ s. d. | BuRKITTS D. S. |
| 3 10 6 | | | 3 6 | 3 7 - | |

| Brief explanation of changes in Columns 12 and 15 | "National Insurance Bene- | £ s. d. |
|---|---|---|
| | fits" excluded for tax purposes. | |
| | Monthly paid staff only. Number of weeks' National Insurance Contributions in Column 15. | 4 |

B.B. Ltd. 51-3087

Dave Birkett's payslip for his first week's work for the post office, 1954.

PC Nigel Brown on foot patrol in Southchurch Drive in Clifton, 1978.

cut. From having almost shoulder-length hair, going to a short back and sides was a tremendous change. Then there was the strictness of the job, having to follow orders all the time, just actually having to work a proper shift pattern, working nights, mornings, evenings or whatever. Having your life almost planned out for you was totally different.

I think wearing a uniform is probably the hardest thing – actually being noticed. When you go out walking for the first time on your own on the streets, you feel everybody's looking at you. And you've got to be prepared that if anybody comes up and asks you a question, you've got to have an answer. You've got to think very very quickly. You've suddenly become the centre of attention. I wasn't fully prepared for that – even the training school can't physically prepare you for it.

One of my most frightening experiences was at a Nottingham Forest football match. This must have been in the mid-1970s when I was very green. I was on duty in the ground, and a large group of people were milling round at the back of the stand and I could see scarves being thrown up – one was an opposition scarf, and then there were some Forest scarves, and people were shouting and larking about, and I thought, 'crikey, there's one of the opposition fans in amongst there!' So I waded in to see what was going on in the middle, only to find a group of lads just enjoying themselves. My helmet disappeared. I didn't get roughed up but my helmet went off, and I never saw it again. And I must admit that was quite frightening, thinking to myself I was stuck in the middle of a group. No other officers were with me, because I'd gone in without thinking really. And that could have been very, very nasty.

But there are some brighter moments – when, for example, you go to a potential serious situation, such as Social Services can't get into a house, and Mrs So-and-so or Mr So-and-so hasn't been seen for a while. You kick the front door down and they're sat there drinking tea and having their morning breakfast, absolutely startled as to why this policeman is stood watching them eat their toast!

*Nigel Brown, born 1953*
*West Bridgford*


## One Heck of a Job!

I was a farmer. It was the Ragsdale Brothers farm in Wellow. My father George Ragsdale was farming it before, and before him it was Matthew Ragsdale and that was 1884. It was farmed continuously right up to my brother dying in 1978. After that the land was sold and then it dispersed to various farmers.

It was horses when you were harvesting and you had to take it right down into Wellow, and that's about a mile. It was one heck of a job. You had a team of three and you had one in the field filling, one on the road going up and down, and one in the stackyard emptying. And you kept that going all day. And then there were two others in the field; they was hooking sheaves up. So it was hard work. That's why you had terrific muscles on you. I've still got them now. I may be eighty, but I could belt anybody!

We started growing sugar beet in the lighter fields during the war. You had to grow it in the war, because there was no sugar coming in from abroad. When we grew sugar beet we had to have a gang from Worksop. Mr Marsden brought a gang of the women out from the slums of Worksop, and they split them into two. We had to plough the beet out and lift it on top and let it wither for a day or two, and when he brought his gang he'd split them up, and half of them would knock the beet together and drop them neatly into rows. Then the other half came along with sharp knives, and we had to have hampers handy at the side of the road, and then they came with a sharp knife and chopped the top off and dropped the beet into the basket. And they could do that without even looking where the basket was. And of course some of them did chop themselves nastily. But Marsden never bothered, he said, 'Carry on working, no stopping. Keep your backs down.' And they worked like slaves. And to keep these hampers empty we had to work like slaves. 'Cos they sometimes got filled right up and you picked up them one-handled baskets, and you'd tip 'em into a horse and cart, which was quite high, so you had lift it about six foot and tip it in. You don't realise what sort of work you did. There were no weaklings on farms then. They were all brawny chaps. Nowadays to drive a combine or a tractor you can be as slim as you like.

Wellow village existed on farming, and there were nine farms. You needed quite a lot of labour on the farms then, of course. We had two men sleeping in the top of our farmhouse. I slept in one garret and two men slept in the other garret. And they snored like hell, these two blokes did – and they had sweaty

64

Bill Ragsdale (far right) oversees a Corrective Training Activity for youngsters, cleaning out Gorge Dyke in Wellow village, in the late 1960s.

feet as well! Every farm had to have quite a few workers on to keep the farm going. These days machinery's made it possible to farm things without so much labour.

The whole system's changed. When the mines were sunk in 1926 – a lot of the mines round here, like Ollerton, started from about that time – they had ponies down the pits then. So the men on the farms who worked with horses, left the farms. There was not much money on a farm you know, at that time. It was only about twenty bob and they often had quite a biggish family. So they left the farms, and then others went to work at the brickyards, because they were taking on more workers as well at that time.

*Bill Ragsdale, born 1918*
*Wellow*

## Learning the Lingo

I left school at fourteen and began work at Herrington Colliery in County Durham. I worked on the surface for nine months and went underground at the age of fifteen. In those days it was usual to be underground at that age. There was no other work in that area except mining.

In 1947, my colliery was looking as though it was going to close, and because I was a colliery official, I decided to move to a brand new colliery which was being opened in Calverton. And Calverton Colliery was just more or less beginning production when I moved here. It was the first of the newer collieries to open after nationalisation.

I'd say about forty per cent of the miners at Calverton were from the North East, about twenty per cent from Yorkshire and the rest mixed, with probably only ten per cent from Nottinghamshire itself.

It wasn't very easy to become part of the community at first. For one thing, when I went down the mine I couldn't understand a lot of the terms they were using. When a man was shouting for his shot-firer, you see, when I first started shot-firing, he'd shout, 'You! Shotty!' I'd always been addressed by my name before that, and I thought well, you don't talk to men like that. But I knew what they wanted, and they'd say, 'Ay up, my duck, I want this firing and that lot firing.'

The collieries up in Durham have their own pit dialect – an entirely

George Richardson looks into a Shearer coal-cutting machine on a management course at Linby Training Centre, 1965.

A team of 'Sinkers' at Calverton Colliery, 1949.

different language down the mine to what we speak on the surface. And you've got the same in north Nottinghamshire. They've got their mining terms and you've got to learn them. We didn't think that you called each other 'duck' for a start, when you were talking man to man. We didn't talk like that in Durham.

It was a long time before I really got into the way of it all – the Nottingham men had different terms entirely to the Yorkshiremen, and of course we also had some Scotsmen among them, and so we had to learn to adjust ourselves to all the different dialects. And gradually they adjusted themselves so that over time we got our own dialect at Calverton colliery – probably different

entirely to what they had at Cotgrave colliery.

*George Richardson, born 1919*
*Calverton*

## Twice the Toil

I was born in Poland. I fought for the British in the war and in 1946 I came to England. We were demobbed in 1947, and we could go anywhere in the world except behind the Iron Curtain, and that was where my home had been. I had been offered a lot of jobs, but these jobs had no money. I said I was not frightened of a job, to go somewhere where there was plenty of money, so

Lance-Corporal Walter Urban, 1946.

Polish camp, waiting for a job. They picked fourteen of us to go to Mansfield Colliery. It was my impression that they wanted to see if we could hold a shovel in our hands. But before we went there, we had to sign a declaration: If any jobs are going, you go first – that's us Poles. So anyway, we had no option. We signed the papers and went to the pit. But before long, when any jobs were going, the Poles didn't go. The other, skiving ones had to go, and it wasn't very nice for the unions. But management was for us because we worked twice as better, twice as much, and the job was done properly, not just skipped. We were working to make everything safe.

*Walter Urban, born 1925*
*Sherwood*

they said there was plenty of money in a coal mine, and there are plenty around here. But when it came to getting a job in a coal mine, they couldn't get us one. The unions were very, very strong, and they didn't want the Poles to work in coal mines. It was terrible. There were Communists in the unions, and they thought we were making propaganda about how bad things were in Russia. They thought different, and they had a grudge against the Poles because in 1926, in the General Strike, they tried to take over, but Poland was selling coal to England, and of course the strike didn't succeed. But what was that to do with me? And they were against the Poles.

We were near Chesterfield in a

## Volunteer Work

I do charity work because I enjoy it. It was something I would never have thought of. I got roped in to start with and it's all gone from that. Macedon House decided to start hiring a van on a regular basis. The van they hired was from Nottingham Community Transport. It's a heavy goods van, and they were looking for someone to drive it as a volunteer, to go and help move people from temporary accommodation into permanent accommodation. I got on well with the chap who was actually organising it at the time, and he couldn't reverse a van to save his life. Having driven vans myself I was taking the mickey out of him, and he said, 'Could you do any better?' and I said 'Yes', and it's gone from there. That was how I became known to Nottingham Community Transport. They now actually book me to drive their vehicles and take disabled people out on trips.

If people didn't volunteer there'd be some work that wouldn't get done as well as it gets done. There's an argument that there would be more people employed but I don't necessarily go along with that.

*Dave Ashton, born 1950*
*Aspley*

## Turning the Clock Back

I was a weights and measures inspector for Notts County Council for forty-five years. The first five years or so I was testing petrol pumps. I tested and stamped every pump in the county outside the city of Nottingham, and Newark (which had their own special arrangements) in the period round about 1930. Then I became divisional inspector, mostly covering the Mansfield, Sutton and Kirkby area and the surrounding villages. I was doing general weights and measures work there, not just petrol pumps.

What I did mostly was false trade descriptions of cars – winding back the clocks and that sort of thing. There was a local firm that did a big trade in old bangers, which they picked up mostly at auctions and so on, and charged about £300 a time, which was quite a lot of money in those days. When people took them to their local garage and said, What do you think of my new car?' the local

Dave Ashton (second from left) prepares toz meet Prince Charles at Macedon's Albion Nightshelter, Nottingham, 1999.

Bill Simpson's assistant, Herbert Nuttall, tests the petrol pumps, *c.* 1932.

garage would say it wasn't fit to be on the road. It was absolutely dreadful. And the trouble was, we were limited to the trade description, so it was only in some cases that you could prove that an actual description had been given. But we did our best and got a few prosecutions. We used to get a call about twice a week, and when we asked, 'Where did you buy the car from?' it was always the same place!

When I first started, in the shops most commodities were either sold over the counter by weight or they were packed in the shop. Practically everything was weighed in front of the customer when I was a boy. And that went on till the war. In the '50s everything changed and practically everything was packed in the factories, and the scales in the shops disappeared.

The first to go was tea. I can just remember one or two shops that had tea scales. They were fastened to a pulley system in the ceiling and they pulled them down, and they had big bowls, which they could lift up and drop down. They were going out in 1930 in favour of pre-packed tea.

When I first came to Mansfield, we used to have an arrangement called stamping stations. We used to go to the villages and the small towns, and take over a building, and the people would bring in all their scales and measures and everything else, and we used to test them. When we went to Huthwaite, we used to have team of about half a dozen of us, and we'd go there for two days, and we were kept busy the whole morning and early afternoon testing them. Shops like Maypole and Burtons and Co-op and

so on would have half a dozen scales and a whole set of weights, and it was a real big job going through these. But the last time I went to Huthwaite, myself and my assistant went for an hour.

*Bill Simpson, born 1908*
*Mansfield*


## No Place like Home

I always wanted to be in the Navy. I didn't want to be like my grandfather and stay in this county all my life. I wanted to see the world. I went in as a mechanic. I joined in 1987 and left in 1994.

I was quite lucky. My first draft was on a brand new ship, which was being built in Clydebank, HMS *Cornwall*. After basic training in Plymouth, I went up and joined the ship in Scotland and sailed it down, and from there on it was great trips on that ship – two Mediterranean cruises and off to the States for ten months and things like that. It was pretty wicked even though I was only a junior! Your first draft is where you learn your trade, so it was all a big eye-opener at seventeen.

Apart from learning how to drink beer in copious amounts, the biggest shock to the system is that you have to be pretty self-reliant. There's very little, if any, sympathy if you mess up. If you mess up, you carry the can – unlike the officers. But I was pretty independent. I was never home-sick apart from on my twenty-first birthday. That was five days or so before the Gulf War started. I was on watch in the middle of the night on my own, which wasn't much fun – and not allowed to drink either! But I was definitely sea-sick. I was never a great sailor.

The Navy gives you an appreciation of different cultures and everything, but I'm proud to be from Nottinghamshire. I still think it's the greatest county in the country. When I said I was from Newark in the Navy, they used to say, 'Where the bloody hell's that?' So I've always said I was from Nottingham. And in the Navy as soon as they find out you're from Nottingham, they say, 'Oh, that's where the women outnumber the men.' And it's that, and the nightclubs, that Nottingham's famous for these days. If the women do outnumber the men, I don't know where they went to. I must have been going to the wrong places. But Nottingham does seem to be full of good-looking women – even though my wife's a Derbyshire lass!

*Mitch Fenton, born 1970*
*Newark*

Mitch Fenton receives his Gulf War medal from the Commander of MCMI Squadron, 1994.

# CHAPTER 6
## *At play*

Off to Wembley for the Nottingham Forest v Tottenham Hotspurs 1991 Cup Final. Geraldine Ellis is on the left at the front.

## A Chance to Let Rip

I got into supporting Nottingham Forest football team following a talk by John Barnwell, who played for Forest in the '60s. He came to the youth club and gave a talk about football. I was seventeen, thought he was a gorgeous bloke and thought I must watch him play football in a pair of shorts. So I clamoured for a neighbour who was a member of the club to get me a ticket for the game, and that was my first chance at football. My first game was the now famous quarter-final at the Forest ground – tremendous game, with a Storey-Moore hat-trick that won it for them, and a brilliant atmosphere. To go to a game that was fully charged of electricity, sort of hyped-up and fans shouting and screaming, I got so involved I just had to go back and then keep going. And that was it, really. I was just starting work in a bank at the time and was finding it rather boring and rather tedious. And to watch football was just a buzz, to get out and really shout and let rip and have a great time.

Walking to a match at the Forest ground on a Saturday afternoon, it was quite a sight in those days as you approached the Trent Bridge area down by the riverside – hundreds, thousands of people just walking to the ground, and people wore red and white scarves more then. That seems to be a trend that's stopped now. But in those days, there were thousands flocking over Trent Bridge. You couldn't see for red and white.

To go to away games, I went on the supporters' coach. There were a lot fewer women when I first went. The buses used to go from Nottingham and there would probably be no more than a dozen women and the rest of them were men, but things have changed over the years dramatically.

If I see the team lose, I'm disappointed, but it doesn't leave me depressed at the end of the day. That would be taking it too far. At the end of the day, it is just a game of football, and you can't take it to the extent that you're going to stop doing things because of it. If they win, it's a tremendous feeling and you get a buzz. It leaves you on a real high. You can feel great emotion, and people will laugh and say, 'Come on, you're grown up, forget it! It's just a game of football.' But Nottingham Forest Football Club is a part of my life and what happens there is part of me.

*Geraldine Ellis, born 1950*
*West Bridgford*

## Cricket-centred Community

Cricket is the only real focal point of Milton. We've no pubs. For such a small village, it's a wonderful thing that we've been able to produce two cricket teams every week in the Bassetlaw League. We started with very humble beginnings.

I went to East Markham school and the headmaster's passion was cricket, so that gave me a good start. We decided we wanted to play a bit of cricket at home here, and we got a few lads from round about and played just over the River Maun bridge, at the bottom of our paddock. Eventually we thought we could scrape a team together, so we borrowed a bit of tackle from the local church school. We used a blackboard for

The cover of Geraldine Ellis' Forest scrap book of 1967-69.

NOTTINGHAM
FOREST
FOOTBALL CLUB
(Founded 1865)

City Ground, Nottingham
Telephone Nottingham 88236/7/8

PRESIDENT :
Mr. G. N. Watson, J.P.

CHAIRMAN :
Mr. A. Wood

VICE-CHAIRMAN :
Mr. H. Levey

COMMITTEE :
Mr. J. H. Willmer
Mr. H. W. Alcock, F.C.A.
Mr. J. Glenn
Mr. F. Chambers
Mr. A. E. Chambers
Mr. B. J. Appleby, B.A.
Mr. N. W. Crammond

MANAGER :
Mr. John J. Carey

SECRETARY/TREASURER :
Mr. Ken Smales

HON. CONSULTING SURGEON :
Mr. J. P. Jackson, F.R.C.S.

MEDICAL OFFICER :
Dr. A. H. MacLaren, M.B., Ch.B.

HONOURS
F.A. Cup Winners—1898 and 1959.
First Division Runners-up—1966/67.
Second Division Champions
    1906/07, 1921/22. Runners-up 1956/57
Third Division Champions—1950/51.
County Cup Winners
    1961/62/64/65/67/68.

a scoreboard and arranged a friendly fixture or two. We did quite well, and actually started as a club in 1949.

We decided we would have to have somewhere to get changed. One morning my neighbour rang my father and said, 'There's a double-decker bus in the market at Newark.' My father said, 'Buy it, and make sure they'll deliver it.' He bought it for £32 and it was towed by lorry across to Milton. It was an old Nottingham bus. It had gone past Trent Bridge many a time, so it was quite fitting for it to come to our cricket ground.

We changed upstairs in the bus and visitors changed downstairs, and we had two young schoolgirls who sat in the driver's seat and did the scoring. One of them, Daphne Johnson, is still our social secretary.

*Derek Footit, born 1925*
*Milton*

## Perfect Pitch

I took on the work of groundsman at Milton Cricket Club when I retired. But I'm still a player too. I played my first match in 1939 for the school under tens, and I turn out regularly for the second team in League matches every Saturday afternoon. My ambition is to play into my eighth decade of cricket.

We have benefit matches for all the top Nottinghamshire players each year, and they've said one of the first grounds they enquire about for a match is Milton, because it's so different from Trent Bridge. It's the other end of the scale. When the players come here, they can bring their children, they can park their cars round the ground, and they know they're going to play on a good surface. They know there's going to be good company after the match. And we have built up this tremendous relationship with Trent Bridge.

Milton Village Cricket Team, with their 'changing-room' bus, 1955. Also visible is Bevercotes Colliery, demolished in the mid-1990s.

Milton Cricket Team, 1950. Derek Footit is second from the right in the front row.

Occasionally, sheep get onto the pitch and make a bit of a mess of the square. And we also have flocks of rooks which arrive in the summer, and although they do a lot of good, they do peck holes in the pitch. Several times on a Saturday I've had to come along and fill in holes that the rooks have dug. These are things that the likes of Trent Bridge don't come across, but it's all part of village cricket.

*Colin Shaw, born 1930*
*Milton*

## Growing up with Green Fingers

We've lived in Nuthall for forty-two years, and we bought the house for the garden. We've got about a third of an acre. I enjoy everything about gardening. As the years have gone by, it's become our main pleasure. We just love gardening and love to see the result, and like to see other people's pleasure when they see it. We belong to the Hardy Plants Society and since we joined that we've learned such a lot more about gardening than we ever knew. We're always wanting to improve the garden, and we're always striving for a bit of change. Every minute that we've got to spare we spend in the garden. We never stop, even in the winter. There's always tidying up to do.

I gardened from when I was a child, because there were no men in the house, so I did the garden. I always enjoyed it and I used to swap plants like other people swap marbles or cigarette cards.

77

Herbert Wybrew and family on their Gedling allotment, in front of the greenhouse he built, in the 1930s. Tomatoes and chrysanthemums were his speciality.

Tom and Margaret Leafe in their Nuthall garden, 1999. The couple regularly open their garden under the National Garden Scheme.

I think gardening's got popular today with the coming of garden centres. Firms that were once very small nurseries caught on to the fact that if they became bigger and bigger and provided cups of tea, and artificial flowers and pots and things, they could attract people who didn't garden a lot, but liked gardens.

*Margaret Leafe, born 1924*
*Nuthall*

## Flowers versus Food

I enjoy working in our fruit and vegetable garden. I wouldn't enjoy working in an allotment. It's simply the pleasant surroundings of the garden being here. In the summer it gives a great pleasure to be in it and walk round it. Another pleasure is the seasons – the fact that each year you start again.

There's always something to look forward to. You do things and then you wait for the result. And if it's not quite what you thought, well then next year you can have another go.

People don't seem to have time to grow vegetables. They've got so many other interests now. And they haven't room, of course. These minute gardens that people have nowadays, they want them as a flower garden rather than a vegetable garden. And I think people are well-off enough not to have to grow them, and that I'm sure is a big difference. Fifty or sixty years ago, people grew vegetables simply because they had to.

We've always grown as many of our own vegetables as we could and they last us through the winter. We don't buy a lot. We had a freezer very early on, before freezers were common. Before that we were growing stuff and bottling a little, but having to give a lot away. We were probably the last of our friends to have a car, the last to have a television, the last to have a microwave, but we were the first to have a freezer! Definitely we were one of the first.

*Tom Leafe, born 1927*
*Nuthall*

## The Joys of the Open Road

I have a 1935 Riley, which I bought in 1961, 'Suitable Scrap or Spares'. It was a saloon, and the whole of the saloon body was rotten. The idea was to

Rebuilding the Riley, with David Cope's daughter Louise in the driving seat, 1963.

David and Ann Cope in the Riley at a rally in Bingham, 1988.

strip it down and build a sports competition Riley out of it and that I did across a six-year period myself – I did probably ninety per cent of the work myself.

What I love about this car is the sheer pleasure of having a fine piece of engineering and as an engineer, it appeals to me. You can 'place it' on the road. It will corner where you want it to corner. You can set her up, and she'll go. Each journey's an adventure. You think, we're going to Yorkshire tomorrow, and you really look forward to that as an adventure. You keep off the motorways as much as possible, and you really do enjoy it. And whenever you go out, people come up to you and you get into conversation.

We belong to the Riley Register, Notts and Derby area, and I probably spend about fifteen hours a week on club activities and I spend a lot of time organising events. For twenty-five years I organised our autumn weekend where we took twelve to fourteen cars away to places like North Yorkshire or the Lake District. I organised two rallies a year, the spring rally and the Thoresby rally.

The club to me gives a marvellous social activity with the stimulation of the engineering aspect and the sheer pleasure of driving a classic car, a car which is made up to a standard, not down to an accountant's cost.

*David Cope, born 1930*
*Wollaton*

## Family Motoring

I love the Riley. It's part of my husband and I. And when the children came along, they've grown up with it. And this is what's so lovely with the club, it's something you can do as a family. We've had many weekends where you went off with all the cars – you had a picnic in Clumber Park, you played cricket. And now our grandchildren ride in it. The other thing is, I always know where my husband is – he's in the garage!

*Ann Cope, born 1934*
*Wollaton*


## Trying to Tango

We went dancing at a place called the Gaiety in Hucknall. You learnt to foxtrot, waltz, and if you were clever you learnt to tango. It was enjoyed very, very much on a Saturday night. Admission cost ninepence, and of course it closed at ten in those days. The girls used to put their long dresses on, and their high heels. You shampooed your hair on Saturday afternoon, curled it in pipe-cleaners and off you'd go to the dance. I used to go with my friend Nora Barker. She lived at Bulwell. Everyone was friendly. The men had their suits on. You thought you was in London dancing. It was quite exciting. Saturday night was the night of the week.

These fellas used to go to the Gaiety. They used to come from Annesley, Newstead, Bulwell, Hucknall, and some of them used to come from Aspley, but the thing was getting home. You hadn't got a car. You didn't have taxis to get home. That was the problem for those people.

It was a large room. It had got three people in the orchestra, as they called it: piano, drums and a violin, but the piano was the dominant musical instrument. They were on like a little stage, three steps up from the floor. They used to listen to all sorts of radio and play their tunes. At the interval we went to the pub and we had port and lemon, and you came back feeling drunk. I don't know what sort of port it was, but it affected you.

Eventually, when I got to about eighteen or nineteen, we went to the Palais, where there used to be a ball in the ceiling whizzing round, giving out light. Ladies would hire gentlemen who sat in the corner, and they paid sixpence to dance with them. They were the professionals. We used to watch them dance and then try and dance like them. This tango business was just coming in. And they used to throw you back, you know – very exciting! That finished at half-past ten.

*Vera Hatfield, born 1917*
*Hucknall*


## Self-taught Strummer

When I was about fourteen I sent away for a wooden ukelele and I think it was about four and sixpence. George Formby was all the rage and I got this ukelele and I got George Formby records, and I used to sit on the table, look in front of the mirror and pick the ukelele up and practise with it. So I learnt to play the ukelele entirely by getting books and listening to lots and lots of George Formby songs, and eventually I got a banjo ukelele.

The first job I ever got was at Ilkeston at the Pioneer Club. I got half a guinea and had to do five little spots of two songs each, and the stage was about six inches high. And from here I used to do shows everywhere. Then I met a fellow called the Nottingham Street Singer, and he took me in hand and

Sixteen-year-old Wally Binch practises the ukelele near Trent Bridge, 1939.

took me to places – I sang to 1,000 people at Coventry. I thought it was great.

Then I joined what was called the Military Entertainments Unit run by the city council. We used to go out entertaining people in the Forces all over the place, and the final one I went to was at Wilford, an Ack-Ack site it was – anti-aircraft guns – and I'd just started singing my numbers when the sirens went. They knocked over their beer, dashed out to the guns, and I thought, this is the life for me!

So I went to the recruiting office at London Road, presented myself to the recruiting sergeant, and I said I'd like to join the Army, and they said, 'How old are you?' I said I was seventeen, and

they said, 'Come back when you're eighteen.' So I came back the next day: 'I'd like to join the army.' 'How old are you?' ' Eighteen.' 'Right, what would you like to join?'

The Sherwood Foresters sounded good to me. So I joined them and wherever I went I took the ukekele. It made great friends everywhere, because a ukelele was very popular during the war. We used to make up songs about what we'd been doing. All you needed was somebody with a mouth organ or an accordion and away you went singing songs.

After the war my brother Dennis and I went into semi-professional entertaining as the Binch Brothers. We used to do all knockabout stuff, sing-songs, do some of the Dick Barton shows and so on, and then we started doing comedy miming, and I can remember how this started. We got the gramophone going in the front room and we got Bing Crosby singing, *Lay that Pistol Down*, and I can remember I used to pop my head through the door and pretend to be singing and this gave us the idea. And we started doing an act and we brought this into it.

There was a competition at the Nottingham Empire, and we went for it, doing this one number, *Lay that Pistol Down*, and we won! We were presented with the prize, and we came home with one of the first television sets in the country – this would be about 1953. We took it to our local, which was called the Millers' Arms, and the next day we sold it to somebody and we had the money between us.

*Wally Binch, born 1923*
*Bakersfield*

## Quick on the Cue

My father managed to get work in Hyson Green as the manager of a billiard hall just off the Radford Road, and that had living accommodation with it, so we occupied that until the war came. It was a rough sort of area. The people who played billards, or more snooker really, were the young lads – sixteen, eighteen upwards, who had very little spending money, and they would have to get a frame of snooker done in fifteen minutes. That cost you fourpence. If you went over to twenty minutes it perhaps cost sixpence. So you had to be a sharp shooter.

Saturday nights and Friday nights were a hive of industry, every table occupied. The atmosphere was largely what you'd expect from a largely under thirties clientele. It wasn't what you'd call a classy sort of place, unlike the Mechanics' Institute, which had a very large billiard room with better tables. With our ones, you just to had to make do, because the takings didn't run to buying new cloths or new cushions, and some of them were quite ancient and covered in grease. There was a down-to-earth atmosphere, and they were rough and ready types, but all quite jovial. Of course, a lot of them were called up in the war and never came back.

In those days, if you bought the *Football Post* on a Saturday night, there were several pages that were devoted to the League Tables of the institutes as they were called. There were hundreds of these club institutes, church institutes, and so on, and they all had

Binch brothers' poster, 1950s. Wally is on the left in the picture.

The Adelphi Cinema in Bulwell, pulled down in 1997.

things like snooker teams, billiard teams, chess, cribbage, whist, dominoes – always competitive. And this was quite a major part of the younger male element's entertainment.

*Geoffrey Oldfield, born 1920*
*West Bridford*

## The Silver Screen

The cinema really took off in the 1920s, particularly in the suburbs. Small cinemas were set up. They used to change the programme twice a week, Mondays and Thursdays, usually a big film and then a minor film and a cartoon and a newsreel, and of course they were completely revolutionised in the early thirties by the coming of the talkies. This developed into quite a thriving industry in Nottingham, such

luxury picture palaces as the Odeon and Mount Street cinemas, the Carlton, the Hippodrome, and a very nice one in beautiful architectural style at Bulwell called the Adelphi. And these, of course, were a bit of a dream world. People used to go twice a week, because there were usually good, comfortable seats, a warm atmosphere, and the things on the screen represented a world completely unheard of till then by most people.

*Geoffrey Oldfield, born 1920*
*West Bridgford*

## First-class Entertainment

I wish they hadn't taken the Granada Cinema away in Mansfield. The Granada had loads of atmosphere. It had a Wurlitzer organ that they could bring up out of the stage. We used to get live shows there. We saw Helen Shapiro heading the bill when the Beatles were number two on the list, and it was a brilliant night. We were all there the next day because the Beatles were coming back, so we were all queuing on the steps to get the tickets for the next show.

There was the ticket offices where they sat behind glass, and it was always ladies wearing these spectacles that sort of go up in the air at the side, and a lot of makeup – I think they thought they'd really made it in life, bless their hearts! And then there would be where you could buy confectionery. You could buy popcorn but not anything like in the quantities that we have it now. And there was actually a restaurant over the top of the cinema where if you were really wealthy you could go for tea first. The decoration was very 'scrolly' –

probably imitation gold leaf, with a red carpet going up a central staircase, and it had a smell that was a mixture of coffee and cigarette smoke. It was really good.

As you didn't go to the pictures that often, it was even more special. I went to see everything that Elvis Presley ever made, at least twice if not three times – and he had the nerve to die on my wedding anniversary! We were at the White Post, probably one of the best eating places in the district, and a friend rang, and the head waiter came and told us, and I was mortified. I don't think my husband's ever forgiven me for that. It was costing him an arm and a leg to take me there, and I went all to pieces!

*Sheena Mabbott, born 1947*
*Edwinstowe*

BBC Radio Nottingham's Dennis McCarthy interviewing under the Tri-sail at an outside broadcast of the Nottingham Festival in the Old Market Square, mid-1970s.

Fantasy figures constructed by John Laing.

## Wired for Sound

Our principal entertainment as teenagers was the radio. Having acquired one in 1936 this was still novelty to us, and we used to spend most of our evenings listening to the radio. Things like Bandwagon with Arthur Askey and Stinker Murdoch, and the dance bands, they were a favourite of mine. Every night from about ten o'clock for an hour or so, there were the major dance bands – Joe Loss, Henry Hall, Jack Hilton, Jack Jackson, usually broadcasting direct from London from the main hotels there.

*Geoffrey Oldfield, born 1920*
*West Bridford*

## Small is Beautiful

I'm a modeller. I've always done model soldiers for war games, and Nottinghamshire happens to be the capital of the world for that. The best known magazine for the War Games industry is published right here in Newark. I also dabble in fantasy figures, that sort of thing, and more recently model railroading.

Most grown men have some sort of hobby that takes them away from the reality of modern life! Modelling is something I've been interested in for a long time. There's the appeal of the craftsmanship in building your model, and also there's the love of miniaturisation. People have built models for years. There seems to be a natural tendency to do things in miniaturisation. I think to some extent some men don't grow up, and they want to keep playing with their toys all their lives.

*John Laing, born 1947*
*Newark*

# CHAPTER 7

# Town and country

A walk along the Trent embankment, early 1900s.

## A County of Variety

When it comes to Nottinghamshire, variety is the keynote of its attractions. There's so much there. There's nothing ugly now, particularly now the headstocks have gone from the collieries and most of the soil heaps as well. They did tend to give it a rundown appearance in the west, especially as the pits got older. But what with that and the largely agricultural elements still in the county once you get away from the Nottingham city centre itself, Nottinghamshire is a very beautiful place. It may be only forty miles from north to south, but there's such a variety in a relatively small area.

*Geoffrey Oldfield, born 1920*
*West Bridgford*

## Marking Time

The Council House clock was designed and built by my father. His name is on this clock along with Bill Hickling and Herbert Smith, and the three of them built it together.

Clocks always represent time, and this is something which goes on long after father passed on: His craftsmanship, his vision to develop a clock of this sort is here as a permanent memorial to father. And it is this ongoing memory and action, almost like the beating of a heart, that seems to have a life of its own. And certainly after father died we had some problems with the clock. I could offer no technical reason for the problems, but for about six weeks after he died it was quite temperamental.

The other side of Nottingham's Council House clock face.

Princess Elizabeth and the Duke of Edinburgh in the Old Market Square for Nottingham's Quincentenary, marking the granting of the Borough Charter to the city.

Every time I walk through the Market Square and look up, I think 'father', every time, and automatically check it against my watch. But it was instinctive to us to always keep an eye on this clock. The Council House clock always had priority in our works. Whatever happened, if the Council House clock stopped, somebody was up here from Lenton within ten minutes.

*David Cope, born 1930*
*Wollaton*

## Witness of Events

The civic clock of Nottingham has overseen so many things: the official opening of the Council House by the then Prince of Wales who became Edward VIII. The clock was built and installed in 1928. Then it saw all the problems of the abdication, death of George V, and the Coronation.

I remember coming here in the war, and whole of the roof above the clock was completely covered with sandbags, so that if incendiary bombs came through they would only land on sandbags. And of course there would be

View across Nottingham's Old Market Square, 1929.

## City Atmosphere

I remember on market days in the Market Square when the old Exchange Building was there, and all the stalls. It was a very busy scene – hustle and bustle, and stall-holders shouting their wares and that sort of thing. And at night it was a very special occasion, because they were all lit by naphtha flares, and these used to burn quite brightly with a hissing sound, and it did give them quite a theatrical sort of appearance.

And of course in those days the trams came into the centre of Nottingham, so that was always a feature of the streets. The thing about the trams was that they had to run on the steel tracks in the middle of the road, and when you went to alight on them, they didn't pull up at the kerb, you had to walk across the intervening ten or twelve feet to get on, but one didn't worry about getting knocked down by motor cars, because they were so few and far between.

Horse-drawn vehicles were still quite prominent and that used to give it quite an atmosphere, because you'd see horses at the side of the kerb waiting, delivery cars waiting to be loaded, and they'd all have their nosebags on eating the corn, and chaff blowing everywhere. And of course they were very useful providers of fertiliser. In the summer months the Corporation, if you had a dry period, they had what they called a watering cart. It used to have to go round full of water and spray the road to keep the dust and the horse chaff et cetera down. One of the things some boys used to do was to try and get behind it with no shoes and

a firewatcher up in the clock room every night, all night from 1940 to '45. Then after the war of course, the huge celebrations, VE and VJ Days, the celebrations for the Quincentenary in 1949, the Festival of Britain in '51, and of course, the various sporting celebrities who've come to the Council House. We were in the square the night that the FA cup came back here in 1959; Torvill and Dean came here for their receptions, and of course there were visiting foreign dignitaries who came here. There have been royal visits – the Queen came here in 1977, her Jubilee year. And all of this overseen by our clock, Nottingham's own.

*David Cope, born 1930*
*Wollaton*

socks on, and get their feet wet.

*Geoffrey Oldfield, born 1920*
*West Bridgford*

## Loss of a Landmark

Nottingham has lost a number of buildings which people would regret losing. I can remember the controversial buildings and looking back, I still believe in my period at the city council, though I was nothing to do with it, that the demolition of the Black Boy was the turning point in conservation in Nottingham. It wasn't in a conservation area. I don't think it was a listed building then. The Civic Society and a few local people objected, but there wasn't a huge furore when the planning application came in. But the moment it came down, people went up the wall. Local people said this is a disaster. What on earth is going on? There was an outcry and people said this must never happen again. That hit the councillors and elected members hard, and they started to have a glimmer of awareness of the importance of historic buildings.

The Black Boy is the biggest tragedy in conservation terms. You cannot believe that anybody would have agreed to its demolition. It was an enormous building. It must have been about seven storeys high. It was a richly encrusted building with lots of details – turrets and frills, overhangs and gables. I remember it being very grimy and somewhat rundown, but it was so rich in its architectural quality. It was *the* meeting place. People who didn't know Nottingham that well but had visited would say they'd been to the Black Boy. Certainly the Forces in the war, they all met in the Black Boy. So it was the heart of social activity in the town. And it was where the horses were stabled that came in from the outlying villages. It was a focal point for Nottingham, so it was an absolute disaster to lose it. I felt very sad when it came down. And I think it was adding insult to injury that a building of such desperately poor quality was put in its place. The Littlewoods building has nothing to commend it at all.

But the Black Boy did not go in vain. Now Nottingham's got twenty-five conservation areas, probably more than any other city of its size, and it's also got a huge number of listed buildings.

*Jim Taylor, born 1948*
*Nottingham*

Demolition of the Black Boy Hotel, Nottingham, 1963.

## Living Above One's Station?

I've lived in West Bridgford almost forty years. It is suburbia, but it's virtually on the edge of the countryside. I live on Musters Road and if I go outside of the front gate and look up the road, I can see open country at the top, the woods and the fields. I do appreciate living close to a town as well, for all the many amenities there.

It's a very pleasant suburb. It's got its own character. The Bridgford people are a very proud, independent race, particularly those who've lived here all their lives and there are a lot who have, and whose parents lived here before them.

The city of Nottingham, since 1912, has had its eyes on West Bridgford and would like to have taken it over as part of the city. When it started to build up as a town about the 1880s, it soon acquired the name of Bread and Lard Island, because it was established as a fairly middle-class suburb. There were covenants on the type of houses that had to be built. They were to be of a far superior standard, for instance to the industrial side in The Meadows. And this led to this unfortunate sobriquet, which rather reflected the idea of the citizens of Nottingham, that if you lived in West Bridgford you were living above your status – you were in a nice house, but you had to live on lard instead of butter on your bread.

*Geoffrey Oldfield, born 1920*
*West Bridgford*

## The Role of the Manor

People had to go out of Epperstone in time because there wasn't so much work in the village with the Manor closing. There wasn't the staff employed

Aerial view of Epperstone village, *c.* 1946.

Eileen, wife of Stanley Bourne, owner of Epperstone Manor, 1933.

as there had been.

The Manor was very important. During the war Mrs Bourne closed it and it was used as a Red Cross nursing and convalescent home. Quite a few girls married the soldiers or sailors that came there.

The Manor was a community within a community. After the war, Mr Bourne died and Mrs Bourne decided to sell up. Eventually it was bought as the police headquarters, but now they've moved to Sherwood Lodge and it's used as a training centre.

The coming of the police hasn't changed the village much, because they don't take all that big an interest in it. They don't give any Christmas parties or anything for the old age pensioners or anything like that. The Manor gave Christmas parties. Mrs Bourne had three boys and a girl, and they always used to do a pantomime at Christmas and she always gave presents. Mr Bourne had a factory and they had several cars and horses and all that kind of thing. They seemed to be the benefactors of the village. If there was anything wanted, they always approached her. Mostly they were very good – she always gave generously, and they were a big help to the village. There was somebody 'in charge', if you know what I mean. There was somebody you could turn to if you were really stuck. That's gone now. There's no-one in the village to turn to in that way now.

*Florrie Radley, born 1917*
*Epperstone*

93

## A Gentle Pace of Life

I was born in Milton. There are very few of the old families left. In my young days there were four farms. Now there aren't any. Most of the people used to live and work in the village. Nowadays they live here and work somewhere else

Milton is a very small village. It's actually a hamlet. In the early days there were no more than twenty houses. There's a road that branched off Main Street through an avenue of trees, where the Duke of Newcastle built the mausoleum, and the vicarage is there, but there's no parson there now. The Revd Crookenden was there when I was a lad. He went all round the village. It didn't matter whether you were Methodist or Church of England, he visited and had a cup of tea. He lived at the vicarage and employed servants. Now it's been changed into four dwellings.

Life was lived at a more sedate pace in my early days. Farming was totally different. You seemed to have time to talk to your neighbours. I started ploughing with horses, and you could get to the end of the field and have a chat to your neighbour over the hedge. Now they're on tractors they just don't seem to have the time. My mother would come across two fields at tea-time with a great big basket of food and a gallon tin of tea, and we'd have time to sit amongst the sheaves and enjoy it. That day's gone.

*Derek Footit, born 1925*
*Milton*

Edwinstowe High Street, early 1960s.

## A Change of Focus

I've lived in Edwinstowe for thirty-two years. It's changed tremendously. Edwinstowe was very much a mining community, though with the mine being out of the village it still retained a lot of its history. It was quite a self-contained village.

But as the mining dwindled, then tourism seemed to take over, and I think this is brilliant, because it's a tragedy to see a place die, and it means that we've just had a change of industry. We've not had something stop, it's just moved on to a new way of living. Some people get a bit uptight about the amount of visitors we have, but it's keeping the place healthy.

*Sheena Mabbott, born 1947*
*Edwinstowe*

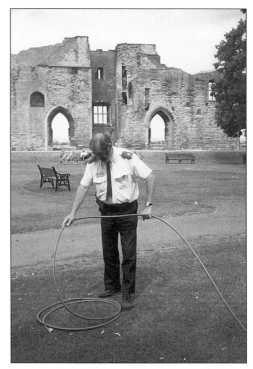

John Laing on duty at Newark Castle, 1999.

## Historic Appeal

I've been living in Newark for eleven years. We came over from Canada. We'd visited Newark previously, and we liked the idea of moving to this town. There were some gorgeous pubs, a bridge over the river, great big castle, old brick buildings, terraced houses, a medieval restaurant and a big market square. It was really quite enchanting, and it was a high priority to look for a place to live here.

We found a three-storey town house with very little front garden and big rear garden. It was just the kind of place I'd always envisaged myself living in. I am very much a 'townie' and I like the shape of my house. It goes 'up' rather than 'out,' if you know what I mean.

What I like about Newark is the history of the town. My present job is guiding people around the castle and various other historical sites in Newark. I'm very interested in history in all its forms. I get endless entertainment working out why the streets are like they are and trying to analyse the form of the town, and talking about it to anyone who'll listen. And I like the pubs.

*John Laing, born 1947*
*Newark*

## Class Divide

Mansfield was a big change from London when I first came. There was so much poverty in the '30s – a lot of unemployment and low wages. A lot of the town was really quite poor. There were a lot of narrow, rather slummy streets in the centre, in places like Westgate and so on. There were lots of little courts running off it with houses in them. They were gradually being got rid of. The council put up the Ravensdale Estate just before I came, and that was to house the people from these courts, but there were a lot of what you would call mean streets. You can see the pattern a bit now, if you go along the Chesterfield Road to Pleasley – the Portland Road, the part running into Pleasley, all those houses with flat fronts straight onto the road. Like most towns, where you've got this poor housing they've been tarted up nowadays, and bathrooms put in where there weren't any and so on, but you can imagine, if you look at it now what it would have been like then. On a Sunday morning you'd see ladies sitting on the step with their hair in curlers. A lot of those houses have been pulled down and rebuilt or refurbished, but there are bits here and there still.

Then of course these big estates have come about, Ladybrook, for instance. I was in digs when I first came, just off Ladybrook, and I used to walk across the fields on a Sunday morning. Now it's all the built-up estate. And all along Oak Tree Lane, there's that huge estate. So it's expanded enormously.

There was a sort of snobby section of Mansfield. With all the miners and the

Leckenby's on Leeming Street in Mansfield, early 1970s. The shop ceased trading in 1973. (From Nottingham City Council: Leisure and Community Services: Angel Row Library, and by permission of the Mansfield Chad)

Construction of the Four Seasons Shopping Centre, Mansfield, 1973. (From Nottingham City Council: Leisure and Community Services: Angel Row Library, and by permission of the Mansfield Chad)

factory girls and so on, they were the underclass (a factory girl got seven and six a week, which is equivalent to fifteen pounds a week, now. Can you imagine that?), so of course the people who owned the factories and the bigger shops and so on, they constituted a superior group of people down Alexandra Avenue and so on, and had little maids. They used to meet at the Borough Club and the Hanley Arcade. The better-off people shopped at Leckenby's and the ordinary people at the Co-op.

We're more democratic now. Streets where you never saw a car now have cars down both sides of the road.

*Bill Simpson, born 1908*
*Mansfield*

## A Mansfield Morning

I have fond memories of Mansfield, because I spent all the latter part of my school life there, and I actually worked in Mansfield for a year as well, before Mansfield 'lost its middle'. When I was at school, Mansfield appeared to be safe, as probably many other places were then. The streets and the shops had character; people owned them, and you knew who owned them. There wasn't a name over the door that you could see in the next town up the road.

Linney's was a family business; John Manners was the school outfitters; there was Jolly's the jewellers, it was a family business; there was tobacconist at the bottom of the street where I worked which was another family business. And in the morning, when I went to work, it was like the town was coming to life. Of course with wheelie bins we don't get the clatter now, but there used to be this sort of friendly clatter of the bins, and people were whistling while they went about their work, and the market on market days was being set up. And although you were working in a town, people shouted 'Morning,' because you did that every morning.

There was lots of alleyways as well in Mansfield which have all gone, all been knocked down and new buildings have gone up, and we've lost the little streets. There used to be at the back of Clumber Street a walkway that went from Woodhouse Road right along the back of Clumber Street. And there was all these wonderful sand cottages. Now they've all gone in the name of a ring road.

*Sheena Mabbott, born1947*
*Edwinstowe*

## Getting Around

I remember when the trams was running from Mansfield, up Nottingham Road, and taking people from to Pleasley and Sutton and all over. There was not a car on the road. And there was lady drivers, 'cos the men was in the First World War.

We used to have to get to Mansfield and back by tram, or we had to walk it. When we walked from Pleasley to Mansfield, we'd only see one house and that was the Toll Bar on the Chesterfield Road.

I think Mansfield's improved, but when it was first all done nobody could find their way to get in when they made the ring road. Every time our lads used

to come they used to carry on alarming, 'cos they used to get lost.

*Daisy Mee, born 1908*
*Mansfield*

## Car Culture

I think the biggest change in motoring has been the concept of the modern car. There are three ages of motoring: leisure, pleasure and necessity. Up to the outbreak of World War One, it was leisure. The leisured class was the only one with cars – the hunting, shooting, fishing people. Ordinary advertising between the wars nearly always showed the car at the golf club or tennis club or something like that. It wasn't used like it is today, mid-week. The car was mainly used at the weekend and for pleasure activities. But after the war it became a tool, what with out-of-town shopping, supermarkets, and people using cars for work.

*David Cope, born 1930*
*Wollaton*

## Changing Connections

We had a good bus service in Epperstone years ago, which dropped off quite a lot because there wasn't the people using the buses. Most people have cars now, so they don't rely on the buses as they did.

*Florrie Radley, born 1917*
*Epperstone*

## Road Revolution

I started with Nottingham City Council in 1971 as a junior planning assistant, and ended my work as director of development in 1998. It was a period of big change.

When I started most of the city was covered by a development plan which had been created in 1952. This was the blueprint that we were starting to try and implement in the early 1970s. After the war there was this idea that more and more people would have cars, and there was a proposal for a primary highway plan for Nottingham, based on predictions of huge growth in car ownership in the city. Nottingham was going to be criss-crossed by urban motorways – going through areas like the Arboretum, Burns Street, St Ann's, and Sneinton, with a huge motorway interchange at the junction of

Mansfield Road and Huntingdon Street. One of the real crackers was Park Way! This was to be an urban motorway through The Park and round the castle. It was going to be on stilts, go across The Meadows, and go into a tunnel coming out at Canning Circus. It's hard to believe that this was even in people's minds less than thirty years ago.

The revolution was in 1972. The first leg of the urban system was being put through a public enquiry, and the Civic Society and some well-known local people were objecting to the building of this urban motorway. And there was a growing concern about the blighting effect of these road schemes on the city, and that quality of the environment would go right down.

Frank Higgins was a councillor who led the revolution in transportation in Nottingham in the '70s, and he and his colleagues said we should have a public

Placing girders on the motorway bridge over the A610 in Nuthall, 1966.

transport-based plan rather than a road-based plan, and now that's what's being said in the '90s. In some ways he was ahead of his time. Certainly the transportation plan for Nottingham was being looked at from across the world, because Nottingham was one of the first authorities to abandon its major road schemes, which were all abandoned overnight in one fell swoop – in one committee.

*Jim Taylor, born 1948*
*Nottingham*

## Just a Curiosity

The motorway came to Nuthall in 1966. When you contrast what people's reaction would be nowadays to what it was then, it's astonishing really, because nowadays if it was proposed to build a motorway through Nuthall, with a great big bridge straight over the main road in the middle of the village, there would be absolute uproar. There'd be people lying down in front of the

bulldozers, wouldn't there? But there just was nothing. And we didn't bother about it. We were just curious more than anything. We used to go up there for a stroll with a camera.

*Tom Leafe, born 1927*
*Nuthall*

## Split Village

I don't think we realised the motorway was going to go right through the middle of the village, and worse than that, there would be a roundabout which would completely divide the village into two and cause the horrendous traffic that there is now.

When the motorway first opened here it was chaos, because all the traffic came off at Nuthall and went down towards the Nottingham Ring Road. For six months the motorway ended at Nuthall until the next section was built, so that was terribly busy, but we thought then that it wouldn't last. And then of course the bridge was built, literally over

Tom Leafe stands on the M1 the day before it opened in August 1966.

Arthur Wybrew's father at Pinxton, 1956.

the village, and the next section was built, so all the traffic roared over the bridge.

The motorway does a great big curve in order to come through Nuthall. If it hadn't been for Stanton Iron works, the road would have been straight. But now Stanton Iron Works is derelict. Nuthall is the only village that the motorway actually goes through.

*Margaret Leafe, born 1924*
*Nuthall*

## Junction Impact

Building the motorway through the village was a dreadful thing to do, but it's building the junction that created the major impact, because that meant that the network of roads was built all around us, and then later on all the factories and office blocks. Developers seem to feel they must build near a motorway junction. The building of the roads which feed the motorway has been the biggest change since we moved into the village in 1957.

*Tom Leafe, born 1927*
*Nuthall*

## Running out of Steam

My father was an engine driver. The railways were the only real public form of transport in those days, and there was a fascination about a steam train that the electric engines and the diesels have never achieved. They were almost alive. You could see them straining, but they eventually did it, sort of thing. With modern diesels or electric they either do it, or they stop dead and don't move at all!

Nottingham Victoria Station, *c*. 1930. The station closed in 1967.

But I saw the railways deteriorate over the years. They just crumbled away. Until the end of the war there was a marvellous spirit among railway men, but then it gradually eroded. Nationalisation was going to do great things for the railway, but it carried on just the same as before, except that nobody was prepared to spend any money on it. And it's been the same all the way through. Reorganisation after reorganisation destroyed the camaraderie among the people themselves.

It wasn't really until Beeching swung his axe that we began to realise what a disaster it was for the railway. What hurt so much was that as soon as the railways were closed, in Nottingham, through The Meadows, the first thing they did was to take the viaducts and bridges down, just to make sure that nobody would bring them back again. Or at least that's the way it seemed. And they've been crumbling away ever since.

There was a lot of manipulation with it. The Great Central Line from Nottingham Vic up to Marylebone was one of the best lines there were. The trains were on time, but when they decided they wanted to close it, they'd alter the trains: The most popular trains, they'd put them an hour later or an hour earlier, and then there wouldn't be any between two and five at night. They just drove the traffic away. And that line had been designed to go to the Channel Tunnel – they were talking about the Channel Tunnel back in the 1880s. It was made to a continental gauge, and all the bridges were that much wider than they would have been to a British standard.

*Arthur Wybrew, born 1927*
*Tollerton*

# CHAPTER 8

# Good times, hard times

George V visits the Shell-filling factory in Chilwell, 1916.

*July 16th 1918*

TELEGRAMS BLIDWORTH.

BLIDWORTH DALE,
*nr.* NOTTINGHAM.

Dear Brooks

I dont know if you are well enough yet to receive a letter, but I wanted to write & tell you how <u>very</u> sorry I was to hear of your suffering & injuries, I do trust you are going on well & improving gradually & have not much pain, & will be much better soon – Im afraid I could not yet walk as far as the General Hospital or I should like to see you, but I am thinking of & praying for you. May God be very near & very real to you in this time of inaction.

Your true friend
E. M. Smith

A letter to Anne Benson's injured father, from a fellow injured police officer.

## Explosion of Grief

In 1916, my father went to work at the Ordnance Depot at Chilwell, because his eldest brother had gone down to take charge of the timber there. And my father cut all the coffin wood for those killed in the Chilwell Explosion.

It was on a Tuesday evening, and my father and my uncle had come home off the train to Ilkeston, and my mother sent me out to fetch a loaf. So I walked down the avenue and saw all this crowd coming out of the middle of Ilkeston station. They were all running out. Well, those who did the shell-filling went yellow – their hands, face, hair and clothes, that was the shell-filling that did

that, and I thought, whatever is all this crowd coming out of the town station for? So I got a loaf and hurried back, and I said to my father, 'There's been something going off at Chilwell – a whole lot of them running out of the station, and some of them were crying!'

So my father finished his dinner and went up to my uncle's to tell him, and they decided to go to see what they could do. And when they got down to Chilwell, my father found on his workbench a skull with long, yellow hair.

*Gladys Dawson, born 1903*
*Farnsfield*

## Never the Same Again

Chilwell was a shell-filling factory during World War One, and nobody knows quite what happened, but on the 1 July 1918, the whole factory just blew up. There were well over 100 people killed, and my father was one of the police officers on duty at the gate, of course for security reasons. And he was very badly injured. A police officer who was nearer to the shell-filling factory was actually killed, and two more policemen who were also on duty there, were badly injured.

But my father was terribly injured – a double fracture of legs, a fractured hand and fractured skull, and he spent the rest of his days having to have a built-up shoe because one leg was permanently an inch and a half shorter than the other. But the police were wonderful. Because he'd been injured on duty, they always paid for his shoes. A wicked price for shoes in those days was fifteen shillings. I was told off very severely, because I'd bought a pair of very good walking shoes – brogues – and paid fifteen shillings. And my father's surgical shoes used to cost the equivalent of seven pounds fifty a time, and he was allowed two pairs per year, so the police were very very good.

*Anne Benson, born 1920*
*Mapperley Plains*

## Nowhere Else To Go

People were pushed into Southwell Union Workhouse because people couldn't afford to keep them. It used to be families in those days. There used to be a lot of men and a lot of families lived in tied cottages, and then if the man did anything wrong and he got the sack, out the cottage they had to come. And there was one family, Hawkins, and he could stay with his parents, but the family had to come into the workhouse. And they was in a long, long time, until he got another job, and got a cottage. That was it with the gentry in those days. They got the people in and if they just didn't behave themselves, out they had to come.

People felt terrible when they realised they had to go into the workhouse. I know Mrs Hawkins did. She'd got the four children there, and her husband used to come and visit her on Sundays,

Inmates at The Workhouse, Southwell, *c.* 1927. (From the Workhouse, Southwell, by kind permission of the National Trust)

Golden Wedding greetings telegram, 1936.

but I know she used to feel awful. They had to work hard and they got very little food.

*Ada Pointin, born 1908*
*Clifton*

## To Mourn or Celebrate?

Nobody liked to see a telegram boy, because they always used to relate it to bad news, and there was very, very few bad ones. Mostly somebody was going to be late on a train or they'd cancelled a visit, or this sort of thing, but there's one particular one I had to deliver that sticks out, one black telegram. This lady's son was in the Army and he'd been knocked over by an Army lorry and killed. And when you think that you're only sixteen, you would think the police or somebody from the Army would knock on the door, but we got this telegram, and it was someone down St Ann's Well Road and down this little terrace street. And the people are stood on their doorsteps, chatting across the street as the neighbours used to do then, and you pull in on your motorbike, and of course all the conversation stops and you knock at this door. And the lady opened the door smiling, and you just feel absolutely gutted because you know what you've got in that envelope, and she said, 'Hello, my duck,' you know, as they did. I passed her the telegram and just waited, and she just looked at me, and I'll never forget that look, obviously not blaming me, but she just went out in the street screaming, and rolled in the road. And all the neighbours came out and they said, 'What's the matter?' and I just said, 'She's had some terrible news, you know,' and I left it to them really. You come away and those days aren't very good at all, but it was just part of being a telegram boy.

But it had its happy side as well. Easter Saturday was *the* day of the year. Everybody who was getting married tried to get married on Easter Saturday, because if you did it was the last day of the tax year and you used to get a tax refund for the whole year.

We started work at seven o'clock in the morning. Everybody was on the full day, so you worked from 7 o'clock till 8 o'clock at night. All the bikes were out. So off you went straight out on the road, 'cos overnight there was quite a lot arrived. Your first delivery was half past seven in the morning, and you'd take two or three telegrams for this particular bride or whatever, and the father would say, 'Come in, lad, have a drink!' Well, at that age you don't refuse anything. And invariably you would go in and perhaps have a quick sherry or something like that, but the drink driving thing wasn't in at all then. And then at the next house he'd say, 'Come in and have a drink or do you want a cake or something?' And you did. Can you imagine what we were like at eight o' clock at night when the receptions had really got going? In the afternoon and in the evening especially you'd go into a church hall and everybody would be saying, 'Oh, it's some more telegrams! Help yourself to the buffet!' and this

sort of thing. But nobody ever fell off their bike and nobody ever hurt anybody, but I dread to think what the breathalyser would have read on today's standards!

*Dave Birkett, born 1938*
*Gedling*

## Cash Crisis

I started work after I left school, aged fourteen, in 1927, as a pawnshop assistant in Brailsford's Nottingham Road shop in Ilkeston. I think the wage was about fifteen shillin' a week. Monday morning we had to start work at half past seven because that were the

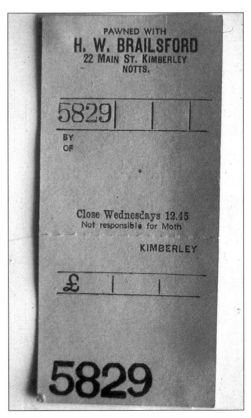

Pawnbroker ticket from Brailsford's, c. 1935.

Brailsford's the pawnbroker's in Ilkeston, *c.* 1935.

busiest day. Folks wanted their money. There were usually a queue outside the shop.

Pawnbroking charges was a ha'penny on every two shillings per calendar month and the article was in pawn for a year and seven days. Then it was sold by the pawnbroker. If the article was over two pound they had to have a special contract, in which case it was wrote out on a separate sheet, and the pawnbroker couldn't sell that object when it was out of date, he had to go to auction. And if the owner of that article came after it was sold, he could claim that extra money, after the pawnbroker had stopped his charges for interest. They were special contracts, but you didn't get many of them, 'cos in them days, with the poverty, a lot of people weren't getting even two pound a week wages.

We used to get all sorts of things in pawn. Most were clothing, but they used to bring shoes, and they had a special arrangement when they used to bring their husband's best suit. They used to wrap it in a brown paper parcel and put it in a drawer, and that was a penny extra. One woman used to always come in on Monday morning with a trumpet, 'cos her husband was in t' Salvation Army and she used to regularly fetch it out on Friday night ready for t' weekend.

People used the pawnshop because they were hard up. The majority of people, they got their wages on Friday or Saturday, and they'd spent it by Sunday night, usually on beer and baccy, and they'd got absolutely penniless on Monday morning and they'd pawn anything to get through. They used to get about four and threepence on a new pair of shoes – if they'd been worn, about two and threepence. People used to bring gold rings in or sovereigns in them days. You used to weigh 'em on scales, to get the exact weight.

You'd got a regular gang of people coming, and they would bring you stuff for other people. And they used to charge the other people 'cos the other people were too ashamed to come. Where we were at Ilkeston, we were just topside of Catholic church, and this Irish woman, she were one o't best customers. And the Roman Catholic priest, he came and fetched all the stuff she'd got in pawn out, and paid for it to try to get her on t' straight, but she were back again next Monday. They couldn't handle money at the weekend. They had to spend. You had the same clientele every Monday; queues of 'em.

*Arthur Plumb, born 1913*
*Kimberley*

## Amateur Cobbler

As a child I lived in Lenton – on Cycle Road, and it was quite a pleasant road to live on.

It was a two-up, two-down terraced house. But you had an attic as well, and me and my brother, we slept up in the attic. In wintertime I think we were colder inside than out. Ice used to form on the fanlight on the inside, and when you picked your socks up in the morning, they were stiff. And when you went to bed at night, we'd got one hot water bottle, a stone hot water bottle, and it was a squabble who had the hot water bottle, and then we'd compromise; one of you'd finish up with dad's Army greatcoat on the bed to keep you warm, and one of you had the hot water bottle. But after a time you'd swap the hot water bottle when the bed had

got a bit warmer. It were pretty grim, looking back.

With your fire, you only heated one room. You heated the main living room, and as kids you'd get red leg. All the fronts of your legs were all burnt from sitting in front of the fire, and yet your back was frozen, your back was shivering through the draughts coming up the cellar and running through the house.

But my family were quite well off comparatively. My dad had got a car and we'd got a caravan at Inglemells. But other people in the Willoughby Street area, for instance, and Radford, all down there it was real poverty. Everybody wore boots. And I didn't get a pair of shoes till I was twelve either. Boots were very robust, very strong, and you used to have the Blakeys in them. But my dad, he went one better. He used to cut up cycle tyres and he'd nail

Tough conditions at Barkergate in Nottingham, early 1900s.

A 1950 ration book.

them on your boots, so when I brought the kids home with me from school, my school friends, my dad would say, 'Get them boots off, you've got all 'oles in the bottom of them boots,' to the kids, me friends, like. And he'd take their boots down the cellar, and he'd repair their boots for 'em, and he'd put this rubber in the boots and give 'em a retread, put a rubber tyre on for 'em!

It's hard to believe that fifty years ago there was so much poverty. We talk about poverty today, but there was no comparison. People today, they get all sorts of handouts and accommodation. They're far better looked after generally now than they were then.

*Christopher Blackamore, born 1943*
*Cotgrave*

## You've Never Had It So Good

Most of the big Nottingham companies were very important in employment, and we were very fortunate. In 1958 you could pick and choose. It was a great time to be leaving school. Everything was happening. We'd had all the austerity of the post-war years and rationing, and it was great to be able to go out to work and earn some money, and spend it on all the things that you could do, like the Palais and Locarno, where they had a disc jockey on playing records. The music was loud and fast – Bill Haley and the Comets, and Elvis Presley. Everything was all so exciting in the late '50s. It was a great atmosphere, and you could pick and choose your job, of course. You went in one job, you didn't like it, you went to another one the following week. As Harold MacMillan said in '59, 'you've never had it so good', and what he was referring to was full employment, and that was the first time everybody really had full employment, so it was great to be at work. Working at Players, I earned three pound five and tenpence a week. I paid a shilling income tax, and four and eleven National Insurance. Your friends who'd gone into apprenticeships were earning around two pound, so I was quite well-off at three pound five and tenpence.

*Christopher Blackamore, born 1943*
*Cotgrave*

## Greatest Joy

My happiest day was the joy when my eldest son Kevin was born, and knowing he was all right, because unfortunately when my wife had Kevin there was one poor dear in the Highbury Hospital who'd suffered through this thalidomide business and the child was born with no arms. And it made you eternally grateful to look at your own child and think, thank goodness the child's all right.

*Bert Stringer, born 1924*
*Sutton-in-Ashfield*

## Unexpected Sadness

Stillbirth is the greatest trauma in being a midwife, because it's exactly the opposite end of the scale. The majority of the work is one of joy and happiness, and then you've got the exact opposite with a dead or an abnormal baby. It's very, very sad. It makes you feel very sorrowful. When I delivered a baby that wasn't alive many years ago, it was in an incubator in the labour ward and the father insisted upon seeing it, and so I showed him. And I stood there with him and he burst into tears and so did I, and I felt abnormal for showing that emotion, because it was not encouraged. It is today and it's right that the midwife who's cared for that mother shows her feelings, unless she judges that the situation would be embarrassing for the mother. But many mothers appreciate a few tears from the midwife, and also today many of the midwives go to the funerals of these babies with the parents, because they've got to know them personally during a very intimate time in their lives. I think it probably helps the midwife as well as the mother to be present at the funeral of these babies.

*Iris Cooper, born 1941*
*Woodthorpe*

A little girl called Laura, in The Meadows, Nottingham, *c.* 1908. She died in the 1918 influenza epidemic in Bulwell.

## Adventurous Eating

I've run the Rhinegold Restaurant in Nottingham for the last eighteen years. I came to England from Spain nearly forty years ago. We're one of the oldest established restaurants in Nottingham.

British food now is excellent. Even here in Nottingham you can try any type of food that you like. The only problem is that people can't relax. They have no time. In the early '80s, there was a little bit of a 'flash of cash' and at lunchtime it was a huge, big entertainment – we could serve good wines and port on the table, and people could drink brandies with coffee and would spend the whole afternoon in the restaurant. And they'd put the bills onto the business, which is now not allowed. Now things have changed. People relax in the evenings, but not at lunch. They have too much pressure.

People know a lot about food and wines these days. I put it down to television and foreign holidays. And eating habits have changed. If you put in here any different type of food or cooking, people will try it. Twenty-five years ago they wouldn't. Now people like to eat out in the evening two or three times a week, and especially at the weekends, and they change restaurants perhaps every time, so you perhaps see them every five to ten weeks. There's a tremendous amount of people eating out every day now.

Alan Trease of Weavers Wine Merchants (on the left), at the launch of Weavers' 'Robin Hood Mead', 1991.

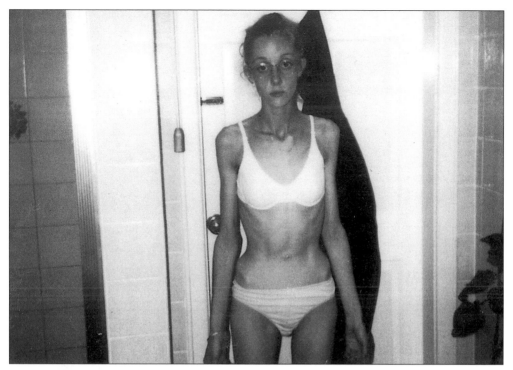

Rebecca Osborn, weighing just over four and a half stone, summer 1997.

In food you can do two things. Either you eat to live, or sometimes you live to eat, which is different altogether. I like to eat to live every day, but occasionally I like to change myself and live to have something excellent to eat, and it gives me great pleasure. And I like to go to all different types of restaurants.

*Roderigo Beltran, born 1937*
*Nottingham*

## Never Thin Enough

I don't really know where it started. When I was fourteen I had a throat infection and I lost a bit of weight, which felt good, and it just spiralled on and on from there. It was just a way of coping with things. Nothing else mattered as long as I was concentrating on my food.

I denied being anorexic for quite a while. I think I knew I was ill, but sometimes I accepted it and sometimes I didn't. I knew it was going too far. I knew I couldn't stop.

I used to wash apples, and wrap 'em up in clingfilm and put 'em in bags away from everybody else's food 'cos I thought fat might get onto 'em, and I wouldn't clean my teeth 'cos I thought there was calories and fat in toothpaste. I wouldn't lick stamps. I wouldn't touch other people's food. I used to cook and cook and cook. I used to cook loads and make everybody else big cream cakes and things that I'd cooked, but I wouldn't touch 'em. I used to be able to sit at a table and get my whole meal into my shoes or pockets and things without people knowing, and my family would find it shoved all over the house.

It got to the stage where my hair was falling out and my teeth were rotting. I felt dizzy. My skin was flaking. Everything was just a mess, but by then I didn't care. I wanted to look as bad on the outside as I felt on the inside. It was horrible. I wouldn't put cream on my face, 'cos I thought it would soak into my skin and make me fat.

You see all these pretty and what you presume are perfect people in these magazines and all of them are thin, so I thought if I was thin, everything would be okay.

I knew that my bones were sticking out, but I still thought I was huge. I just looked in the mirror and I absolutely hated what I saw. There wasn't anything that I liked about myself.

*Rebecca Osborn, born 1982*
*Retford*

Rebecca Osborn, September 1998.

## Appetite for Life

I loved food before I was ill, especially chocolate and sweet cakes and things like that. I still haven't been brave enough to eat them again yet. Now I love bread and all sorts of food. I still eat low-fat stuff, but I'm getting better and I do try other things. I love food now. I wouldn't give it up again. I don't eat chocolate or cheese or chips. My mum still says I don't eat normally and I suppose I don't, but it scares me sometimes, because if I get tub of ice-cream or a cake, I eat the whole thing, rather than just have a portion of it. I don't know why I do it, but I can't stop till it's all gone, which isn't normal.

I look at myself sometimes and think I need to lose weight here or tone up there, but I have to pull myself round, because I'm scared of dieting and it all going downhill again. I haven't been on scales for seven months – I used to weigh myself twenty times a day. I don't need to know how much I weigh now, and I'm never getting on a pair of scales ever again in my life. I hate them.

I don't want to worry about what I eat. I've still got to work on eating chocolate. But I'm getting there. I'm living life as fully as I can now, because I so nearly lost it. I wouldn't wish anorexia on anyone. I've got my life back. Thin isn't perfect. It's what you think about yourself, not the way everybody else sees you that's important.

*Rebecca Osborn, born 1982*
*Retford*

# CHAPTER 9

# Community

VJ Day street party at Godfrey Street in Nottingham.

## A Sense of Community

I've lived in Arnold all my life, and I've never left it apart from on holidays. I wouldn't leave it. I've always loved Arnold, and I've got fond memories. Looking back, there was real sense of community. It was a different world entirely.

Every birthday, it didn't matter whose birthday it was, there was a street party. With it being rows of houses, communal, all of them as lived close to wherever it was the birthday came to the party. The parents, they'd be there and the kids would have the party and then they'd all have a turn to do. You had to do something. Everybody joined in with sing-songs, and somebody would do a clog dance or something out in the yard. Of course there were barrels of ale down the cellar, you know. It was ever so cheap to buy a barrel of ale. And as you got bigger you got the job of fetching the ale up in big jugs. The main things were weddings, wedding anniversaries and birthdays. And your twenty-first birthday party, the whole street was in that! That was looked on as a stage of life.

Everybody knew everybody else, and everybody knew everybody's business. Anything that happened, the whole street would know about it. If somebody had got done for something, they'd see he were having a hard time and they'd have a collection for him. If he got fined two pound, it were a fortune – it were a week's wages. You got less than two pound at the pit. So they'd have whip round, so as the kids didn't go short.

The community life was really good. There was people as weren't in it. They weren't in the community, didn't want to be in it, and they worked against it – there were some right villains. And some of them as were well-off and were a bit 'how d'ye do' didn't belong, because they thought they were a bit above it. It depended whether they'd got big families or not. If they'd got four or five children, yes, they were in it. If they'd only got one who was going to go to 'high school' or 'be a doctor' or whatever, and they were a bit aloof, they were out of it. But it didn't do them any good.

*Jim Turton, born 1909*
*Arnold*

## Keeping Law and Order

There was nothing official about the Elders. It was just a group of men that looked after Arnold. The people picked 'em out. My father, he was one. They were people of consequence in the community, and they used to meet in the little snug in the Cross Keys every Friday night and Sunday morning. And people used to go with their complaints. P'raps somebody had been knocking kids about or something like that, you see, and they used to say, 'Well, he wants teaching a lesson, and the only lesson he'll understand is violence.' Well, there was a lot of street fighters in Arnold. They were as hard as iron. And they'd p'raps give 'em a couple of shillin' and say, 'Now, teach this man a lesson.'

Round where I lived in Gedling Road, Worral Street was the area. If there was anyone round there, they used to drag 'em onto Worral Street and give 'em a right beating, the street fighters.

116

The Cross Keys pub in Arnold, *c.* 1910. (From Nottingham City Council: Leisure and Community Services: Angel Row Library)

And that's where they used to teach 'em a lesson.

We watched them and we all used to cheer. He only got it because he deserved it. He'd perhaps been hitting children or something like that, or hitting his wife. And sometimes it'd be the women, and they'd get on one there, and they used to knock 'em about a bit, knock another woman about a bit. It's true.

The police kept out of it. They used to stand on the pavement and watch and then they'd say, 'Come on, I think he's had enough now.' The police never interfered, but if the street fighters was giving one a right good beating, they'd p'raps take him somewhere and wash him – the man that had done it! But the Elders only dealt with domestic affairs. The police dealt with everything else.

It had started all before my time, and for long as I can remember when I was little. It went on after the war, till about 1920 or '22. Arnold was only a village then, and they had their own rules, and if anybody broke them they was in trouble. The police had an easy job!

*Jim Turton, born 1909*
*Arnold*

## Community Building

We were among the first to move onto the Clifton Estate when it was built just after the war. I ran a Cub pack and my husband ran the Scout troup belonging to St Francis' church, even though we hadn't got a church building. We were meeting in a hut that Wimpeys the builders had actually given to St Francis', to be used as a church until such time as we had one.

117

A young winner for the Best Bird in the Nottingham Bird Show, 1928. The bird was the rare Cinnamon Blackbird, and the prize was a side of bacon.

We were quite a big community belonging to St Francis' and we all decided that we did want a building. We had a very forward-looking priest, the Revd Verney – he eventually became a bishop. We found out that amongst our church community there were people who were builders, people who were plasterers and plumbers, and if you couldn't do any of those skilled things, at least you could dig. So we decided to build our church for ourselves. And we did. I'm very proud to say that there's one complete drain that my husband and I dug.

But we did struggle and work hard. And the people who perhaps couldn't work physically were working in other ways. They were organising bazaars and selling cakes, or having whist drives, to raise money to help to build the church. It was hard work but it was so rewarding. You really felt that you were doing something so worthwhile. And of course you had all the joy of the companionship while you were working. It really was wonderful. And that was how the feeling of the Clifton estate was at that time.

*Mavis Harrison, born 1928*
*Clifton*

## Mining Melting-pot

We live on Bellamy Road Estate in Mansfield. It was very cosmopolitan when we first came. People came from Scotland, Yorkshire, Durham, Northumberland, Wales, Ireland, Lancashire, you name it, they lived here. Everybody who lived here worked for British Coal. So it was one big family – one big happy family. Today, out of the seventy-five properties up this top end of Bellamy Road (Barton Court, Bramcote Court and Bradmore Court), all of the seventy-five households, there's only seventeen of the original people left.

*Maureen Wilkinson, born 1933*
*Mansfield*

## Common Ground

Everybody round here that came at that time were miners and their wives and families. That made it more interesting, 'cos we were all in the same boat. They built Bellamy Road Estate for miners that was being transferred from other parts of the country. And it's amazing how we all got on. You were all on the same level. You could talk to your next-door neighbour and the men used to chat pits all the time. We'd all come together, all strangers to each other, apart from one or two. We just all became friends and it was absolutely brilliant.

When we first moved here, there was nothing. The estate was built on fields. And so there wasn't even a shop, and we didn't even know how to get to Mansfield to shop. It was that sort of place. We didn't know what we were coming to. There wasn't even any roads, so of course we just all ploughed in together, and that's what made it better. Things were serious, but we were happy.

*Mary McGarrigle, born 1933*
*Mansfield*

## Taking a Stand

We had to take the children up to Southwell Road to get the bus for school and it was a very busy, very dangerous road, because there was no other road through at all, and the bus company didn't run buses.

People got so exasperated about having to take children up here in these dangerous conditions, that we got all these placards, made them, put them on, took the children in the pushchairs and the prams, and we went and stopped the traffic on Southwell Road! And we had the traffic stopped for

Calverton Miners' Welfare activities advertised in the *Notts and Derbys Club Review*, 1970.

about three miles. The police came up and weren't very happy, but it worked. We won. We got a bus down here to pick the children up from where we lived and take them to school, which was the main object. We've had to fight hard for everything here.

*Maureen Wilkinson, born 1933*
*Mansfield*

## Good Neighbours

It's lovely knowing your neighbour. In this day and age you're a bit nervous of who you're going to get living next to you. But I've been neighbours with Maureen for thirty-one years – we've been together since day one here!

If I wanted to go into Maureen's, I'd just open the door and walk in and vice versa, but I wouldn't go and do that in anybody else's house. I don't know the other neighbours very well.

Maureen lost her daughter when she was thirty-one, and I was there for her all the time. And I was glad to be there. I thought that if it had happened to me, I would have wanted Maureen, just the same. We've had very bad times, but we've had very good times too.

*Mary McGarrigle, born 1933*
*Mansfield*

## Locking your Doors

Things have changed a lot. Years ago when we first lived on the estate, you were so safe. That was the key word – safe. You never thought that anybody was going to hurt you. I've been on the bus and I've been going down town and I've suddenly thought I didn't lock the door, but that didn't worry me at all, 'cos I knew that when I came back everything would be as I left it. Now that has all gone. It's hard even to go to Mary's next door and not be tempted to turn the key in my lock. That's how it is these days.

*Maureen Wilkinson, born 1933*
*Mansfield*

## Camaraderie Underground

In 1988 when Mansfield Colliery closed I moved to Bilsthorpe, and I was made redundant when Bilsthorpe Colliery closed in June of '97. Now I work for a local firm making marquees.

I knew redundancy was coming on me. The media knew it. Everybody knew it. It's one of them things, in't it? Everybody's being made redundant all the time. At one time of day it wasn't an accepted thing, but now it is.

The closing of the pits broke up communities. A hell of an amount of my friends I'd known for years and years at Mansfield Colliery, from day one I've never seen half of them ever again. You'd see 'em virtually every day for twenty-two years, and then it just goes. It's just sad to miss your friends. It were one of them things you never expected to happen.

You could have laughs and jokes, you knew all the family life of each other, and you used to tell each other your tales about your wives, and what had gone off, 'Guess what my wife did to me yesterday', and all things like that. And

Nottinghamshire miners support Polish miners in a march from Forest Fields to Nottingham's Old Market Square, in aid of the union – Solidarity, 1980. The money donated was sent to Lech Walesa.

you'd say, 'Is the wife still talking to you?' and they'd say, 'No, she's stopped talking to me again.' And that were it.

I think it were a friendship special to the pit. You could actually say things to people where if you was on the surface you couldn't say it to 'em. You could say terrible things. You could say, 'I fancy your wife, what's the chance of having her?' and things like that, and it was just a bit of a laugh and a joke type thing. But if you say it to somebody else in a pub, it's a fisticuffs job, in't it?

You were mates, you were working together and you relied on each other. You'd just got to rely on each other for your safety and everything, and when one bloke were doin' something, he made sure he did it right for you and vice versa. It's just a different walk of life. You look after people, you're friends, you're mates. You can have an argument, but you're best of pals two minutes later. You'd 'elp each other. If somebody wanted something, you'd get it 'em if it were possible.

There was definitely a community spirit. You used to go drinking together, and all kind of things like that. We had a social club at Mansfield Colliery. We used to go on trips, have fishing competitions. We once went down to Bognor Regis on the train.

I was talking to a young lad yesterday and I said to 'im, I says, 'Over there that used to be Sherwood Colliery,' and he says, 'Was there a colliery there?' He couldn't even remember. I says, 'Yeah, there were collieries everywhere.' Now that bothers me. It's important to

121

remember the collieries, because the mining's actually produced all the power for the country and the steam trains and all that. They produced all the coal. And they used skills down the mines that people haven't got these days now and they'll never have again.

*Trevor Tuffley, born 1946*
*Mansfield*

## Ex-Pat Postman!

I'm still a Canadian, but I feel I belong in Newark after eleven years here. I feel very much at home. When we arrived in Newark, we found the people very friendly – much more open than North Americans. We got to know people quite readily, and had no trouble getting 'on board' in the town.

I soon became involved in what we called the King Alfred Cake Society, which was a group that met at the old Kings' Arms pub of a Tuesday night. The object was that all the men in the group had to bake a cake, and then all the women in the group had to judge this thing. The idea was that the men were going to make a flat burned cake like King Alfred did, but of course the object was to make some sort of culinary creation which everybody could enjoy. I don't know, maybe I killed it, but I was the last winner before it ceased to meet! My initial job didn't work out as I'd hoped, and after a year I had to get another job. In fact I got a job in the post office carrying letters, and that did me an awful lot of good, because it brought me into contact with a lot of people that I wouldn't otherwise have met. It meshed me into Newark in another way entirely and to this day I know half the postmen in town.

*John Laing, born 1947*
*Newark*

Canadian John Laing arrives at Harcourt Street, Newark, 1987.

Wellow Village Show, in the 1950s.

## Friendly Faces

I've lived in Epperstone all my life. I'm the fourth generation to live here. My children are the fifth. My grandfather and his father were the village blacksmith and they used to do a lot of the wrought iron work round the village and for the Epperstone Estate.

The village is nice and friendly, there's open spaces, good community relationships, and lots of times we all get together and have superb fun. Whereas I think when you're out in the town, they're mainly out at work, aren't they? They never have time for their social life like we have here. We have the Village Produce Show once a year; gardens are normally open; we have a village ball once a year, and everybody's just so friendly. You can walk down the street and people always speak to you.

The village hasn't changed that much, because there's not been many houses built at all, except we've had a new village hall built. It's still very friendly. The only difference is, I don't think the children are as close as we were, because the village school closed down. When I was young, a lot of the mums didn't work, but some of the new villagers that have come in are business people, so I suppose during the day everybody's not as close as what they were. Most of the ones that come into the village just seem to settle down into village life. People go out of their way when somebody new moves in, if it's their next-door neighbour, to introduce them to what people are already in the village.

*Pauline Henshaw, born 1955*
*Epperstone*

## A Spiritual Home

I remember the Albert Hall from being a tiny child. We were taken to the Sunday school there as beginners and young children, my brother and I. My father was caretaker, so we were always there.

The morning and the evening services were extremely well attended, and I can remember being taken in as children when we old enough to sit still. They used to queue to come in, in the evening, and we had a full hall which seated at that time about 2,500. We had a marvellous choir of about 100, and they used to do a lot of the major works. And we had lots of things happening there.

On a Saturday evening we had quite a few people who were in service and belonged to the mission, and we used to have a room there with a fire for them to come into and meet people, to have

Waiting to attend on the May Queen in Wellow Village, 1951. (By permission of the Mansfield Chad)

NOTTINGHAM
METHODIST
MISSION
1967

METHODIST
MISSION

"WE
CONQUER ONLY
IN THAT SIGN"

Nottingham's Albert Hall Institute Building, which formed part of the extensive Albert Hall premises.

somewhere to go and somewhere to sit. And we used to have tea and magazines there as well. There was quite a lot of them at one time. Then we had a used clothes store, and people in poor circumstances used to come in and they were kitted out. Also in the building we had a Jewish Club, which seems funny in a Methodist church really, doesn't it? They had a room on the top floor that they used as a club room. Later it was made into a chapel.

It was a family church and it had a family feeling. We had a lot of visitors and non-members come in, but that didn't matter. They were there, and they were with us.

I don't think I could describe exactly what it felt like in a hall of that size to be full. It used to be completely full, right up the sides of the organ, and it really takes some believing when you see church congregations these days. I don't think it'll ever come back.

We had a huge Sunday school back then, and when we had Sunday school anniversaries, we used to fill the centre choir. My brother and I sat on each side of the minister on the platform, and it was when ministers wore tailcoats. My brother had the watch to pull his tailcoat when it got to a certain time, to tell him that it must be time to stop. That was in the days of the Revd Luke Wiseman. But we had some marvellous ministers, and they held the congregation. You really felt you'd been to a service when you'd been there.

We used to let out our premises, so we lost out when the Concert Hall opened. We lost revenue, and the congregation was dwindling. But I think it was a great tragedy when we had to sell in 1985. People knew the Albert Hall and what it stood for. I think it meant a lot to a lot of people, and it was

125

Activities at the Albert Hall from its 'Wartime Mission Report', 1915.

heart-breaking to have to come to the end of a chapter of Methodism there. When I go back now I feel horrible. I feel as if I've lost something. The Albert Hall was a spiritual home, that's all you can say. I know the church is not the building – but the building helps.

*Irene Dove, born 1915*
*Mapperley Park*

## Being Alongside

When the Franciscan Friars first came to St Ann's in 1930, their primary objective was to provide religious services for the Catholic community. We still do that, but we've branched out in many directions. We try to, at any rate. It's all very well to say we're working for the poor, we're living with the poor; it's another thing to do it in reality.

There is still a lot of poverty and human need and a lot of suffering in this area. St Ann's is, one could say, a place where all life happens. We find ourselves engaged a lot in perhaps what would broadly be called counselling – being with people, listening to people who are in trouble or distress.

When I came to St Ann's, there was a lot of talk about a sociological study that had been published by Penguin. It had made a great impression in the academic field of sociology: a study of inner city deprivation here in St Ann's. Now the city had acted on this and had largely pulled down the whole of St Ann's and rebuilt it. This brought in a lot of Irish workers, so by the time I came here I think there was a very large Irish presence in Nottingham. And also people of other ethnic origins have come in, so there's quite a big mix.

In the '50s we built a social club, and that was a very thriving centre of social life – it went with a bang. Over the last decade it has been thriving very much less, because the nature of the local community has changed, and their social and entertainment patterns have changed too.

You hear people speaking in glowing terms of the good old days, but when

Demolition of St Ann's, Nottingham, 1970. This was the view looking across St Ann's Well Road towards Northumberland Street.

you actually hear about the living conditions, they don't sound so good. Life was hard physically, but it bred community. As we've become a lot more opulent that has eroded, so it is very much harder now to build a sense of community.

*Quentin Jackson, born 1930*
*Nottingham*

## A Bonnet in the Bar

I joined the Salvation Army through knowing this Salvation Army bandsman. He invited me to his home where the family used to talk about the Army activities, and I became interested, because it was very different from the Methodism I was used to. And I thought that God could use me perhaps outside, to contact people in a

Dorothy Bird as a new recruit to the Salvation Army, 1946.

127

Dorothy Bird sings *The Old Rugged Cross* in Nottingham's Britannia pub in the 1970s.

on you. But by going regularly week after week and singing to them, perhaps *The Old Rugged Cross* or *Jesus Wants Me for a Sunbeam* – little simple things I thought they might remember – we got to know each other, because most pubs have what they call regulars, and after a while they used to look for me and welcome me.

I was going round the Nottingham pubs till about twenty years ago. I used to go to the Duke of Cambridge and the Duke of Devonshire and the March Hare and the Old Dog and Partridge. I never really wanted to give it up. I still sometimes drop in the pubs and talk to the licensee or the landlord, because all the regulars like to see me. I enjoyed it very much.

*Dorothy Bird, born 1900*
*Nottingham*

way that I'd perhaps previously been sheltered from.

I was made a soldier in the Salvation Army, and they used me straightaway by giving me a bunch of Army literature and a collecting box and sending me to the nearest Britannia pub, which is right next to their hall in Nottingham. I stood on the threshold and I said, 'Lord, you're with me now, give me confidence, and courage, and go with me,' and He did and I've never looked back.

A Salvationist going into the pub in her uniform, with a bonnet on, she was different from the rest, and you'd find all eyes looking at you. And they'd be saying, 'What's she come for?' and some of them would greet you and welcome you, and others would turn their back

# YOUR WAY TO WINNING GOLF

## David Graham
with Larry Dennis
Introduction by Jack Nicklaus

Stanley Paul
London   Sydney   Auckland   Johannesburg

Stanley Paul & Co. Ltd

An imprint of Century Hutchinson Ltd

62-65 Chandos Place, London WC2N 4NW

Century Hutchinson Australia (Pty) Ltd
88-91 Albion Street, Surry Hills, NSW 2010

Century Hutchinson New Zealand Limited
191 Archers Road, PO Box 40-086, Glenfield, Auckland 10

Century Hutchinson South Africa (Pty) Ltd
PO Box 337, Bergvlei 2012, South Africa

First published in USA by Golf Digest/Tennis, Inc. 1985
First published in Great Britain 1986
Reprinted in paperback 1987, 1988

© Golf Digest/Tennis, Inc. 1985, 1986

Printed in Great Britain by Scotprint Ltd, Musselburgh

British Library Cataloguing in Publication Data

Graham, David
    Your way to winning golf.
    1. Golf
    I. Title   II. Dennis, Larry
    796.352'3        GV965

ISBN 0 09 172645 X

Photographs by Stephen Szurlej
Illustrations by Bob Giuliani

# THANK YOU

*To my wife, Maureen.* Without her, none of this would have happened.

*To Bruce Devlin,* who made me the player I am today. He instilled in me the confidence to come and play in the United States and gave me invaluable advice and friendship at a time when I most needed it.

*To Mike and Marion Marinelli,* for instilling in Maureen and me the meaning of American hospitality, a sense of the real American tradition, and for being true friends and god-parents to our sons, Andrew and Michael.

*To B. M. (Mack) Rankin Jr.,* a gentleman in every sense of the word who has taught me the values of life and has been a loyal friend. The world needs more of this kind of Texan.

*To Bill Saxon,* whose support and kindness are appreciated more than I can say.

*To Gary Player,* who has been an inspiration to me and to golfers all over the world.

*To Jack Nicklaus,* a perfect gentleman and without a doubt the greatest player in history, who started my 12-year relationship with the MacGregor Golf Company and gave me the opportunity to design his Limited Edition and Muirfield model clubs.

*To Hughes Norton* of International Management Group, my agent for 15 years, for the professional way in which my business has been handled and for his friendship.

*To the late George Naismith,* whose teachings remain an important part of my life.

*To the late Eric Cremin.* Without his advice to leave Tasmania and try to develop my abilities as a golfer, it's hard to say where I would be today.

*To James Paul Linn of Oklahoma City,* a close friend and advisor for whom I have the utmost respect and admiration.

*To the members of Preston Trail Golf Club,* for allowing me the honor and privilege of being a part of their club.

*To the City of Dallas, Texas,* for its friendliness, kindliness and opportunity.

*—DAVID GRAHAM*

# CONTENTS

# 8 HOW TO LEARN
Drills and other thoughts that will make your practice
more efficient and your learning more productive. . . 116

# 9 START WITH THE RIGHT EQUIPMENT
A well-fitted set of clubs may or may not make you play
better, but it will eliminate one variable, and the more
variables you eliminate,the more consistent you are. 126

# 10 GOLF, THE MIND GAME
There are two aspects to golf's mental side, one
played from within, the other played from without. 146

# SECTION TWO

# 11 THE EARLY TRIALS AND THE AWFUL CHANGE
From my start as a left-hander to becoming a right-
hander—and a professional—at the age of 14. . . . . 156

# 12 FROM TASMANIA TO PORTLAND
My first head job as a professional was a disaster
. . . but it led to the Alcan and the United States. 162

# 13 BREAKTHROUGH AND BREAKDOWN
From blossoming as Australia's newest star to humility
and frustration in the U.S. . . . . . . . . . . . . . . . . . . . 170

# 14 THE REBUILDING
After Bruce Devlin told me I didn't have anything that
would work, the process of revamping took me—
after a long, long time—to the PGA Championship. . . 178

# 15 THE REWARDS
Winning becomes easier, and Dallas, Texas, USA,
becomes my home. . . . . . . . . . . . . . . . . . . . . . . . . . . 188

# FOREWORD

Co-authoring a book, as I have discovered in more than a decade of doing so, is akin to marriage. You develop the same sense of intimacy and ride the same emotional roller-coaster that couples often do. Writing a book is, after all, somewhat of a baring of the soul, regardless of the subject matter. The two who share that experience—author and writer, teller and listener—become inextricably bound by a tie that, no matter the years or the distance, never loosens. It had been that way for me with each of my previous collaborators, and it has been so with David Graham.

Sharing authorship was not a new experience for the two of us. Since David won the U.S. Open and joined the Golf Digest staff in 1981, we have been the perpetrators of his popular column and his instruction articles. But a book requires a deeper commitment, one that is both more frustrating and more satisfying . . . . and infinitely more work.

That was particularly true of this book. This is an instruction book of a different sort. In it, Graham not only records his considerable knowledge of the golf swing and how to play the game, he also tells us about his life, the fascinating story of a youngster who overcame some incredible odds to become one of the world's best players. Even when one is purposely relating his own story, there is a tendency to hide, to shield oneself from the awful truths that sometimes arise. It was my job, on occasion, to break down the barriers.

I had known David Graham the player for many years, and for the last several of those we had been friends, at least as much as two individuals who live almost a continent apart and see each other only a few times a year can be friends. But during the collaboration on this book—the listening, the occasional pleading, once or twice the yelling—I came to know David Graham the man. I learned what drove him in those early years—indeed, what possessed him at times—and what motivates him now. As with most stars in sports or entertainment, Graham allows the public to see only part of him. Much more lies beneath the surface. As with any of us, some of it is less than loveable. But I found a great deal more that I liked.

I hope that what I have learned about the private Graham and how he has grown over the years comes through in the following pages. In particular, I hope it is made clear how much David's wife, Maureen, has meant to his success, both as a golfer and as a human being. One of my personal joys in doing this book is that I've had the chance to spend more time with Maureen. She has been involved in the research and she has shown that she cares. She's a neat lady, and I thank her for her help and friendship.

My thanks, and David's, go also to the staff and membership at Preston Trail Golf Club in Dallas, where David is a dues-paying member and where this book was researched and most of the photographs were taken. Preston Trail is possibly the wealthiest golf club, per capita, in the world and is most probably the friendliest and most down-to-earth. I have been stopping there occasionally for more than a dozen years, and have never received anything but the warmest welcome. In a world wherein money and trappings too often breed *hauteur,* it is a pleasant oasis.

I think you will enjoy David Graham's story, and I'm sure you will benefit from what he has to tell you about golf. You won't get Maureen's secret for marinating ribs (she won't even give that to me), but you will get David's secrets for hitting better shots and preparing yourself to better play this awesome game.

Larry Dennis<br>
Huntington, Connecticut<br>
June, 1985

# INTRODUCTION

The thing that impressed me the most about the young David Graham was his almost obsessive desire to learn. When I first met David in Australia back in the late 1960s, he was an intent watcher of the better players and not at all bashful about picking their brains—mine, Gary Player's, anybody who would share his ideas with him.

I suspected then that David was going to be a successful player. Anybody with just a normal amount of talent who has that much dedication is bound to go places, and I guess there's a lesson there for all of us.

I once told David that his best future was as a club designer. In saying that, I was paying tribute to his skills in that area rather than intending to imply he didn't have a future as a player. Two major championships and victories around the world have proved his playing ability beyond all question. To me, those accomplishments were the result of his willingness to make changes in his swing and work on the improvements until he had built a game that was totally repetitive and reliable. I've had to make changes, and I'm fully aware of how difficult it is to do so. If there is one major point that comes through in this book, it is that everybody has to keep thinking and working to get better at golf.

Observing and changing and working to improve develops a sound knowledge of the golf swing and what makes it effective. David has that knowledge, and along with it he has also gained exceptional knowledge of what makes a golf club effective. I discovered this talent many years ago and was intrigued enough to want him as a member of our design team at the MacGregor Golf Company.

David's knowledge of swing and club is passed on in full here, along with the interesting story of a young Australian who overcame long odds to make it big in professional golf. The result is a book that is both instructive and entertaining, and one that I'm sure golfers everywhere will thoroughly enjoy.

Jack Nicklaus
May, 1985

# THE RECORD

**1967** — Queensland PGA, Australia
**1970** — Tasmanian Open
      Victorian Open, Australia
      Thailand Open
      Yomiuri Classic, Japan
      French Open
      World Cup (with Bruce Devlin)
**1971** — Caracas Open, Venezeula
      JAL Open, Japan
**1972** — Cleveland Open
**1975** — Wills Masters, Australia
**1976** — Chunichi Crowns, Japan
      Westchester Classic
      American Golf Classic
      Piccadilly World Match Play, England
**1977** — Australian Open
**1978** — Mexican Cup
**1979** — PGA Championship
      West Lakes Classic, Australia
      Air New Zealand Open
**1980** — Memorial Tournament
      Heublin Classic, Brazil
      Rolex World Mixed Team Championship
      (with Jan Stephenson)
      Mexican Open
**1981** — Phoenix Open
      U.S. Open
      Lancombe Trophy, France
**1982** — Lancombe Trophy, France
**1983** — Houston Open
**1985** — Queensland Open, Australia
      Dunhill Nations Cup, Scotland
      (with Graham Marsh and Greg Norman)

# SECTION ONE

# CHAPTER ONE

# THE TRIUMPH

**From Wattle Park to Merion**

*Here I'm holding my first trophy, emblematic of the Wattle Park Junior Championship that I won in Melbourne as a 13-year-old left-hander, and my most significant, awarded for winning the 1981 U.S. Open at Merion.*

**T**he last time I had cried on a golf course—perhaps the only time—had been in 1968, after a penalty had cost me a chance to win the Australian PGA championship. Now, on a June day in 1981 in Ardmore, Pa., a world away from my roots, I was crying again. I had just tapped in a nine-inch putt to become the United States Open champion, from a skinny 13-year-old working in a golf shop in Melbourne and playing with left-handed clubs to the winner of the most prestigious championship in the world. With thousands watching around the 18th green at Merion and with the television cameras focused on me, the tears came. My wife, Maureen, was crying, too. She had come all that way with me, and she knew what was going through my mind.

Never had all the years of perseverance, all the hours and the hundreds of thousands of shots on the practice tee, the willingness to make traumatic changes in my golf game, seemed so worthwhile. I had done it so I could play better, so I could reach the top in my profession, and now—however momentarily—I had. Whether your goals, in golf or in life, are as lofty, or whether you are after more modest success, it's a lesson that should not be lost.

I was in the middle of a change even during the Open. Gary Player had told me several weeks before that my swing was too short and that there was no way I could play consistently well unless I lengthened it. He had told me that about three years before, too, but I hadn't paid much attention. Now I had made myself a weighted club and practiced swinging it and hitting balls with it to stretch my swing.

A month before, I had collapsed on the 10th fairway at Muirfield Village and had to withdraw from the Memorial Tournament, where I was the defending champion. I was plain worn out from what was diagnosed as a potassium deficiency, so I went home and spent the next three weeks on a strict diet, relaxing and working a couple of hours a day on my game.

I arrived at Merion early and played a practice round on Sunday with Player—ironically, I also had played a practice round with him before I won my other major championship, the PGA at Oakland Hills in 1979. Gary said to me, "It's unbelievable. I cannot believe that one man can change his swing that quickly. There is no reason you can't win more majors." It was nice of him to say that, and it got me thinking in the right direction that week. I started hitting the ball well, and I really liked the golf course. It was a fun golf course to play, a precision course, not a "beat a drive and beat a 2-iron" kind of course. It was difficult, but we had had a little rain and the greens were not unputtable. I told Maureen before the championship started, "My longer swing is good, and I've really started hitting some good shots."

On Thursday I shot 68, two under par, not playing particularly well but putting like an absolute dream. I had an up-and-down round the next day—I think I made two pars on the back nine—but managed another 68 to stand second, a stroke behind George Burns. On Saturday my game flip-flopped. I hit it as well as I'm capable from tee to green and putted just awful. I shot 70 and went into the final round still second but now trailing Burns by three.

In the final round, all the years of preparation paid off. I just wanted to play a solid, steady round of golf. My emotional state was pretty good—I felt my swing was repetitive, I was driving the ball well and thought I was putting well despite Saturday's problems. So I just kept swinging and hitting, swinging and hitting, not really keeping track of how many fairways and greens I was hitting.

In a situation like that you don't think about your swing. You think about the type of shot you are trying to hit and where you want to put the ball. And when you have the ability to hit it there, your golf course management becomes so much easier. You don't get on the tee and say, "Don't go left," because if you do, you go left . . . or so far to the right that you are in even more trouble. You simply walk on the tee and say, "There's the middle of the fairway, get your checkpoints right, go ahead and swing the club."

I'm not sure what it is that allows you to get into such a state of mind in a championship situation of that nature, whether it's a combination of knowing you are swinging well and are playing a course you enjoy, or whatever. I *do* know, however, that it's impossible to achieve mental stability like that if you don't have a golf swing that is fundamentally sound, one that you trust to hold up under pressure.

In any event, I ended up missing the first fairway by three feet (and making birdie on the hole) and hitting every one thereafter. I technically missed three greens by inches but putted the ball from the fringe every time. Some say it was the most precise round ever played in the final round of the U.S. Open. I'll leave that

**Victory Shared**
*Maureen and I hold up the U.S. Open trophy after the final round at Merion.*

**From Trouble to Triumph**
*The famed (or notorious) Scotch Broom in Merion's bunkers gave me some trouble in the third round (above), but everything came together on the final day. At right, dismay as my record-tying putt on the 72nd hole rolled over the lip was quickly replaced by the satisfaction of knowing that the U.S. Open championship was mine.*

for others to decide. All I know is that when I got to the 18th tee with a two-shot lead over Burns, I went nervous. Had I not been very repetitive at that particular time, I'm not sure I could have handled it.

The 18th at Merion is awesome, a 458-yard par 4 where you must drive the ball over a gaping chasm and through a narrow chute...and you must drive it well to have any chance of reaching the green with your second. At this point I had enough composure left to go through my system, to say, "Pick out the spot in front of the ball, put the club behind the ball, go through your waggle, make sure you are comfortable, don't hit until you do your system, then go ahead and make your swing." Still, it's an incredible feeling when you start your downswing thinking you need four to win and are playing a hole like that.

George had hit first and had driven it into the right-hand rough, and that helped me a little. I made a good swing, and the moment I hit my tee shot I knew I could win. I hit an enormous drive, the best drive I hit all week, into the left center of the fairway, but even walking to the ball I was telling myself, "It's not over yet. Don't get too excited. Don't show too much jubilation because you haven't won yet."

I got my yardage—I had 184 yards to the front of the green, 202 to the flag—and my caddie, Wayne Beck, was keeping me cool, telling me to relax. I hit a 4-iron that carried well onto the green and trickled to within 20 feet of the pin. Then I knew I had won the golf tournament.

I still had to two-putt. Burns had hit a phenomenal second shot and had really been a bit unlucky, because the ball ran about six feet over the green into heavy rough. But he was only 25 feet from the hole and

could have chipped in from there. He didn't, eventually winding up with a bogey, and it was only after he hit his chip that I thought momentarily about the U.S. Open record of 272. I could hole my putt to tie the record Jack Nicklaus established the year before at Baltusrol. As it turned out, my putt ran over the edge of the hole and I knocked in the second one for a 67.

It wasn't until later—after the champagne party in the press tent, after the trip home to find our house decorated by our friends, after the thrill of being announced at the White House—that it all began to sink in, that I began to realize what I had done. It might surprise a lot of people who have known me during my career, but I'm a sentimentalist. The thing I liked so much about winning the U.S. Open is picking up the trophy and seeing all the immortal names on it, the legendary and the contemporary greats. I keep thinking about those days on the little nine-hole course at Wattle Park in Melbourne, cleaning clubs, sweeping the floor, picking up range balls and having a good time some 20 years ago. I think about the dozens of people who told me to forget about golf, that I was never going to be any good. I look back at what my father did to me and at what my mother did for me to make my career possible. I look at my wife and the transition of getting married and taking on that responsibility. I look at the problems I had getting my life organized and making my game respectable, and at getting screwed up and having to start over again.

Then I look at my name on that trophy with all those great players, and nobody can ever take it off. It's something I'll have for the rest of my life.

It's a hell of a deal.

81st U.S. OPEN CHAMP

# CHAPTER TWO

# LOOK AND LEARN

Golf always has been difficult for me. I feel as if I'm a manufactured player. I had to manufacture my golf swing from the ground up, mechanically. Nothing has come naturally, probably because of my start from the "wrong" side of the ball . . . wrong for me, that is.

One of my greatest assets in the manufacture of my swing has been my ability and willingness to "look and learn." By that I mean I have made it a point to seek out the best players and best teachers, to watch them, to listen to them and to learn from them.

Whenever international stars would come to Australia while I was learning the game, I'd bug them to death. When Jack Nicklaus came, I'd sit on the end of his golf bag and watch him practice. I wanted to look at his clubs, find out what kind of grips he used, find out everything I could about his equipment and his swing. When Gary Player would visit Australia, I was his shadow. I remember a day during the 1971 Australian Open at Victoria Golf Club. It was pouring rain and the day's play had been canceled. Player was having lunch, and I simply invited myself to his table so I could pick his brains about the

American tour, about his exercises, his running and whatever else I could find out from him.

I was never backward about trying to go forward. And while some of my peers may have resented this a bit, I think the Gary Players of the world respected me for it. Certainly there never has been a person more dedicated to learning and to improvement than Player. Listening to him and playing practice rounds with him taught me about tenacity, determination and the will to achieve.

Playing a practice round with Nicklaus in 1971 prior to the Australian Open at Royal Hobart also taught me something . . . in fact, it gave me my first true shock in golf. It showed me I was about one-eighth as good as I thought I was. Fortunately, that made me all the more determined to work harder.

During my career I have looked at and learned from the players I consider to be the best mechanically. I have examined their grips, their setup positions, leg movement, shoulder turns—every facet of their swings. I personally believe that the most knowledgeable people in golf are those who have had success as players. I find it very difficult to have confidence in

anyone who has not had the ability to go out and do it himself. And those who have success are those who are fundamentally correct, a point I'll explain more thoroughly in Chapter 4.

I've been fortunate enough to have teachers who fit my rather rigid criteria. George Naismith and Eric Cremin were respected players. Alex Mercer had the best swing of any player in Australia but couldn't putt. Bruce Devlin, of course, was a great player.

In 1981, just prior to The Masters, I arranged to have Norman Von Nida flown to the U.S. to stay with me for about a month. Selfishly, I wanted him to help me with my game. But I also felt the man had never received the acclaim in Australia that he should have, and it looked as if nobody was going to step forward and recognize what

he had done in the past.

Not only was Von Nida a great player, he's a great teacher and a great human being. He always supported me in Australia in his newspaper columns, and he has done much for other young Australian golfers. He has always been around to help, to slip a kid $50 if he needed money, to give him a golf lesson, to go to a sporting goods company and get a set of clubs made, to get him some balls.

As a small repayment for all that he had done, I felt I wanted to bring Norman over here and take him to Augusta, where he had been a competitor in The Masters, to see all his old friends.

That's the way it worked out, but not without some anxious moments. Air New Zealand, the airline I had represented for about four

*Learning from Nicklaus . . .*
*Watching and playing with Jack Nicklaus always was—and still is—a learning experience.*

**. . . and Player and Devlin**
*I took advantage of Gary Player (top) and Bruce Devlin, but it paid off, and I really don't think they minded.*

years, flew Von Nida to Dallas. I picked him up at 2:30 in the morning and took him to our house. The very next morning, at the breakfast table, he suffered a fibrillation of the heart and passed out on the floor. Fortunately, our housekeeper had been a registered nurse, and she knew how to handle it. We got Norman to the emergency ward at Dallas Medical Center, and when I walked in, the young doctor on duty asked me if I was David Graham, the golfer. When I said I was, he asked who was on the table. I said, "His name is Norman Von Nida." He said, "You mean Norman Von Nida, the golfer? I can't believe it. I'm an absolute golf nut. I've read about this man. He's the best bunker player in the world, isn't he?"

I said, "Yes, but right now he has tubes up his nose and needles in his arms, and you'd better get him out of here and take care of him."

"He'll be all right," the doctor promised. "He'll get absolutely the best attention." And he did.

During one of my visits to the hospital a day or so later, the phone rang in Norman's room. It was Ben Hogan calling, and the two old friends spent a lengthy time talking.

Three days after he had passed out at my breakfast table, after undergoing some rigorous tests, Von Nida was out of the hospital and on the practice range with me at Preston Trail, sitting on a chair under an umbrella and working on my game. He was helping me with my bunker play and making a couple of small refinements in my full swing. Most important, he was helping me develop some confidence, something he was very good at. At one point during the session he said, "David, I'm sorry I got sick. I kept thinking about what people would say if I died at your house. But, you know, I could

not think of a nicer place for that to happen." That touched me.

We went to Augusta, and Norman saw all his old friends and had a great time. Then he returned to Australia, where he's still doing his thing. And two months later I won the U.S. Open.

Though my reasons for bringing Von Nida over might have been mainly altruistic, I really did want him to help me with some refinements I wanted to make in my game. That's the point of the story—I know that it's never too late to learn, that you should never stop trying to get better. Jack Nicklaus made a rather drastic swing change, for him, when he was almost 40 years old and after he had won 17 major championships. He has won two more since. Gary Player, nearing 50 as this is written, is still working hard on his game, making changes and refinements, and he's playing about as well as he ever has. Virtually every good player I know has made working on his game a lifetime commitment. I assure you I'm still trying to get better, working with my weighted club to stretch and strengthen my muscles so I can hit the ball farther, learning new little shots, refining old skills. When I quit doing that, I'll be ready for the scrap heap.

The same philosophy holds true for any golfer at any level. When you quit trying to improve, you go backward. Everything is a matter of degree, of course, but unless you can put in some time working on your game, making some changes and refinements, you not only won't get better, you won't stay as good as you've been. The fact that you're reading this book leads me to believe you want to improve.

I urge you to start your improvement the same way I did—by looking and listening and learning from good players and good teachers. You probably won't have a chance to sit on Jack Nicklaus' golf bag, and you may not be able to fly in Norman Von Nida from Australia. But you can expose yourself to the better players at your club and in your area. You can seek out competent instructors and develop a relationship with one you find who can help you.

The purpose of this book is to help you understand what it takes to make that improvement at golf, to tell you of the changes I made over the years, the effort that went into those changes and what I now think are the fundamentals of a good golf swing. Equally as important as the changes in my golf swing were the changes in my attitude, my emotional control and strategic ability as I learned over the years to really *play* this game rather than just swing a club at a ball. Finally, I have learned quite a lot about equipment and how important it is to have the correct tools in your hands, and I'll try to pass that along to you.

In the first part of the book I'll tell you what I've learned and how you can apply it in making your own game better. In the second part I'll describe what I went through in learning all this, relating the story of a driven, stubborn, hot-tempered kid who went all over the world trying to become successful at the only thing he ever wanted to do.

You don't have to put up with the frustrations I did. You don't have to beat 1,000 balls a day until your hands are sore, as I did. You don't have to tinker incessantly with your equipment to make

it perfect, as I have done. After all, golf is a *game* for most people, not a livelihood. You are supposed to have fun with it, not fight with it, and you can enjoy it at any level of skill you choose.

You will find my explanations in this book simple, I hope, because I believe that the simplest way of playing is the best way. But this will not be "golf made easy." Learning is never easy. I hope to convince you that *any* improvement demands *some* intelligence and effort. If you want to get better, in whatever degree, you're probably going to have to make some changes in your approach to the swing and the game, and you definitely will have to put in some work to make those changes playable. How much of that you put in will determine how much improvement you make. You don't find many free lunches around, and for sure you won't find any in golf.

I hope that my story will inspire you to do that work, challenging you to take the time and make the effort it takes to achieve any worthwhile improvement.

Reading a book like this about the golf swing and how to play the game can be helpful in developing the correct concept, in getting your thinking started in the right direction. It can provide guidelines, a blueprint for improvement. But to truly get better—and I repeat—you need a good, sympathetic instructor, one who is in tune with what you are trying to do, who can see if you are or are not doing it and can help you unravel the problems.

The blueprint follows. The rest is up to you.

# CHAPTER THREE

# RIGHT IS MIGHT

The first change I made in my golf swing was much more traumatic than any that you, hopefully, will have to make. I had to change the side from which I swung at the ball. Maybe it was just preordained that nothing was going to be easy for me in this game.

The first clubs I picked up—and I'll explain all this in Section II—were left-handed. I was 12 years old and knew nothing about golf at the time, so I didn't know the difference. Thus, although I was a natural right-hander, I began playing left-handed. It was a natural mistake but a mistake nonetheless. In the years since I have learned that a naturally right-handed person should play golf right-handed, just as a natural left-hander should play left-handed. The reason is simple: there comes a time in your golf swing when the mind tells the body to "hit," and that's when you try to apply the power. Now, the sides of your body have different degrees of strength. If you are right-handed, perhaps 60 percent of your strength lies in that dominant side. When your subconscious demands that you "hit," you automatically exert power from your strongest areas.

If you are in the situation I was, a right-hander playing left-handed, that power would come from the right hand pulling on the grip end of the club. That means the right hand and the grip end would get to the ball before the clubface. Forgetting for the time being the path of the club, whether it is coming from inside or outside your target line, the simple fact remains that you are asking about 40 percent of your body's strength—the left side—to override the stronger side and try to get the clubface square at impact. It's logical to assume that the stronger side will override the weaker every time.

Let's look at the reverse of that situation and examine natural right-handers, playing right-handed, who have been told that golf is a left-handed game and that the left hand and arm should dominate, pulling the club through on the downswing. He or she is being asked to exert more power with the weaker side and sublimate the stronger side. Invariably, the act of pulling down and through becomes a pull across the body, which accentuates the fact that the right hand is not being allowed to square the clubface in the first place. It's not difficult to see why so many golfers slice, is it?

The simplest analysis of why the stronger hand should be below the weaker on the club was given to me by George Naismith, a former Australian Open champion who was my earliest teacher. He pointed out that the hand on top, nearest the end of the grip, controls only the area of the club that it is holding onto. The bottom hand controls all the rest of the club and thus should be your strongest hand. *That has become one of the main foundation blocks of my swing philosophy.*

Ben Hogan has been quoted as saying he wished he had three right hands. I wish I had six . . . well, almost. There is no doubt the left hand, arm and side have their roles in the golf swing. Golf is no more a right-sided game (for a right-hander) than it is a left-sided game. It is a two-handed, two-sided game. The right side can do its job only if the left is working properly and, especially important, if your angle of approach to the ball is correctly from the inside of your target line. I'll get more explicitly into that in Chapter 5.

Yes, there have been natural left-handers who have been successful in golf playing right-handed. Johnny Miller is a prime example. But most of these have been tour-caliber players where other factors—like natural talent, desire and the willingness and opportunity to practice long and hard—have come into play. There probably have been even more natural left-handers who have been ruined, maybe lost to the game, because their fathers or early teachers told them that the greatest golfers in the world played right-handed and they should, too.

**The Right Side Controls**
*The left hand, arm and side remain firm through impact, but the right side is definitely controlling the club and applying the power.*

# CHAPTER FOUR

# THE FOUNDATION

In 1972, unhappy with the way I was striking the ball and playing, I started working seriously with my good friend Bruce Devlin on changing my swing. The first thing Bruce did was to emphasize his philosophy, which is that the best way to play golf well is to play it the way it is fundamentally simplest and easiest.

It is a philosophy I embraced completely and to which I adhere today, mainly because I've never seen a really good player—consistently good over a long period of time—who was not technically sound. Many players, from the handicap levels to the professional tours, have decent, even good, golf swings that are not quite fundamentally correct. There are players who have won tournaments on the PGA Tour whose fundamentals are not that solid. They have the talent, the eye-hand coordination, to get away with it and hit a lot of good shots. But they come and they go. Somehow, the player with the correct basics holds up better under extreme, long-term pressure. The player with the questionable fundamentals more often than not deteriorates under the heat of competition.

Somewhere along the line, if a player with incorrect fundamentals wants to improve, he or she has to decide which route to take—to get better by improving the fundamentals or maintain the status quo and hope to get better by just pounding golf balls.

The latter route doesn't offer you the best chance to improve. If your fundamentals are not correct, or not as good as they should be, a couple of problems are generated. In the first place, the effectiveness of your swing and consequently your golf score is extremely dependent on your timing and the pace of your swing, factors that can vary greatly from day to day in the best of players'. Secondly, when you have a bad round, or play badly over a period of time, you lose your confidence more quickly. Because you know your swing is not that sound to begin with, you begin to doubt it, and that compounds your problem.

A major reason good fundamentals are so important is that they give you checkpoints. When you do start playing poorly, as we all do more often than we'd like, you have something to return to, some guidelines that can put you on the right track again. With poor fundamentals in the first place, you're just groping your way out of trouble.

If you go through your golfing life with incorrect fundamentals, there undoubtedly will come a time when you tell yourself that maybe you should have tried making changes, that two or three months of not playing well while making them may have been worth it in the overall. There are no sadder words than "what might have been."

Once Devlin had his little chat with me, I had that decision to make. I chose to become more technically sound as a player and to try to become a better player at the same time. I was a perfectionist, and I didn't want people saying, "There's David Graham with the bad grip or the funny swing or whatever." I wanted to be known as a basically sound golfer with good fundamentals and good technique. I also figured that being that kind of golfer would help me at the pay window.

Your pay window may be just the $2 bet payoff on the 19th hole, but I'll wager you like to be on the receiving end more than the giving. Just follow me.

## THE GRIP

The ability to play golf consistently well begins with the grip. That is the only connection you have with the golf club. You must have your hands positioned on that golf club in the correct relationship to the face of the club. If you can do that, it is like having a car with no slack in the steering mechanism. It is much easier to drive with precision than a car that has a lot of slack in the wheel.

*The grip is the steering apparatus of your golf swing.* To be able to aim the face of the golf club, then swing it from a starting position and consistently return it so you can strike the ball down your line of aim requires that you have your hands on the club properly. The great players

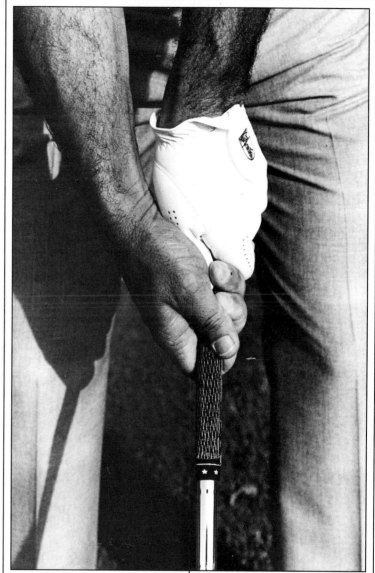

—Hogan, Nelson, Snead, Palmer, Nicklaus, Watson and all the others—have great grips, and the basics of their grips are the same: their hands are placed in a more-or-less "neutral" or palms-facing position, aligned with the clubface so they can return that face square at impact without having to make a lot of adjustment. I know players with excellent golf swings who have faulty grips, and they are simply working at cross-purposes. If they return the club to square at impact in any given swing, it is purely happenstance.

### The Old Grip
*This is the way I started as a right-hander, with a grip that was too strong, both hands turned too far to the right. It's difficult to steer straight with a grip like this. What usually resulted was a low hook.*

**How to Form the Grip**
*With the clubface aimed straight down the target line, (right), place the left palm against the left side of the shaft, the shaft running diagonally from the middle joint of the forefinger to a point just under the heel pad, so that pad sits slightly on top of the shaft (1 and 2). Curl your fingers around the club so the pressure from the fingertips is against the right side of the shaft and your thumb is sitting on top of the shaft or just slightly to the right side (3 and 4). The grip should be more in the palm than the fingers, and the V formed by your thumb and forefinger should point somewhere between your right shoulder and your chin. Set the right hand with the club resting at the base of the two middle fingers (5), then curl the fingers around the shaft. The right forefinger is slightly triggered and the thumb sits on the left side of the shaft, the V thus formed matching the V of the left (6). The completed grip (7, 8 and 9) is formed by hooking or overlapping the little finger of the right around the left forefinger.*

It is often said that the grip is the most neglected fundamental in golf. I think it is not so much neglected as it is misunderstood. Too many players grip the club in a way that they feel gives them more strength. They grab onto it with both hands turned too far to the right, thinking, "I've got hold of this sucker and, boy, I feel like I could chop wood!" And that's just what they proceed to do.

I'm not snickering, believe me. I fell into the same trap. I was pretty small when I started playing, and a "strong" grip—left hand on top of the shaft with all four knuckles showing, right hand under the shaft—felt powerful, made me feel like I could hit the ball farther. Unfortunately, I never could return the golf club to the ball the same way twice in a row. Couldn't even put my left hand on the club the same way twice in a row, in fact. And did I ever hook the ball! But, alas, never the same amount twice in a row.

The truth is, *your hands are not put on the golf club to increase your strength. They are there to control the face of the golf club,* to develop a relationship between your body and the club so that when you swing your arms and turn your body, the position of your hands in relation to the clubface will return to the correct position at impact to hit the golf ball straight. The power of your swing, the clubhead speed you generate, come from your arms, your legs, your shoulder turn, your inherent strength, the shaft of the club. Your hands are there simply to guide all that back to the ball.

A so-called strong grip, one in which the left hand is turned too far to the right and placed too much on top of the club, puts too much pressure on top of the shaft with the palm of the left hand and too much underneath the shaft with the fingers of the left. Of course, then you also have to turn your right hand too far under the shaft so it will fit with the left. All of this usually results in your swing plane being too flat and your hands turning over too much through impact. The usual result is a hook, often a big one. Or you could eventually overreact to those big hooks and not release or turn the hands over at all, which causes you to block and slice the ball.

In my case, the other problem created by the strong left hand was that my left wrist was too cupped or angled inward, which in turn put my hands too far behind the ball. Ideally, you don't want to come into the ball at impact with your left wrist cupped, so having it cupped at address simply adds another variable to your swing.

To eliminate as many variables as you can, your hands should be aligned as closely as possible with the leading edge of the club at address. Stretch your arms out in front of you and clap your hands together. Now look at them. That will give you a pretty good idea of the relationship in which your hands should fit together on the golf club. This puts the pressure from the left palm against the left side of the shaft and from the left fingers against the right side of the shaft. The pressure from the right hand is just the opposite. If you imagine that the shaft is square instead of round and has a top, a bottom and a left and right side, it may help you envision where the pressure should be. In effect, both hands and the pressure from both hands should be aligned with the face of the club—the palms more or less facing each other and with the back of the left hand and the palm of the right facing in the same general direction as the clubface. This simplifies the task of returning the clubface

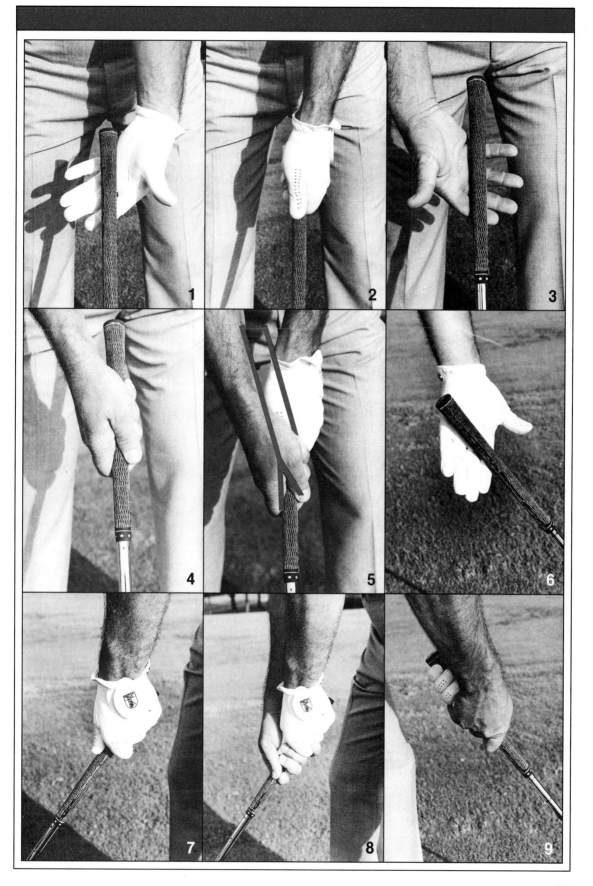

to square at impact.

*The left hand*—To my mind, the most important factor in setting the left hand properly on the club is the position of the left thumb. First, make sure the clubface is aimed straight down the target line, then place the palm of the left hand against the left side of the shaft. Then set the thumb on top of the shaft, rather than over on the right side. I like to feel that the tip of my thumb is pointing at the middle of the clubface. *I want my left thumb to be squarely underneath the shaft at the top of my backswing, so I want it squarely on top of the shaft at address.* Ideally, so should you.

**The Grip Reversed**
*This upside-down view of the completed grip shows especially well the triggering of the right forefinger and how the right little finger is laid over and hooked around the left forefinger.*

The shaft should run from the middle joint of the forefinger diagonally up the palm so the heel pad sits slightly on top of the shaft. The pressure of your palm is against the left side of the shaft. Your fingers curl around the club so the pressure from the fingertips is against the right side of the shaft. You should feel as if the grip is *more in the palm than in the fingers.*

The sensation you want is that the back of the left hand is aligned with the face of the club and is facing down a line parallel to your target line. Actually, because of the way the hand is made, there will be a very slight cupping of the wrist, and the back of the hand may be pointing slightly right of that parallel line or upward. But you will be close enough. *One checkpoint is that the V formed by your thumb and forefinger should point approximately between your right shoulder and your chin.*

*The right hand*—The position of your left hand pretty much dictates how your right hand will fit on the club, because you want the left thumb to fit into the channel between the thumb and heel pads on your right hand. The pressure of the right hand is applied to the right side of the shaft at about the base of the two middle fingers, which makes the right hand grip slightly more in the fingers than in the palm. The thumb, again, sits about on top of the shaft. The forefinger is triggered and extends slightly down the shaft, and this is important, because it gives you maximum control of the golf club. In the normal Vardon or overlapping grip, which I use, the little finger overlaps or is hooked around the knuckle of the left forefinger. This helps unify the hands during the swing.

This positions the two hands so that the left can lead without breaking down (the left hand and wrist turning over or cupping too quickly through the impact area), while the right hand, with the pressure on the right side or behind the shaft, applies the power. And because both hands are essentially aligned with the clubface, everything can get back to square at impact without any funny manipulations of the hands.

If you are used to a grip that is too strong, you'll have the same problem I did at first. The correct grip actually feels weak. When you go from four knuckles showing at address to only one or two in sight, you'll feel you can't hit the ball anywhere. You'll also tend to slice the ball for a while until you get used to the new position.

Actually, you will have put your hands in a very strong position on the club. All you have to do now is learn to swing from that position. I say "all" laughingly, of course. I know how difficult it is to change your grip and adapt to the new one. I bit the bullet and made my change all at once after Devlin got after me . . .and it took me three or four months to get used to it. If you don't get a chance to hit balls as often as I do, it probably will take you longer. And you can count on not playing to your usual standards for the length of time it takes you to do it. But if you want it badly enough, the improvement will be worth the sacrifice. Just keep telling yourself that, although it's not working now, you know that your grip is better and when you learn to apply your power properly from a different angle, you will eliminate the slice and begin to play better golf.

You can, if you wish, go at it more gradually by moving your hands to the left a little bit at a time. You may end up not wanting your hands in the same position in which I have mine. I'm pretty strong (yes,

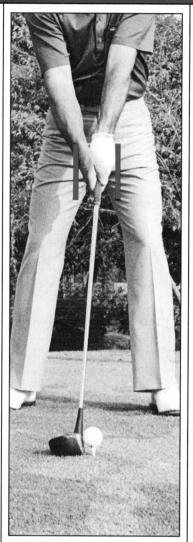

I've put on some weight and muscle since those teen years) and I release the club very quickly through impact. So I tend to keep rotating my grip farther and farther left to reduce the chances of hooking the ball.

That may not be your problem. You may need to set your hands a little more to the right to facilitate rotation through impact and help you hit your shots with a right-to-left draw. Experiment to find the best position. Just keep in mind the basic premise—the closer your hands are aligned with the clubface, the more consistently you can return the face to square at impact.

*Grip pressure: how light is*

### Hands Aligned with Clubface
*At address, both hands should be generally aligned with the clubface (below). The back of the left hand, the palm of the right and the face of the club all should be pointing in about the same direction.*

29

1

### Stand Erect and in Balance

*Correct posture will have you standing as erect as possible, your knees flexed slightly and your weight shaded toward your heels (1). You should bend from the waist, your buttocks protruding slightly and your back as straight as possible. Your arms should hang naturally but will extend or reach with the longer clubs, such as the driver here. Your weight should be distributed equally between both feet (2) and your stance should be wide enough, depending on the force of the swing you are going to make, to allow you to stay in balance.*

*light, how tight is tight?*—If you have read or listened to much golf instruction, you have been given advice on grip pressure ranging from treating the club like it's a bird to gripping it in a vise. Each is a bit exaggerated, but I lean more toward tight than light.

Very simply, *the pressure of your grip has to be great enough that you never lose control of the golf club.* You cannot afford any movement between your hands and the grip of the club. If you have movement, the angle of the clubface will change during your swing. Then it becomes a guessing game as to which way it's going to be at impact. The hands should be the direction-finder for the face of the club, and they should be able to hold onto that club so that there is no space or slack between your hands and the

grip. Then, if you do aim the club properly and put your hands on the club properly, you will have no loss of control, no unwanted movement of the clubface. You will have a better chance of returning the face to the position it was in at address.

That's why I think gripping the club a little too tightly is better than not gripping it tightly enough. You can see the veins in Jack Nicklaus' arms when he swings the club. You can't pull the club out of Tom Watson's hands at address. When Arnold Palmer grabs hold of the club, it's like putting it in a vise.

Admittedly, these players have more strength than most amateur players, and they know how to control it. You can strangle the club so tightly that you tighten up the other muscles and inhibit them from acting properly.

Still, holding the club "like a bird" is going to produce a lot of golf balls going in a lot of different directions. It's up to you to determine how much pressure you need, but always bear in mind the need to have your hands on the club securely from start to finish.

George Knudson once showed me a good drill (I think he borrowed it from Ben Hogan) to determine your proper grip pressure and keep it constant. He would line up three balls on the ground, then hit all three without moving or readjusting the grip and without consciously changing his grip pressure. It's a great exercise to teach you how to keep control of the club.

# POSTURE

I like to see a golfer stand erect, to play with as much height as possible. By that I mean you should bend from the hips and not slump forward from the shoulders, which could make you too top-heavy and cause you to lose your balance. The best way to find your correct posture:

•Stand to your full height with your legs straight, then flex your knees slightly to take the pressure out of your legs. This in turn should cause the buttocks to protrude a bit, and you should feel a little pressure in the small of your back.

•Bend from the hips, keeping your back straight and your chin up, until your arms hang down naturally. Keeping your chin up makes it easier to make a backswing turn, because your left shoulder can get underneath your chin. How much you bend and the angle at which your arms hang will depend on what club you have in your hand. With a 9-iron, you will bend a little more, your arms will hang straighter down and you will be closer to the ball. With a driver, you will bend less, your arms will be slightly extended and you will, of course, be farther from the ball, because the club is longer. As I will discuss in the chapter on equipment, having the correct lie on your clubs is critical to a good setup position and standing the correct distance from the ball.

•Distribute your weight equally between each foot for normal shots. (For special shots—high, low, etc.—the adjustments are simple and will be discussed in another chapter.) I prefer that the weight be shaded toward the heels rather than toward the toes. My heels are pretty firmly planted, because I find this keeps you in better balance and helps you swing the club down correctly on a path that comes from inside the target line. (That's a point I'll deal with later in much greater detail, because it's another critical factor in the golf swing.)

•Adjust your stance width depending on the club you have in your hand. Your guideline is simple—your stance should be comfortable and should allow you to stay in balance for the club you are using and the force of the swing you will be making. With a driver, my stance is about an inch narrower than my shoulders, measured from the insides of the heels. It will get progressively narrower as I go down through the bag and as the force of my swing becomes less. You should experiment to find your correct width. In general, I prefer a stance that is slightly narrow rather than slightly wide. However, that may not be good for a smaller person, who needs to create more coil on his backswing by restricting his lower body. He may want his stance a bit wider than normal for better balance. The bigger, stronger player can afford to play from a narrower stance because he

**1**

**2**

### Body Tilt Varies with Club

*The angle or tilt of your upper body and the angle at which your arms hang changes with the club in your hand. Notice as I move from a driver (1) to a 2-iron (2) to a 6-iron (3) and finally a pitching wedge (4) how my upper body tilts progressively more from the hips and my arms hang straighter down and closer to my body.*

can rely more on his arms and upper-body strength to create clubhead speed.

## AIM AND ALIGNMENT

I find it's best to aim the leading edge of the golf club at the target, then align your body to the face of the club. Thus it becomes critical to aim the club correctly. If you are trying to hit the ball straight, you don't want the clubface open or closed to the target line at address, because then you have to make some compensations during the swing to get it square at impact.

The most effective aiming method is to use the leading or bottom edge of the club and align it perpendicular or at right angles to your target line. It's of great benefit to use an "intermediate spot" to do this, simply because it's easier to aim at something close by than far away. Pick out a divot or other mark a few feet down your target line and aim the face at that mark.

With the clubface aimed, align all parts of your body perpendicular to the clubface or parallel with your intended target line—that's assuming you're planning to hit a nor-

3

4

mal straight shot. One trick I find helpful is to use my knees to establish my body alignment. If you want your body parallel to the target line for a straight shot, set your knees parallel to that line. If you want to close your stance to hook the ball, set your right knee slightly behind your left. To fade or slice the ball, the right knee will be slightly ahead of your left, closer to the target line. With your knees thus positioned, the entire body should follow and your alignment should be correct for the type of shot you are planning to play.

## BALL POSITION

Playing the ball from the same position in your stance is critical to making good shots consistently. Unfortunately, most players have a difficult time with this. I know I did after I switched from the left to the right side. I played for years with the ball too far forward in my stance and aiming too far to the right, because I was looking at it from a different angle. I even went through a period in 1975 when I practiced with a patch over my right eye just to get an idea of what it was like to see the club straight up and down out of my left eye. And the problem is not restricted to those few of us who have switched sides. If you are right-handed, you probably are right-eyed, and you may have the same difficulty without being aware of it. I had to find a way to get my body and my eyes attuned to the same ball position every time, and you must do that, too.

My solution was—and is—to stand to the ball with my feet together when I first take my address position, the ball positioned directly in the middle of that very narrow stance. If you then want the ball positioned off your left heel, simply move your right foot the prescribed distance for the correct stance width. If you want the ball, say, a couple of inches inside your left heel, first move your left foot those two inches toward the target, then move your right foot in the opposite direction the distance you want, depending on what club you are using. That's a lot more precise than to move willy-nilly and start fiddling with your feet, because your eyes will tend to fool you and make it difficult to get the ball in the same place consistently.

On almost all my full swings, I will play the ball in the same position, just inside my left heel. This holds true

1

whether I'm swinging a driver or a 9-iron. The only difference is the width of my stance, which will change the look of the ball position in relation to the right foot but will leave it the same relative to the left foot. The game is hard enough to learn to play without having to learn a whole lot of different ball positions for different clubs. Narrowing the variables makes it simple and gives you a better chance to be effective.

You should, of course, change your ball position for different types of shots. If you want to fade the ball or hit it higher than usual, play it farther forward in your stance, more toward the left toe. If you want to hook the ball or hit it lower than usual, move it back, more toward the right foot. In all cases, *establish ball position with your left foot, then adjust your right.*

For all normal shots, I like to set my hands just over the ball. I don't believe your hands should be in front of the ball at address unless you're trying to hit a knockdown shot or play a special chip shot. If you want to play with the true loft of the club, which you do in most cases, the shaft should be straight up and down at address and should be returned to that position at impact. The moment you put your hands a little ahead, you have delofted

3

### Adjust Knees to Shape Shots

*In general, your body alignment determines the line on which you swing the club. This, in conjunction with clubface aim, determines the shape of your shots. The easiest way to adjust your body alignment is with your knees. For a basically straight shot, align your knees—along with your feet, hip and eyes—on a line parallel to your target line (1). To fade the ball from left to right, set your left knee back or away from the target line (2). To draw the ball from right to left, pull your right knee back (3).*

### To Find Your Ball Position

To find your correct ball position consistently, start with your feet together and the ball directly between them (1). Then establish your ball position by moving your right foot (2). Here I'm setting up for a draw with the driver, the ball a bit farther back than normal in my stance. After setting the left foot, the stance width is established by moving the right foot (3 and 4).

the club and probably opened the face at the same time.

When we get into the discussion on angles in Chapter 10, you'll be better able to understand how ball position affects ball flight and trajectory. For now, just trust me.

## ROUTINE

The most important factor in tying together all your pre-swing fundamentals and in getting your swing started is a routine, a system. This gives you a trigger for your swing and also provides a series of checkpoints to which you can return when you start playing poorly. A good preshot routine gives you a repetitive way to aim the club, set your grip, get the ball in the correct position, get yourself balanced, get your alignment correct,

give your muscles the feel of the swing . . . and then swing, *almost without thinking about it.*

In my particular routine, I start from a few steps behind the ball, where I visually establish my target. I move into the ball and aim the face of the club. I put my left hand on the club to establish the relationship with the clubface. I put on the right hand to complete the grip. I adjust my left foot for ball position, then the right foot for balance and comfort. Then I waggle, look at the target, then look back to the ball. I do this three times, and as I finish the final waggle I go into my swing.

*The waggle is important* —It is vital that you waggle to set up your swing. I prefer to do it with my hands, moving

the clubhead away from and back to the ball to give myself the feeling of swinging on the correct path. It is important that whatever type of waggle you use takes the pressure and tension out of your arms. This makes it easier to start your swing under pressure.

I don't happen to use a forward press to start my swing. When I complete my final waggle, I start. Most good players do incorporate a forward press, making a slight forward kicking movement with the right knee, a slight forward movement of the hands or, as in the case of Jack Nicklaus, just a slight leaning of the body to the left . . . anything to set up a rebound motion that will trigger the backswing. My approach to the swing is deliberate

enough and systematic enough that I've never seemed to need a forward press, but it probably is good for most players, in that it gets them into motion a little more easily. If you feel you need it, then practice it enough that it becomes an instinctive part of your system.

Your system, your waggle, your forward press or lack of it, need not be the same as mine. You must, through practice and experimentation, find what works best for you. But once you establish your routine, your system of checkpoints, it should never vary, no matter what the club or the situation. Your waggle might be a little shorter and quicker if you are planning to play a little punch shot, for instance, and it might be longer

**Place It Inside Left Heel**

*The normal ball position for a driver is just inside the left heel. For most amateur players, any error in position should be toward* back *in the stance rather than too far forward.*

and slower for a drive. But your checkpoints always should come in the same sequence, in the same rhythm and at the same pace, and your number of waggles always should be the same.

The major mistake most players make under pressure is changing their routines. You almost always can tell when a player is panicking, because suddenly he starts doing things differently than before. That's because the situation, the shot at hand, has become more important than those that preceded it, and he forgets what got him this far. If you have a solid routine, trust it when you walk up to the ball leading the tournament and must hit a good shot. Tell yourself that

your system got you this far. Resist the temptation to change, to hurry your preparation and your swing. Never speed up your checkpoints. I concentrated on my system when panic was striking on the 72nd tee at Merion, and it carried me through.

Eventually you will find that, no matter how pressure-filled the situation, your swing becomes mostly a reaction to your repetitive preshot routine. As Bert Yancey once said, a good routine "eliminates that awful moment when you have to take the club away." And your shots will be consistently better for it.

### The Waggle Sets Up Your Swing

*The proper waggle gives you the feeling of the path on which you are about to make the full swing. While I waggle, I also identify my target line by looking at the intermediate spot I've selected (1 and 2). I prefer to waggle with my hands, moving the clubhead away from and back to the ball (2).*

# CHAPTER FIVE

# THE SWING

The purpose of the golf swing is to propel the ball in the right direction and for the correct distance. Assuming proper alignment, the golf swing can only do that if the club is traveling on the correct path. Regardless of what the swing looks like, regardless of speed or length of backswing, to strike a golf ball consistently well the shaft and clubhead must be consistently on the right track coming into impact.

That seems pretty obvious, but getting the club on an *incorrect* path, for one reason or another, probably ruins more golf shots than any other single factor.

Learning to put the club consistently on the right path requires some practice, some training of the muscles. But once you've done it, you will have opened up a whole new world. You will be able to swing at different speeds and hit different kinds of shots. By releasing your hands at different points in the downswing and by doing some other manipulation, you can do some wonderful things in shaping your shots. You can do this because you have laid a solid foundation for your swing—the club is always coming into the ball the same way.

You also might be amazed at the improvement in the tempo or rhythm of your swing. Poor tempo, usually defined as pace that is too fast at the wrong time in the swing, is emphasized—or probably caused—by the club getting on the wrong track at some point in the swing. When a player gets off track and hits a bad shot or two, somebody usually tells him, "You're swinging too fast." But if he's on the right track and swings fast and hits a good shot, nobody will say, "You swung too fast." They'll say, "Good shot!"

## THE CLUB COMES FROM THE INSIDE

The correct swing path is simply this: *on the downswing, the club should be traveling on a path inside or behind the path it took on the backswing.* Notice I didn't mention anything about target line, that imaginary line extending through the ball to your eventual target. In most cases, your downswing *will* be coming from inside the target line ("inside" being the side of the line on which you are standing, "outside" being the other side of the line). But there can be an exception, which I'll explain in a moment.

### The Swing Is Clockwise

On the backswing and the forward swing through impact, the swing travels in a clockwise direction. If you stand on this giant clock, facing 12 o'clock and aiming at 9 o'clock, your clubhead should start back toward 3 o'clock. As your body turns on the backswing, the clubhead moves toward a position between 3 and 4. When you start down, you should feel that the clubhead is coming from close to 4 o'clock. It might not be quite from there, but it should feel like it. At the very least, it must have traveled in a clockwise direction and be starting down from inside the backswing path.

**The Inside Swing**
This view looking down the target line shows that after I've reached the top of my swing and have established the plane of my backswing, my hands remain just inside that plane and the club comes from behind me on

*the forward swing on the way to impact.*

43

**Downswing Inside Backswing**
The backswing path (left) starts straight back, moving up and to the inside as the body turns. (Below) the clubhead path on the downswing comes from well inside the backswing path, approaching the ball from inside the target line and moving down that line through impact.

Imagine, if you will, a giant clock on the ground. Your ball is teed in the middle of it, where the hands join. You are facing 12 o'clock. Your target is 9 o'clock. Now I simply want you to think of swinging—from takeaway to impact—in a *clockwise* direction. Start the clubhead back toward 3 o'clock. As your body turns on the backswing, the clubhead will swing inside or away from the target line as it travels back and up. Let's say that halfway back the club is at 3:30. At the top of your backswing it might be at 4 o'clock. When you start your downswing, the club must be traveling on a path inside or after the 4 o'clock mark. At the very least, it must be coming down from 4 o'clock. If the club starts its downward motion outside the backswing path, or counterclockwise—at 2 o'clock, for example—you will be outside the golf ball and you will not play golf properly.

All of the good and great players I have seen make a very noticeable movement at the top of the swing, either with their arms or legs or both, to get the club started down inside.

Let's go back to the clock. If you want to fade or slice the ball (this is the exception I mentioned earlier), you probably will stand a little open to your 9 o'clock target, your feet and body set left of the target instead of on a line parallel to it. Let's say you start the club back toward 2 o'clock and bring it back down from 3 o'clock or just short of there. You will be cutting across the ball slightly and this, in combination with your clubface position, will impart a left-to-right movement to your shot. But, because you still are coming down inside your backswing path, you will be hitting with power.

If you want to hook the ball more than usual, you might

### Outside Is the Wrong Side

*This is an example of how not to swing into the ball (left). My shoulders are spinning, the right shoulder moving outward, which forces the clubhead to come into the ball from outside the target line at too steep an angle. The result can be a pull, a pull slice, a pop-up or other disaster. In any event, it will be bad.*

1

aim a little more to the right, which would start your backswing toward 4 o'clock. That means the club should start down from about 5 o'clock.

In general, *the path on which the club is traveling on the downswing dictates the line on which the golf ball starts, while the position of the clubface determines how much the ball will curve.* If the face is square to the target at impact while the clubhead is traveling straight down the target line, the ball will start straight and go dead straight. If the face is open while the clubhead is moving straight down the line, the ball will start relatively straight and slice right; if the face is closed, the ball will start relatively straight and hook left. If the face is square with the club-head coming from the inside,

the ball will start right and hook back. If the face is square with the clubhead coming from the outside, the ball will start left and slice back. With the clubhead traveling in either of those directions, the open or closed position of the face will affect the curvature of the shot just as when the clubhead is going straight to the target—the ball will start on the path of the club and curve either left or right. So there are nine possible directions in which the ball can fly and curve, with an infinite variety of degrees for each.

In all cases, the golf ball is your teacher. By noting where it starts, you can tell what you are doing with the path of the swing. By noting how it curves, you can tell what you are or are not doing with your hands and arms to properly

3

**Legs Move First Starting Down**

*The first movement on the downswing is with the legs, as you can see in this three-picture sequence. Note the position of the club and the legs at the top of the backswing in Picture 1 and see how much relative movement there is through Pictures 2 and 3. My knees have returned to a position almost parallel to the target line in Picture 3, while the club has moved hardly at all.*

release the clubhead.

So the problem in hitting a golf ball straight revolves around getting the path of the club reasonably straight (but always from the inside) and the face of the club square at the moment of impact. Sounds simple enough, but an awful lot of people have put a lot of time, effort and money into trying to make this happen, often with very little success.

Why is it so difficult? I think one of the major problems is a myth that keeps being perpetuated, the one that says golf is a left-handed, left-sided game. This creates in a player the tendency to pull the club down from the top of the backswing with the left arm. Unfortunately, he or she usually pulls it across the ball instead of keeping the club inside and applying power from

behind. In addition, the mindset that is telling the player to swing with the left hand and arm also inhibits him from releasing or turning the club over through the impact area. He just keeps pulling it along, the butt or grip end of the club stays ahead of the clubhead and the clubface never gets back to square.

That's the major reason nine out of 10 handicap players slice the ball. There are some other causes, of course, but almost all of them stem from an incorrect concept of the swing, the path it should take and how it should be executed.

You already have learned my concept of swing path. Now let's look at my ideas on how the swing should be executed within the guidelines of that concept. Bear in mind one factor—while we're going

**Left Guides, Right Hits**
*The left hand and arm must remain stable and guide the club during the swing (above) while the right hand and arm apply the power through impact (opposite page).*

that your mind can visualize and your body literally can feel, time after time. If you do less, you will create frustration and rob yourself of much of the enjoyment that this game can bring.

With that proviso in mind, let's break down the swing into these categories:
• The role of the sides, left and right.
• The role of the arms and hands, back and through.
• How to release.
• The role of the legs, back and through.

## THE ROLE OF THE SIDES

The simplest way to describe what the two sides do in the swing is to say that the left side guides while the right side applies the power. (That's assuming you're a right-hander. If you're a *natural* left-hander, just the opposite would be true.) Of course, that means that both sides play an equally important role. I've explained how the left hand should be aligned basically with the face of the club and should lead the clubhead into impact. At the same time, the right hand —your stronger hand—should be *hitting* the golf ball. I realize that the thought of *hitting* the ball can cause all kinds of problems with many amateur players, that *swinging through* the ball can be a more effective mental key. Well, whether you are hitting or swinging, you are going to have to apply whatever power you have with your right hand if you are to achieve your full potential. Remember the advice George Naismith gave me, that the strong hand must be on the bottom because it controls most of the golf club.

What you must do is find a way to *control* that application of power, to keep the left hand guiding and stable while the right hand hits against it. The left has to be strong

to have to dissect the swing, breaking it down into parts and examining what each part does, eventually you will have to put all the parts together and develop a *feel* for your swing. If you cannot generate a feel for your swing that will be reasonably repetitive over a period of time, you never will play golf to your potential. I'm not asking that you develop into a potential U.S. Open winner. I'm just saying that whatever your level of physical skill and whatever amount of time you feel you can devote to improving your golf game, it will be better fulfilled by understanding the parts of the swing and blending them into a motion

**Left Firm at Impact**
The left hand, wrist and forearm remain firm through impact, although they are rotating at this point and the hand will begin to recock and move the club upward very soon after impact.

enough and moving fast enough that the right doesn't overpower it. If the left hand breaks down or cups inwardly too much in the impact area, you will either hit a big hook, if your club is coming from the inside, or an even worse pull hook if it is coming from the outside. Setting your hands properly on the club, so that the left hand doesn't easily break down, is the first step. Being aware of the path the club should take during the swing is the next step.

Finally, train the right hand and arm to work properly during the swing. Your feeling should be that you are throwing the clubhead with your right hand, much as a second baseman makes an underhand toss to first. Watch the tour pros when they take practice swings without a club prior to hitting a shot. Almost always they will be swinging the right hand —they are practicing "back and hit."

On the downswing, then, the clubface becomes nothing more than an extension of the right hand. If you want the clubface to rotate, to turn over, you do it with your right hand while the left hand is guiding. Again, that only works if the club is coming down from the inside.

Once you have incorporated those concepts, you are on your way.

# THE ROLE OF THE ARMS AND HANDS

The arms swing the club, and the hands, in coordination with the arms cock the club going back and release it coming through impact.

I mention that the arms swing the club only because you hear a lot of talk about shoulder turn in the golf swing. I'm guilty of it myself. The reason is that we feel the shoulders turning. In my case, I often use the distance my left shoulder travels as a subconscious checkpoint in

my swing. Yet I never think of my shoulders, because if I swing my arms back, my shoulders have to turn with them. I haven't yet figured out a way to make a full backswing with my arms and leave my shoulders still.

At the start of the backswing, you can establish a mental picture of taking the club back on the correct angle by envisioning the angle at which you move your left forearm, whether outside, in-

**Clubface an Extension of Right Hand**
*On the downswing, the clubface responds to the action of the right hand while the left hand guides—and the swing is coming from the inside.*

51

**The Arms Turn the Shoulders**
I've never found a way to swing the arms without turning the shoulders. The shoulder turn follows the swinging of the arms. so that's what you should concentrate on.

52

side or, ideally, straight back.

I like to *start* the arms, hands and clubhead back together. You are asking for trouble if either the hands or the clubhead travel too far without the other. *However,* I like to feel the clubhead getting up higher than the hands rather soon into the backswing. This sets the angle between the shaft and your left forearm. It gets the shaft more vertical and on plane sooner, which in effect changes the weight of the club and makes it feel lighter. All of this gives you better control of the club.

There is no doubt that the hands cock the club up in this manner, but I don't like to feel that I'm making a conscious effort to do so. If I say to myself, "Get the clubhead up," it will happen. I prefer that approach and recommend it, because I find *it's always better to think of the clubhead and be aware of where it is during the swing rather than think of what the various parts of the body are doing.*

The length of your backswing will vary with the club you are using. For a short-iron shot, where distance is not the prime objective, the left shoulder may only get turned *to* the ball. With a driver, when I'm trying to hit the ball harder, I like to feel my left shoulder being pulled as far behind the ball as possible on the backswing. This gives me the full turn I want.

But *length of backswing is not nearly as important as control.* You must maintain a firm hold on the club and you must maintain the radius of your swing by keeping your left arm as straight as possible at the top . . . without having it rigid, of course. Some players are more flexible than others and can take the club back farther under control. We hear a lot about getting the shaft parallel to the ground at the top, but if the only way you can get it to

parallel is to collapse your left arm or loosen your grip, or both, you're much better off taking the club three-quarters of the way back and keeping it under control. You will gain accuracy and quite likely distance, too. A good example is Dan Pohl, who has about half a backswing and still is one of the tour's longest hitters.

As I stressed earlier, it's very important to feel, at the beginning of the downswing,

**Get Club Up Quickly**

*On the backswing, think of getting the clubhead quickly up above your hands. This gets the shaft on plane sooner and makes the club feel lighter.*

### Shorter Club, Shorter Swing

*The shorter the club in your hand, the shorter your backswing can be. You don't need to strike the ball with as much effort and are looking more for precision and accuracy.*

that the arms, hands and club are moving to the inside of the backswing path. The farther back you swing your arms and the more your shoulders and body turn, the more inside the club gets. In starting from the top, I find it helpful to think of my hands moving toward my right knee as the arms swing down. At all costs, you must avoid swinging the arms *away* from the body as you start down. It's far better for most players to be too much inside than to get the club coming down from

the outside. All you're going to do is hook the ball a little more, and that's preferable to the big banana ball.

## HOW TO RELEASE

One of the great mysteries of this game seems to be release, both the term and the action. Depending on the extent of their indoctrination, golfers think release means anything from turning the clubface over at impact to throwing the club down the fairway.

Release essentially means

### Control Most Important

As a generalization, the three top-of-backswing positions shown above are (1) too long, (2) too short and (3) just right, parallel to the ground. However, how far you take the club back depends on your flexibility and your ability to control it (to be honest, I rarely get it back to parallel myself, even with a driver). If you have to err, do so on the side of short, because control is your No. 1 goal.

releasing or straightening the angle between the left forearm and clubshaft that was formed on the backswing, thus helping bring the clubface back to a square position at impact, as it was at address. *When* the club is released during the downswing will vary from person to person and will vary with other factors, such as ball position, weight transfer, speed of swing and so forth. Just keep in mind that your purpose is to get the shaft of the club vertical and the face of the club square at impact.

The task of learning a good release becomes much easier if the club is coming in on the correct path, because then the ball always will tell you how effectively you are releasing. If the ball starts to the right or slices, curving to the right, you have failed to rotate the clubface enough and have left it open. If the ball starts to the left or hooks, curving to the left, you have rotated the face too much or too quickly and got it too closed at impact.

Remember, I said earlier that the clubface is simply an extension of the right hand. With that in mind, my key thought for a good release is to *get my right forefinger pointing at the ball at the same time the clubhead gets there.* That assures that I won't get my left hand or the grip end of the club past the

### Start Hands Toward Right Knee

*One of the keys that helps me start the downswing correctly is to feel that I'm starting my hands toward my right knee. This helps insure that I will bring the club into the ball from inside.*

ball before the clubhead gets there. If that happens, you get a shot that is pushed or sliced to the right.

The action of the hands and arms during and after impact is this: as the hands uncock and straighten the angle between forearm and clubshaft, the right hand and forearm begin to rotate over the left. Ideally this will start happening about the time the hands reach waist-high, but you should make no conscious effort to delay the action. Nor should you attempt to accelerate it unnaturally. Again, the flight of the ball will tell you if your release is being timed properly.

The hands also begin to recock on the other side of the ball. The left hand does not break down or cup backward but recocks basically through the same range of motion as in going back, only in the opposite direction. You should think of your follow-through as a mirror image of your backswing. As in the backswing, the head end of the club should quickly get higher than the grip end in the follow-through. As the right arm extends, the left arm will fold into your side and your right forefinger will become the highest part of your hands as the club comes up. As I said before, just thinking about the clubhead coming up should cause your

57

**Right Forefinger Points to Ball at Impact...**
Thinking of making your right forefinger point to the ball at impact can help you bring the clubface squarely into the ball.

*... and Then Comes Up*
*Getting the clubhead higher*
*than your hands quickly*
*after impact is important,*
*and thinking of getting your*
*right forefinger up will help*
*you do that.*

hands to do the job.

Release may sound pretty complicated, but it really is not. As you swing down, just feel your right arm passing over the left. Try to get your right forefinger to the ball at the same time as the clubhead, and make the clubhead come up after impact.

The extension of your right arm and the clubhead coming up will let you swing to a good, full finish without thinking about it. If you keep the hands higher than the clubhead too long into the follow-through, you are inhibiting a full, free release, and it will show up in the form of a restricted follow-through. That can be a good checkpoint for you.

Finally, it is important to keep your grip pressure constant and relatively the same in both hands. Gripping the club too tightly with the left hand may prevent the right hand from being active enough. And too much pressure with the right hand

**Swing to a Full Finish**
*The thought of getting the clubhead up after impact as you extend your right arm will let you swing to a full, free finish.*

could break down the left and keep it from doing its job.

## THE ROLE OF THE FEET AND LEGS

The action of the feet, legs and hips during the swing is one I liken to opening and closing a door. On the backswing, the hips turn as your left knee moves behind the ball. This opens the door and effectively transfers your weight to your right side. On the downswing, the first move is with the left knee, although I like to get my weight off my right side by trying to get the right knee as close to the left as I can. At the same time, the hips are *turning,* closing the door. If your hips slide too much laterally, toward the target, your swing will come inside too much, your lower body will run out of speed and stop and you will have to finish the swing with your hands alone. The turning of the hips lets you increase your arm and hand speed through impact.

On the backswing, your weight will go to the inside of your right foot, tending toward the heel, while the left heel comes off the ground. On

**Open and Close the Door**
Liken the action of the feet, (above) legs and hips to opening and closing a door.

They open or turn to the right on the backswing, then close or turn to the left on the forward swing.

### Weight to Inside Right, Left Heel Up on Back-swing

On the backswing, your weight should transfer to the inside of your right foot while your left heel is pulled off the ground, depending on the amount of your flexibility.

the downswing, the left heel goes down, the weight goes first to the inside and then to the outside of the left foot, winding up primarily on the outside of the heel as the right foot comes up on its toe. I like to feel that when I complete my swing I could take a step forward with my right foot and just start walking.

One of those long-ago changes I had to make was to narrow my stance so I could transfer my weight more effectively and get my knees working better, the left knee moving behind the ball on the backswing and the right

working more toward the left on the downswing. My stance was so wide I couldn't do that effectively. That's why I like to see a stance that is as narrow as possible while letting you maintain your balance.

A caution here—keeping the weight slightly on the inside of the right foot at the top of the backswing is a good way to avoid swaying, but don't overdo it. *A slight lateral movement that gets your whole upper body behind the ball is much better than trying to keep your head too steady, leaving too much weight on your left side and leaning to the left.* If you do the latter, you'll come across the ball from the outside every time. The slight sway, in fact, might be preferable for most golfers.

## THE ALTOGETHER SWING

Let's try to coordinate all the parts from start to finish. I like to put everything in motion at the same time, starting the clubhead straight back with my left hand and my left knee. The clubhead moves up and inside as the shoulders and hips turn. The weight goes to the right side and the left knee moves behind the ball, opening the door. As the top of the swing is reached, the knees move laterally to start the downswing as the arms and club move more behind or inside the backswing path. As the weight goes left, the hips turn and the arms swing down. The right

**First Move Down Is with Left Knee**
*At the start of the forward swing, the first move is the lateral motion of the left knee, which causes the hips to begin turning and eventually closing.*

63

### Keep a Narrow Stance

*I like to keep my stance as narrow as possible while still being able to maintain my balance during the swing I am about to make. Here, with a driver, my stance, measured from the insides of my heels, is a bit narrower than the width of my shoulders.*

### Start Everything Back Together
On the takeaway, I feel that all the parts move in unison as I start the clubhead straight back with my left hand and my left knee.

forefinger points to the ball at the same time the clubhead gets there. The right hand and arm cross over the left, the right arm extends as the clubhead comes up. The weight goes to the outside of the left foot as the hips finish turning, closing the door, and the arms swing on to a full finish.

As I indicated earlier, I don't worry much about keeping the head still during the swing. In fact, I don't think about the head at all. The head is going to rotate and move a little bit on the back-

swing and a little bit on the follow-through. The arms are moving the shoulders and your head is attached to your shoulders. Trying to keep the head absolutely still just ties you up and costs you freedom and speed in your swing.

I do, however, make a very conscious effort *to keep my body at the same level during the swing, to maintain the height that I have established at address.* This helps you avoid hitting the shot fat, striking the ground before you do the ball, which usually is caused by dropping your

body and with it the arc of your swing. It also helps avoid the thin shot, contacting the ball too high, which usually is caused by raising your body. You can use a couple of different images to accomplish this. The first is to imagine that you have a board across your shoulders and you are just going to turn under that board. The other is to control your height with your knees, especially by keeping the right knee at the same flex on the backswing. However you do it, keeping your body at the same height is vitally important.

I also think it's important to look at the ball during the swing. As obvious as that sounds, many golfers don't do it, at least with enough concentrated effort. I want to be looking at the back of the ball, and specifically the back *inside* of the ball, the quarter of the ball closest to my right toe. That's the specific place I want the club to strike. It's like hitting a nail with a hammer. If you concentrate on looking at the head of the nail, you can consistently guide the hammer to hit that spot.

Don't stare at it too long as

### The Way the Feet Move
*On the forward swing, the left heel goes down, the weight transfers to the inside of the left foot, then rolls to the outside. Meanwhile, the right foot initially rolls to the left and then comes up on its toe, but not so far that the right heel spins outward.*

**The Altogether Swing**
As you study this sequence of the full swing with a driver, note my address posture (1) and how everything starts back together (2). The clubhead comes up quickly (3 and 4) as I swing to a near-parallel position at the top, my shoulders fully turned and my left knee behind the ball (5). The first move down is with the left knee (6 and 7).

*Note the release of the clubhead (8, 9 and 10) and the swing through to a full finish (11 and 12). Study the action of the feet throughout, and especially be aware of the flow of the swing, all the parts moving in coordination.*

**Maintain Your Height**

One of the keys to making consistently good swings is to think of maintaining your head, and the rest of your body, at pretty much the same height you establish at address. I like to do this by thinking of keeping my

knees level, neither
straightening nor dipping
during the swing. Or you
can imagine that you have
a bar across your shoulders
and are simply going to turn
under that bar.

2-IRON

**The Iron Swings Compared**
As you examine these sequence pictures, the first (above and overleaf) of a 2-iron, the next (on the following pages) of a pitching wedge, note the differences in the bend from the hips, the distance one stands from the ball and the angle of the plane—flatter

for the 2-iron, more upright for the wedge. These are factors you should be aware of, but you must remember that the differences occur naturally because of the length of the club. You don't have to consciously alter your setup or swing. Just don't try to fight these changes that occur with clubs of different lengths.

PITCHING WEDGE

**Look at the Ball**

*Once you get ready to swing, keep your eyes on the* back inside quarter *of the ball, just as you would look at the head of a nail you were trying to drive.*

you go through your preshot preparations, because that can freeze your mind and body, but once you get ready to swing, pay attention to hitting the nail.

*Open the door, close the door. Get the club up, bring it down inside, point the finger at the ball, turn the arms over and get the club up.*

It sounds simple . . . and it is. But nobody ever learned the golf swing only by reading about it. These are simply the directions, the blueprint. Now you must take this blueprint to the practice tee—hopefully with some professional help —and use it to build a swing that you can *feel,* one that you can execute consistently. I've said that before, but it cannot be emphasized enough.

# CHAPTER SIX

# GOLF AND ANGLES

This will be a short chapter but an important one, because it will give you an understanding not only of what causes the ball to be hit straight but why it travels in any other direction, shape or trajectory.

Very simply put, golf is a game of angles. To be more geometrically precise, it is a game of angles, circles, arcs and planes. But you don't have to worry about that. You need only be concerned about the angle at which the clubface strikes the ball, whether it be an up-and-down angle or a horizontal angle. Those angles determine how the ball flies. *If you know how to preset those angles, you can produce a lot of different and valuable golf shots without changing your basic swing.*

The different angles at which the clubface comes into the ball are determined by several factors—your ball position and weight distribution at address, your alignment relative to your target and the path on which you swing. As I pointed out in Chapter 4, ball position at address is an important function of striking the ball well. You must find out where the ball should be positioned in relation to the optimum point of release in your swing—the ideal impact position. I suggested guidelines in Chapter 4, but they are only guidelines. You could be making a good swing, but if the ball is too far forward or too far back in your stance, the release point is going to come at the wrong time. The clubface won't be square at impact and your shots likely will go astray. The only way you can really determine the best ball position for *you* is by experimenting in practice.

Assuming you can find your correct ball position for a normal swing, let's work on some refinements. I'm not going to dwell long on how to change the shape and trajectory of your shots, how to hook and slice the ball or hit it high and low. You do that mostly by changing your alignment, your setup position and, again, your ball position. These changes can affect your swing's path and plane —the angle at which the club swings around your body in relation to the ground—but you make very little adjustment in the swing itself.

## HOOK AND SLICE

If I want to hook the ball, I aim the club at the target as usual but align my body more to the right and move the ball back in my stance. This makes the path of my swing even more

inside in relation to my target, but I really haven't changed the swing at all. If I want to slice the ball, I open my stance, aiming the club at the target but aligning more to the left, and move the ball forward. If I just want to fade the ball a little, I'll go ahead and make my normal swing from that alignment. If I really need to slice the ball, around a tree or a dogleg, I'll make sure I don't get the club very much inside, so I will come across the ball from the outside, and I'll keep the left hand moving a little longer without turning over to make sure the clubface doesn't close through impact. In that case, I have to remember that the ball won't go as far.

## HIGH AND LOW

The up-and-down angles are critical in hitting the ball higher or lower. In general, when the ball is on the ground and you want to hit it higher, you position it more forward in your stance and adjust your weight so that it is more centered or even tending toward your right side. This means the club will come into the ball on a shallower or more sweeping angle and the clubface will have perhaps slightly more than its true loft. With an iron or fairway wood, when the ball is on the ground, you don't really want the club coming *up* at impact, but you want it as close to that point as possible. If the ball is in the rough on a cushion of grass, an inch or so off the ground, you definitely want the club coming up to get the ball higher.

To hit lower shots, again when the ball is on the ground, you do just the opposite. Position the ball back in your stance and set your

### Adjust Ball Position For Fade and Draw

*Not only should you open or close your stance for a left-to-right fade or a right-to-left draw, you also must adjust the ball position. Play the ball more forward in your stance for a fade or slice (left), farther back for a draw or hook.*

### To Hit a Fade

To fade the ball, hit it in a left-to-right shape, do the opposite of what you did for a draw—set your stance open, your left foot pulled back from the target line, aiming the clubface at the target. Then swing normally. Your

stance adjustment will cause you to swing down a bit from outside to inside the target line, applying the spin that will create the

fade. Each case, the fade and the draw, becomes a matter of angles.

81

**To Hit a Draw**

To hit a draw, a right-to-left shot, set up with your stance closed, the right foot pulled back, as indicated here, while aiming your clubface at the target. This automatically makes you swing back more to the in-

82

side and down, into impact, more from the inside, producing the inside-to-outside swing that gives you the right-to-left action you want.

## Up for High, Back for Low

To hit a higher shot, set up with your weight equally distributed or even slightly on your right, the ball positioned slightly more than normal toward your target (above left). When you swing, make sure you stay well behind the ball and don't release the club quite as much (above right). For a lower shot, set the ball farther back in your stance, your weight toward the left side (below left). Don't emphasize staying behind the ball when you swing, although don't let your upper body slide forward, and release the club more fully (below right). The differences in setup and swing usually are slight, as they are in these pictures, but golf is a game of nuances and those differences make a big difference in the type of shot you hit. Depending on how dramatically you want to change your shot trajectory, the differences also can be severe, but be careful not to overdo it.

weight more to your left. This will bring the club into the ball on a steeper, more downward angle, which effectively takes loft off the club and creates the lower trajectory.

To put it in perspective, you want to feel your body more *behind* the ball for higher shots, more *in front* of it for lower shots.

## FROM A TEE

The "rules of angles" I have just prescribed apply to any shot, whether short or long, where the ball is on the ground. When the ball is on a tee, most often when you are using a driver, the rules change. A steeper or more descending blow with a wood club will cause the ball to fly too high—often it will be popped up. The ideal angle of approach when the ball is on a

tee would have the clubhead coming into impact on a level or, even better, a slightly upward angle. This will start the ball off on a slightly lower and better trajectory, resulting in more carry and roll.

You will have to experiment on the practice range. I can't tell you what minute adjustment will produce what result. That you will have to find out for yourself, using the guidelines I've given you, because the possibilities are truly infinite. But that's what makes golf such an exciting challenge—there *are* infinite possibilities. And by being aware of how to shape your shots—with setup and alignment changes rather than by using a lot of different swings—you are narrowing the variables and making the game a lot less complicated.

### *Swing Up With a Driver*
*When you have a driver in your hand and the ball is on a tee, your most efficient angle through the ball is upward. Set your head slightly behind the ball at address and keep it behind the ball as you swing through, insuring the upward path of the clubhead through impact.*

# CHAPTER SEVEN

# THE SCORING SHOTS

**D**uring a luncheon I had with Ben Hogan a few years ago, he told me that if he had his life and golf career to live over again, he would do nothing but practice the 9-iron, pitching wedge, sand wedge and putter. The point he was making is that there is no substitute for a good short game. You don't need to drive the ball 300 yards. What you *must* do to score consistently well is capitalize on your good shots and recover from your bad ones...and you do this by becoming a good pitcher, chipper and putter.

I've seen players, from Jack Nicklaus on down, play magnificent ball-striking rounds, hitting 16 to 18 greens in regulation...and shoot 72. I've also seen players hit the ball all over the golf course, miss more greens than they hit...and shoot 65. In the first case, the players did not take advantage of their good shots by holing the putts. In the second, they *did* recover from their bad shots, and then some.

The optimum combination is to be a player with Jack Nicklaus' ability to hit greens and also to be one hell of a good putter. In fact, when Jack was winning everything in sight, that's exactly the kind of player he was.

The reality, however, is that even the most consistent ball-strikers on the PGA Tour hit barely 70 percent of the greens during a round, which means they are missing five or six greens every time out. Yet they average a shot or two below par. It's apparent that whenever they miss a green, most of the time they are making pars, and that they are capitalizing on their putting or other short-game skills to make enough birdies to overcome the occasional bogey.

In a sense, all shots are "scoring shots," in that each stroke counts the same. But for our purposes here, the scoring shots will be those that let you capitalize when you get into position to make a par or birdie. This includes pitching, chipping, sand play and putting—the short game.

I will give you my basic techniques for playing these shots. I've learned and polished my short-game play through my association with some players and teachers whom I consider the best in that area—Norman Von Nida, of course, and Phil Rodgers in recent years, plus Bruce Devlin, also a Von Nida student who is an absolute genius out of bunkers. But, again, these are only blueprints. There are many ways to strike any of these shots. In fact, you *must* find different ways to strike them within the basic technique if you are to be a successful short-game player. The short shots require good eye-hand coordination. They require that indefinable ingredient called "feel." And, perhaps most important, playing them successfully requires the knowledge and the ability to *play the right shot at the right time.*

I cannot give you that knowledge. That you must acquire yourself, through practice and experience. You must learn what *you* can do with a particular shot, what your strengths or limitations are, and how great or small your chances are of pulling off shots under special circumstances. This knowledge also gives you the ability to *improvise,* to be able to dream up a shot that will work when there appears to be no shot at all.

Tom Watson's chip-in from greenside rough on the 17th hole at Pebble Beach during the final round of the 1982 U.S. Open exemplifies the importance of imagination, practice and skill. Facing an almost-sure bogey that would have dropped him out of the lead, he made a magnificent shot that turned potential defeat into victory. But give the man credit. I've seen Tom Watson practice shots like that more than any other part of his game. So if there is any justice, any reward for effort, it prevailed there. Most golfers, especially amateurs but even some tour professionals, do *not* spend that much time practicing the short game. At many courses, including a lot of those at which the tour plays, the facilities for practicing short shots are inadequate. As a result, those shots get no more attention than the grip, which is unfortunate, for they

are every bit as vital as the grip.

You can use many different clubs for the many different short shots you will face. Picking the correct one for each situation is something you must learn. But I urge you, above all, to develop proficiency with the sand wedge, both out of the bunkers and from the grass. It is most likely the most versatile club in the bag. You can hit the ball high or low with it, pitch or chip-and-run with it, use it from 80 yards down to six feet or so, play it from hardpan, good lies, heavy rough, just about anywhere. Use it! Learn to love it! You will be glad you did.

Contrary to popular opinion, I don't necessarily feel you always should get the ball down onto the green as quickly as possible and let it run to the hole. Obviously, for a little shot from the fringe with no trouble in your way and a smooth, relatively flat putting surface between you and the cup, the chip-and-run would be the one to play. But don't make that your guiding philosophy and close your mind to other options. Actually, most of the time you have more control over the ball when it is in the air. You can't always control the bounce and the roll on a chip shot. Judging distance and controlling spin also is easier when you elevate the ball. You just have to learn to get it in the air at the right distance and height to have it finish close to the hole.

## HOW TO MAKE YOUR CHOICES

The basic short shots are:

•*The chip*—the ball travels on a low trajectory and usually rolls on the ground farther than it flies in the air.

•*The pitch*—the ball flies higher and usually carries in the air farther than it rolls.

•*The putt*—the ball rolls on the ground all the way.

• *The sand shot*—one of the few shots in golf (there are some others) where there normally is no club-ball contact. The ball simply flies out on a cushion of sand.

Before you play any of those shots, you need to know something about the area you are playing them to or on—the green. And you must be aware of what is between you and the green. Those are the factors that you consider in choosing which shot to play. Before you make a decision on a short shot, you should walk onto the green, if you are close enough, to determine the firmness of the green and the speed and texture of the putting surface.

Having done that, assess the trouble in your way. If you have only a few feet or yards of flat turf to carry before your ball will land on the green, the chip shot with a 7- or 8-iron is perhaps the correct choice. Land the ball a few feet onto the green and let it run to the hole. However, if there is a yawning bunker between you and the putting surface, an entirely different shot is called for. You must loft the ball into the air, carry it over the bunker and stop it relatively quickly.

Those are the two basic choices you must make, the two basic shots you will face from grass. And there are about nine million variations that lie in between. Again, learning how far a ball will fly and roll with one club as opposed to another club, learning when to apply each shot or a variation thereof, is a matter of experience. And remember that it's just as important to know, at any given time, what shots you *can't* play as it is to know those you *can*. Don't try to do something you can't do at the moment. Choose a safer course, then get to the practice tee and learn the shot that you wanted to hit in the first place. In all cases, the more you learn before you get on the golf course, the better off you will be.

# HOW TO PLAY THE SHOTS

*The chip*—Set up for the chip shot with your stance slightly open, your left foot pulled away from the target line a bit, and your weight more on your left side. Grip down on the club, because the closer your hands are to the clubhead, the more control you will have. Position the ball closer to your feet than you normally would, almost as if it were a putt. This will tend to set your hands higher, with a little more arch in your wrists, which will give you more freedom in your swing and also more control. The club may almost be sitting on its toe.

Position the ball back in your stance, toward your right foot, which puts your hands slightly ahead of the ball. I like to put my left hand on the club in a weaker position, turning it slightly to the left or counterclockwise. This restricts the action of the wrists. I don't like a wristy swing, because under pressure you can get nervous, twitch a bit with the hands and make inconsistent contact. So I recommend you basically adhere to the pendulum theory when you stroke a chip shot, using very little body movement and very little cocking at the wrists.

In making the stroke, take the club straight back and straight through and think of "scraping" the ball. By that I mean you should not hit *at* or *to* the ball. Don't take much, if any, divot and try to make your follow-through the same length as your backswing. If you take the club back two feet, follow through two feet. Think of swinging the club back and through low to the ground, although don't do anything unnatural to keep it low. Remember, you basically

***Turn Left Hand to the Left***
*For the basic chip shot, put the left hand into a "weaker" position by turning it slightly to the left or counterclockwise (opposite page). This prevents your swing from being too wristy and twitching a bit under pressure. It allows you to make solid contact more consistently, leading to more consistent shots.*

### Arch Wrists for Chipping

*For the chip shot, arch your wrists (first picture), setting the club slightly on its toe. This gives you the freedom to swing the club back and through without excessive wrist action. The feet and body are set open or to the left of the intended starting direction. Note how still the head and body remain throughout the stroke.*

are making a pendulum stroke. I just don't want you picking the club up too abruptly on a normal chip shot.

In general, distance is a result of the length of your swing. The longer your chip-shot swing, the more clubhead speed you generate and the farther the ball will go.

*The pitch*—You want this shot to fly higher than the chip and run less after landing. To accomplish that, use a more lofted club (as I said earlier, I prefer the sand wedge for most pitching situations) and then take advantage of the true loft of the club. In other words, you don't want your hands very far ahead of the ball at address, if any at all. If your hands are way ahead of the ball, you've simply delofted your sand wedge into a 9-iron. For a normal pitch, position the ball more forward, just inside your

left toe, so that the shaft is basically straight up and down. Your hands will be even with or maybe slightly behind the ball. Instead of the weaker left-hand grip, which stifles hand action, use a stronger grip, the hand turned more to the right or clockwise. This encourages the hinging at the wrists that you want for a pitch shot. Your stance should be slightly open, as for the chip, but now your weight should be equally distributed between the two feet. Setting the weight too far to the left will give you too much of a descending blow, again delofting the club.

For the pitch shot, break your wrists a little earlier in the backswing, getting the clubhead higher than the hands rather quickly. On the forward swing, your key thought should be to *return the club to the same position it was in at address, the shaft*

*straight up and down.* On the follow-through, the clubhead again should come up quickly as your right hand crosses over your left.

The normal pitch shot, whether it be five yards or 85 yards, is made with simply a miniature version of the full swing. I feel I just cut short my normal golf swing for those shots. The length of your swing will determine the distance the ball goes. It's not unlike having a golf ball in your hand and throwing it a certain distance with an underarm motion. If you want to throw it 12 yards, you can pretty well determine, instinctively, how much arm motion to give the toss. If you want to throw it twice as far, your arm instinctively will go back farther. You want to develop that same feeling with a golf club in your hand.

The shot does not require power. A good rhythm and even pace are the necessary ingredients to develop the distance judgment and touch you need to successfully pitch the ball. Again, that comes only with practice and experience.

To play a higher-than-normal pitch shot, one that gets up quickly and comes down very softly, you simply exaggerate everything slightly. Play the ball slightly farther forward in your stance, placing your hands a little more behind the ball to add loft to the club. Feel like you are getting the clubhead up even more quickly, both on the backswing and follow-through. Rather than extending the club away from your body in both directions, feel as if you are sticking the clubhead in your right ear on the backswing, your left ear on the follow-through. You have more control if the club is swung in this manner. As

Phil Rodgers says, "Keep the handle of the club pointing to the ground on the backswing and keep it pointing to the ground on the follow-through."

A thought I find especially helpful in playing the extra-high shot is that *the back or trailing edge of the sole strikes the ground first.* I don't like to feel that I play any pitch shot with the leading edge of the club. That thought can lead to sticking the club in the ground behind the ball. Instead, visualize the arc of the swing flattening as it comes into the ball so that the back of the sole strikes first. We're almost talking about a scoop. With some practice, the method can be incredibly effective, producing extra-high, soft-landing shots.

When I play a pitch shot, and especially the extra-high shot, I feel that my arms are loose, to the extent that my left elbow is a little bent. This takes the tension out of the arms and the swing. To achieve this, *don't put the club on the ground at address.* Hold it slightly in the air. This will give you a better feel for the clubhead and the swing you are about to make. It also will help you strike the ball without taking a big divot. The best way to spin the ball is to make clean contact with the clubface. Grass or dirt between the clubface and the ball will take the backspin off.

Phil Rodgers has an especially good drill to help you ingrain the feeling you want for this shot. He simply has you hit chip and pitch shots from a piece of plywood. This eventually gives you the feeling of being more of a picker rather than a gouger, catching the ball cleanly the way you want.

While your arms should feel

loose, your grip should be solid and firm with every finger (not viselike, however). I think you especially need to feel that you are controlling the club with the index finger of your right hand. That eliminates any looseness and wobble in the swing.

Don't try to eliminate body movement on the pitch shot. The body should move naturally, turning on the backswing as the left knee moves behind the ball and the weight goes to the right side, then the return to the left side on the downswing. The amount of body movement, of course, will depend on the length of the shot at hand.

Of utmost importance on this shot is that you *keep your body at the correct height throughout the swing. Do not let it move up and down.*

It is equally important to concentrate on following through, keeping the speed of your swing consistent through impact and to the finish. If you don't emphasize this, you'll tend to start decelerating *before* impact.

The same drill I suggested for the full swing is applicable here—line up three balls and hit them all without removing your hands from the club. This teaches you the value of a follow-through and the value of a good grip, and it helps you learn to maintain control of the club.

*The greenside sand shot—* The technique for this shot is basically the same as that for the pitch, except that in this case you swing the club through the sand and do not strike the ball with the club-face. It's really not difficult if you remember to keep the arc of your swing in the same relationship to your body that you do for the pitch shot from grass. In other words, if you address the ball, grip the club

### Scrape the Chip Shot
*You should feel as if you are scraping the normal chip shot, swinging the club back and through low to the ground and not taking a divot. But remember that you don't make any unusual manipulations to accomplish this.*

### The Chip Is a Pendulum Stroke

*The chip shot should be played with the hands set ahead of the ball at address. It should be executed without excessive use of the wrists, much as a pendulum stroke, the length of the backswing equal to the length of the follow-through.*

at a certain length, set your body at a certain height and maintain that height throughout the swing, the club should enter the sand at the proper point.

The biggest mistake—aside from panicking—that amateurs make in the sand is to address the ball the same way they would a pitch or chip shot, standing on top of the sand the way they stand on turf. That means that if they make good swings, the club will hit the ball without taking any sand, usually sending it well over the green. Or they panic at that thought and make some compensating

move that causes the club to dig too deeply into the sand and leaves the ball in the bunker.

The solution is simply to bury your feet in the sand a half-inch or so. Bend your left arm slightly at address to keep the club from touching the sand before you swing, which is a violation of the rules. Then make your normal swing. The arm will straighten naturally coming back down, the clubhead will strike the sand behind the ball and slide through under the ball, and the ball will ride out on a cushion of sand. Once you convince yourself that

will happen, the sand game becomes relatively easy.

After that, your technique is very similar to that employed for the pitch shot. The good bunker player has the face of the club open in relation to his stance but square in relation to the hole. In other words, he aims the club straight and sets his body open or to the left of his target. As with the pitch and chip, I prefer to grip down on the club an inch and a half or so for better control. Again, don't position your hands in front of the ball, because this brings the leading edge of the club too much into play and can cause

it to dig too deeply into the sand, spoiling the shot. Put your hands even with or slightly behind the ball, set your weight evenly and think of the back of the club skidding through the sand underneath the ball. Actually feel as if you are pulling or lifting the leading edge out of the sand rather than jamming the club down into it.

You must figure out how much sand you want to cut out from underneath the ball. To a great extent, that will depend on the texture of the sand. In general, sand that is coarser, heavier or more firmly packed requires an easier,

slower swing to send the ball the same distance as softer, fluffier sand. The type of shot you are facing also has a bearing. The less sand you take, the closer you come to the ball and the more spin you put on it. Thus the quicker it will stop on the green.

There actually is a great deal of margin for error in how far behind the ball your club can enter the sand. Anywhere from two to six inches can be acceptable, depending on the texture. With practice, you can determine what is most effective for you. For the sake of consistency in your bunker shots, I do recommend you try to enter the sand about the same distance behind the ball every time. I try to do that, varying my distance only with the speed and force of my swing. Just don't try to be so precise about it that you tie yourself up and make a bad swing.

When you need to hit an extra-high bunker shot, your method is the same as the extra-high pitch. Set your weight more to the right and cock the club up more quickly on both the backswing and follow-through. The swing becomes almost V-shaped. You should take less sand and concentrate on getting the club up as quickly as possible on the follow-through. Feel as if the ball were glued onto the face of the club and you were tossing it high out of the bunker. You want to feel that, as soon as the clubhead enters the sand, you are trying to stick it in your left ear. Get the right index finger up higher than the left hand immediately.

For the long bunker shot that is not yet a fairway bunker shot, don't bury your feet as deeply in the sand. Make a shallower swing and take less sand from under the ball. The longer the shot, the less sand you want to take

4    5    6

and the more like a normal full swing you should make.

To acquire more versatility with both short and longer bunker shots, practice picking the ball out of the sand, hitting less and less sand until you are literally catching the ball first. This will help you develop touch and judgment that will serve you well in any sand situation.

*The fairway bunker shot*—The shot from a fairway bunker actually is the same as a golf shot from grass, with some reservations. The first is that you should take a club that is lofted enough to get the ball over the lip of the bunker. The worst possible thing that can happen is that you leave the ball in the bunker and face the same shot again.

Dig your feet into the sand to assure that you don't lose your balance, but don't bury them too deeply because that lowers your swing arc more than you might want. Again,

grip down on the club for better control. If the lip allows, take more club than you need for the shot—a 5-iron instead of a 6-iron, for example—and make an easier, shorter swing so you can make better contact.

The common advice for a fairway bunker shot is to play the ball back in your stance to assure hitting the ball first, but there are some dangers here. If you position the ball too far back, you will be hitting it too much on the downswing and tend to top the ball and drive it into the sand.

I much prefer to position the ball normally and try to pick it out of the sand with a sweeping motion. Depending on the height of the lip on the bunker, you usually are better off hitting the ball too thin than too fat. Of course, if you have a terrible lie, you must accept that and just beat down on the ball to get it back in play. But if the ball is sit-

**Return Shaft
to Starting Position**

*To play the normal pitch shot (above and overleaf), stand to the ball with your weight equally distributed and your hands about even with the ball (1). On the backswing, break your wrists a little earlier than normal and get the clubhead up rather quickly (2 and 3). Your key forward-swing thought is to return the club to the same position at impact that it was in at address (5). On the follow-through (6), the clubhead again comes up quickly as your right hand crosses over your left. Note that the leg action, while minimal in a small shot, nevertheless exists. Never try to play the pitch shot stiff-legged.*

97

**The Pitch Is a
Smaller Swing**
The pitch shot (above and
overleaf), whether short or
long, is simply a smaller,
cutoff version of the full
swing. The swinging of the
arms and hands and use of
the legs are the same, ex-

cept that the motion is shorter and easier. Note again how level the knees and the body stay until the finish of the swing.

ting reasonably well up on the sand, the pick shot is a better play.

An excellent way to develop a feel for this type of shot is to practice hitting balls off tees in the sand. That lets you make contact easier and gives you the feeling of the sweeping or picking motion needed.

*Putting, the other game—* All of the golf technique that we have talked about to this point has been concerned with getting the ball to fly through the air in one way or another. Putting, however, is the other game in golf. Now we want to roll the ball along the ground. Quite literally, the player who has the ability to *roll* his putts smoothly along the green surface, as opposed to having them pop up and bounce about, is the one who has a leg up on getting the ball into the hole more often.

How does one do that? Well, the only thing you can say with any confidence about putting is that it is very individual. The best putter is not necessarily the one who is mechanically the soundest. The best putter is the one who gets the ball in the hole, regardless of how he or she does it. Ben Crenshaw has a smooth, flowing stroke. Gary Player jabs the ball. Tom Watson gives it a firm, quick rap. All are outstanding putters.

So I can't tell you how to putt. I will tell you how I putt and give you guidelines that will let you pick the mechanical method that works best for you. All the while, you must keep in mind that having good mechanics, while important, is only one factor in being a good putter. Good putting comes from having the ability to judge speed and distance and to read the slope of the green, then having the ability to hit the ball on the correct line. Far too many players pay too much attention to the mechanics of putting and neglect training themselves to read the putt. A well-struck putt hit on an incorrectly read line won't go in. If you spend more time trying to figure out the speed and the break of the putt, you will be better off. Then you can hit the putt with a jab, a long stroke, with loose wrists or firm wrists or whatever . . . as long as you start the ball on the correct line at somewhere near the correct speed, you have a chance to make the putt. We have players on tour who have magnificent putting strokes but lack the ability to read greens, so they don't make putts. And we have players with very unorthodox strokes who can read greens and judge speed unbelievably well, and they hole the putts.

Equally important is having a system or routine that will let you get your stroke going the same way every time. It's probably more important in putting than in the full swing, and I'll discuss that at some length in this chapter.

I said that I can't teach you how to putt. I can outline mechanics and suggest a routine that will help. But I cannot, for the life of me, figure out a way to help you learn to read greens, to judge speed and break, to compute the effect of grass length, grain, moisture and the other factors that go into determining what a putt does. That simply requires a lot of work on the practice green and experience on the course.

The whole business of putting demands work, if you are going to be any good at it. I can't give it to you any other way. Believe me, I know. I was a much better putter as a kid in Australia than I am today. I'm not quite sure why, except that when I started to play, that probably was the best way I could make a score. Whether I hit the ball straight or sideways, and it often was the latter, I was driven to make a number, so maybe I was a good putter out of des-

peration. I've seen that phenomenon in other players, too. Also, I spent endless hours on the putting green, a fairly common thing with youngsters who don't have that much access to the golf course. As a result, I was an excellent putter when I was young.

Then I began to realize that I couldn't make a living just by being a good putter, because any time I had an ordinary or a bad day on the greens, I was going to shoot 74 or 75. So I started paying much more attention to the mechanics of my full swing, to being a better striker of the golf ball. That required so much time that I neglected the area of my game at which I was already very good. As a result, I wasn't that good anymore. I guess there's a lesson there for all of us. Don't ever stop trying to become a better putter. Working on the practice green is boring, but it pays off in the long run. I've realized that and have worked hard in the last 10 years to improve my putting. I'm not as good as the young David Graham, but I'm better than I was 15 years ago.

Let's look at the mechanics:

**Grip**—The most effective putting grip is one in which the palms are facing, basically straight up and down on the handle of the putter. The handle fits into the left hand along the lifeline, between the thumb and the heel pads. The left wrist should be slightly arched. The right hand goes on parallel to or facing the left, and both thumbs should be positioned on top of the shaft. The other basic difference between this and the conventional full-swing grip is that the left forefinger overlaps or lies across the fingers of the

### The Sand Shot Setup

To set up for the normal greenside sand shot, work your feet into the sand so you have a solid foundation and have set your feet low enough that you can make a normal swing and strike the sand instead of the ball (left). Your stance should be open or set left of your intended starting direction (right). As you can see in both pictures, the clubface will be open or set to the right of your stance line but should be square to your target.

### The Sand Shot Is a Pitch Shot

Once you have set your feet half an inch or so into the sand and established your stance and clubface position (p. 105), the bunker shot becomes simply a pitch shot. The keys are to main-

tain the same height
throughout the swing, feel
as if the back of the club is
skidding through the sand
and that you are pulling or

lifting the leading edge of
the club out of the sand
rather than down through it.
Above all, don't panic.

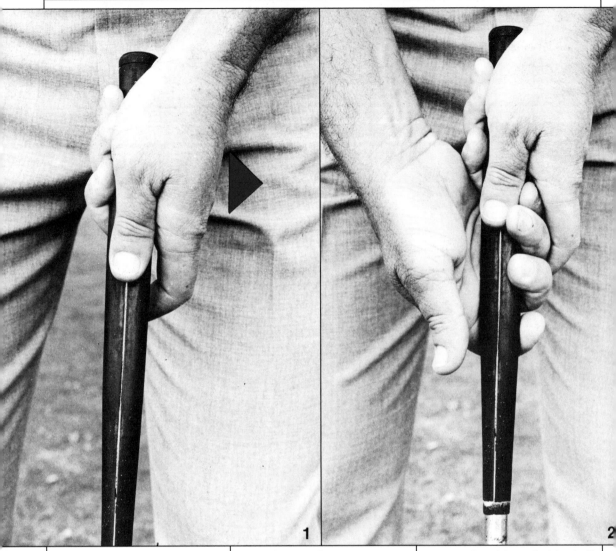

right hand—the common reverse-overlap grip. I feel this grip gives you control over the clubface so you can bring it back squarely to the ball consistently. This is the vital ingredient you need to be a good putter.

**Setup**—As I mentioned earlier in this book, for years I had a problem with hand and eye alignment as a result of switching from the left to the right side. With a putter, I've worked hard on getting my hands at least *to* or even with the back of the ball at address. I've also worked hard on getting my feet the correct distance from the ball so my eyes are over the target line. I want to be able to hold a ball between my eyes and drop it on the target line. This means my vertical vision is on top of the golf ball, which is the thing most good putters concentrate on. That way you are looking straight down on the ball and not at an angle, which gives you a better visual line to the cup. It's also important to have your eyes square with or parallel to the line of your putt. Getting them cocked one way or the other will almost always result in misaiming the blade.

I pick out an intermediate spot in putting just as I do for full shots, and it's best, when you are looking at that spot

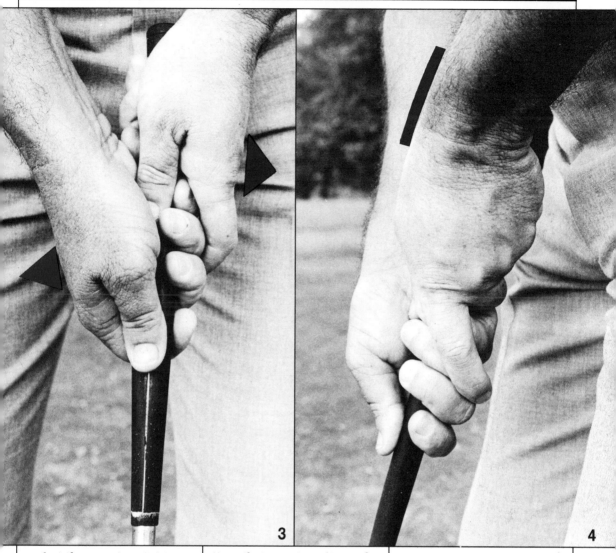

3

4

and at the cup, to rotate your head and eyes instead of lifting up.

I set my feet square to or parallel with the target line, about 12 to 15 inches apart. My weight is equally distributed between both feet and set toward the heels for stability. My knees are flexed, and I feel a slight pressure in the area of my tailbone. My arms hang naturally, both elbows flexed, and my wrists are slightly arched to keep them firmer during the stroke.

My basic thought at address is to be comfortable, within the parameters of a correct setup position. Any contor-

tion that creates discomfort will keep you from putting your best.

**Stroke**—I grip the putter with equal pressure in both hands, which means the hands are not fighting each other. I grip as firmly as I feel I must to have the control I want, and I try to keep that pressure constant from address to finish. It works the same way as in the full swing. Used correctly, a little tension can be good. A little tension that makes you firmer is a lot better than having no tension and being sloppy, or varying the tension throughout the stroke. A sudden surge of tension on the forward stroke

### The Putting Grip

*To form the putting grip, set the back of the left hand facing parallel to the target line, the handle of the putter fitting against the lifeline between the thumb and heel pads (1). The right hand is placed with the club lying across the base of the fingers (2) so that when closed the hand is position parallel to or facing the left, both thumbs on top of the shaft (3). The left forefinger overlaps the fingers of the right in the common reverse overlap position and the left wrist is slightly arched (4).*

### Set Eyes Over Ball

*I try to get my feet the correct distance from the ball so that when I assume the correct setup position my eyes are directly over the ball and the target line. I check this, as you can, by taking my setup position and dropping a ball from the bridge of my nose. If that ball doesn't strike the ball on the ground or somewhere closely inside it, I have a problem and so will you.*

ruins more putts than anything else.

But while I believe in firmness throughout the stroke, I do not believe in rigidity in trying to keep your wrists unbroken and your hands and arms moving exactly as a pendulum. The pendulum-type stroke is fine, but not if it costs you feel. I have always been more of a "feel" putter, allowing myself to putt more with my hands, because that's where most of my feel is. I don't have much feel in my shoulders and elbows, but I do have a lot of feel in my fingertips. I like to feel that the putter is an extension of my hands and that the feel I generate goes from my hands to the putterhead. Whether you do that with some hinging at the wrists or with perfectly straight wrists makes no difference, in my opinion, as long as you don't stifle the feel you have in your fingers.

As with the full swing, my putting stroke is governed by my right hand and forearm. I find if I concentrate on my right forearm, my left wrist won't break down. Many good putters do concentrate on the left hand. Whichever works best for you is correct.

On short putts, I will concentrate on taking the putter straight back and straight through down the line to my target. In practice, I concentrate on the toe of the putter to let me know what I'm doing with my stroke, whether I'm taking it back inside or outside the line. *You can really see what the club is doing if you watch the toe rather than the center of the blade.*

On longer putts, I concentrate primarily on the distance I want to roll the ball. In all cases, I try not to alter the force of my swing. In other words, I don't "pop" short putts and stroke long ones. The speed of my stroke remains the same and I vary only the length of it to accommodate the distance. I do,

however, feel that I accelerate the putter at a uniform rate on the forward stroke. My tendency used to be to decelerate coming through, which would cause my left wrist to break down. The feeling of a smooth acceleration overcomes that. My left wrist still hinges slightly as I swing through impact and into the follow-through, but this is simply because I allow the putterhead to "release" naturally. I think this produces a smoother, more consistent stroke than if I were to try to keep everything rigid.

**System**—The most important thing you can build into your putting program is a system or routine that will allow you to approach and stroke your putts the same way every time, no matter what the circumstance. Kel Nagle was always a master of this. He had a very repetitive stroke and would do the same thing on a six-inch tap-in as he did on a 20-foot putt. I've tried to develop the same kind of system, and so should you.

Just as with the full swing, a consistent routine allows you to make your stroke almost automatically. Everybody gets nervous at one time or another on the golf course, whether he's contending for the U.S. Open championship or simply has a couple of $10 presses riding on the last hole. Controlling your nerves under pressure becomes the key to success, especially in the delicate, exacting business of putting. That's why a repetitive routine is vital. It becomes the ignition to your stroke. It prevents you from freezing over a putt, giving you an automatic trigger that gets the stroke going. It lets you concentrate on *where* you are going to hit the putt rather than *how* you are going to hit it. It keeps you from getting apprehensive and ruining your stroke, because if you are following your routine you have neither the time

nor the room in your mind for apprehension. The more you can make your routine a habit, the more like a robot you can become, the better chance you have of making a sound stroke no matter how great the pressure. At the ultimate level, the stroke is made and the ball is away without your having thought about it.

It isn't that simple, of course, and you're going to have to work hard to develop that kind of repetition, but the rewards will be worth it.

In my pre-putt routine, I first mark the ball and hand it to my caddie for cleaning. Then I walk to the other side of the hole and back, up one side of the line and down the other. When it is my turn to putt, I replace the ball—I don't like to see any writing when I look down at the ball, so I align the seam of the ball with the line of my putt.

I take three steps backward, squat down to line up the putt and lay my putter on the ground to help me with that aligning. For example, if the break is left to right, I angle the shaft to the left of the hole. This gets me thinking in the correct direction.

Then, because I have calculated the number of steps I took away from the ball, I can walk back to the ball and end up with my left foot in the same place in relation to the ball every time.

I stand slightly away from the ball with my feet together and always make two practice strokes, simulating the actual stroke I will make. This also helps relieve the tension a bit. I put my putter down in *front* of the ball, which helps me aim it, then take my stance. When I'm ready, I will adjust

my grip, lift the putter back behind the ball, put the toe of the putter to the ball, then move the center or sweet spot of the putter behind the ball. I take one more look at the hole, look back to the ball and stroke.

Those happen to be my habits, my 1-2-3-4 system. Yours can be different, but you need to have one that will work in just as repetitive a fashion. And you can't just decide you are going to work on it on the golf course. You must ingrain it on the practice green, just as with your full-swing routine.

Just as important as your physical pre-putt routine—perhaps more so—is the mental routine you go through at the same time. To begin with, I find that remembering to breathe properly helps control the nerves. When your

heart beats faster, your breathing gets shorter and faster. When I line up putts, I like to take very deep breaths and exhale all the air from my lungs. It's a great way to relax.

Secondly, you must try never to think of the consequences of the putt. You can't be thinking, "Boy, if I don't make this putt I'll be four over," or, "If I make this putt I'll be the U.S. Open champion." Nor can you think, "It's a right-edge putt but if I pull it a little I'll miss it below the hole." If you're thinking about missing a putt, you'll usually find a way to do it.

That's why a repetitive system is so valuable. No matter how important the situation, you simply remind yourself of the things you have to do. Follow your system, and that will take your mind off the

### Be Firm but Not Rigid
*On shorter putts, the stroke should be straight back and straight through (above), although the longer the putt is the more the stroke swings to the inside on the backswing and back to the inside on the follow-through. Your arms and hands should be firm without being rigid (overleaf). I like to feel that the stroke is controlled by the right hand and forearm. This keeps my left wrist from breaking down until it hinges naturally as a result of my "releasing" the club on the follow-through.*

consequences of the putt. You will be able to put yourself into a mental state that will conquer your nerves and let you make the sound stroke that will get the ball in the hole.

# CHAPTER EIGHT

# HOW TO LEARN

**W**hether you are a beginner trying to learn golf from start to finish or whether you are an advanced player just trying to fix a particular element of your game, it's important to narrow the learning process. In other words, work on one thing at a time.

Ideally, we all would be able to go to experts to learn the various parts of the game—to Phil Rodgers for the pitching game, to Norman Von Nida or Gary Player for the bunker game, to Billy Casper or George Archer for the putting game. But none of us, including me, realistically has that opportunity. So the next best thing is to find the best available instructor who can help you with all phases. Sometimes that's even difficult for a lot of amateurs around the country. So—if you are to improve—you must be able to pinpoint why you are not improving, what areas of your game you need to work on. You must develop an awareness of your strengths and weaknesses and deal with them accordingly, hopefully with an instructor but by yourself if you have to. But the awareness and the willingness to do something about it come first.

For example, we have a member at Preston Trail, my club in Dallas, who is an immaculate player from tee to green but is awful on the green. So he spends his entire life on the driving range and not three minutes on the putting green, then wonders why he is not a good putter. Unfortunately, that's true of most of us. We practice what we do best, because it's fun to be successful, rather than improving what we don't do so well, because that is work.

On the other hand, a touring professional who hits three indifferent wedge shots during a round is likely to go to the practice tee afterward and hit 100 wedges. If he has sliced the ball two or three times off the tee, he will find out why he did that and how he can correct it. He is learning from his failures, overcoming his weaknesses.

If you fear hitting a driver, don't automatically give in to that fear and switch to a 3-wood. That's a viable option, of course, and although you are giving up distance it might work all right in a particular situation. But in the long run you are simply avoiding the issue. What if you are afraid of pitching the ball? There is no way you are going to be able to get around the necessity for hitting pitch shots several times during each round. The best alternative in either case is to suck it up and go out and learn to hit any club that is giving you trouble. No less a player than Ben Hogan used to take just one club to the practice tee and learn to hit it the way he wanted to. Somehow there's a lesson there for all of us.

To improve at golf you have to commit yourself to improvement, even if it means regressing for a while. If your professional tells you that you must change your grip to be a better player, then make up your mind to take a couple of months and change it. Don't be looking for quick fixes, because they last about as long as they take to give.

I have a friend who was an 11-handicap player and came to me for help. Fortunately, he has a lot of time to spend on his game. I changed his grip, his ball position and the plane of his swing. But he had the patience and the confidence in me and he wanted to do it. He would have tried to walk on water if I'd asked him. That's the optimum pupil, and it paid off for him. His handicap now is 5.

You cannot learn golf quickly, nor all at once. You must break the game down into categories—the wood game, the long irons, the middle irons, the short game, the bunker play, the putting. If you concentrate on one of these categories at a time, you'll be amazed at how much better you will get at each. It's like putting together a jigsaw puzzle—you have some pieces missing, so you search for each of them at a time. You make improvement and put that piece into the puzzle. Eventually all the pieces fit together.

Tour professionals do that all the time. You will see a player on the practice tee one day hitting four buckets of balls with a pitching wedge. The next week he is hitting four buckets with a driver, the next week with another club. Suddenly he will win. He has pieced his game together and is physicaly and mentally ready to win a tournament.

An amateur player can do that, too, within his range of ability. If you are a beginner, you simply need to build your game from the ground up. If you are a more advanced player, you need to define your problems and work on them. The best way to do this is to take a scorecard with you on the course and methodically analyze your weaknesses. Find out where you are wasting strokes. Be realistic about it—if you hit a bunker shot 50 feet from the hole and then three-putt, the problem is not so much your putter as it is your bunker play. If your analysis determines that this is your worst problem at the moment, go to your professional and ask him for help out of the bunker. Get that problem solved before moving on to something else.

Even if you have an addiction for hitting golf balls, which I do, practice in general can be boring. So you have to figure out a way to make it fun. I often bring a portable radio to my practice sessions so I can have some music (I have a relatively secluded practice situation at Preston Trail— make sure your music doesn't interfere with others). And bring a thermos full of ice water or other refreshment.

The golf swing is much more tortuous to the body than most people realize, so you should start every practice session with some stretching and warm-up exercises. Stretch your leg muscles, do some turning movements to loosen up the trunk, swing your arms to loosen your shoulder muscles, any-

thing to increase your flexibility.

I find my weighted club to be a great stretching tool, and you might, too. But be careful. Don't make it too heavy at first, maybe 25-30 ounces, and swing it easily until your muscles get used to it. The weighted club is especially beneficial in getting you to swing down from the inside—it's very difficult to bring it over the top—so I'd recommend it if you are working on your swing path.

No matter if you are working on a specific part of your game or just having a general practice session, it's best to start by hitting short shots. This lets you stretch your muscles gradually, puts some feel into your fingers and gives you some much-needed work in an area of the game that is too often neglected.

Follow your warm-up session with work on the specific part of your game that needs help, if that's your objective on this day. If your purpose is simply a general tune-up session, here are some suggestions for making it more fun and more productive:

*Vary your shots.* Practice hitting some hooks and fades,

some high shots and some low ones. Hit pitch shots, then hit some tee shots with the driver. Then hit some short irons. That way you get a feel for mixing swings the way you'll have to on the course.

*Always practice to a target.* And be conscious of your distance with each club. If possible, walk out on the practice range and measure the exact distance to the flags there. Or set out your own distance guides. That way you will find out exactly how far you are hitting each club. You also can practice swings that will send the ball a specific distance, so you'll have that swing in your system when it's called for.

I have several drills I work on that you might find helpful, depending on what particular problem, you are having with your swing at the moment:

*For Weight-shift Problems—* If you have trouble getting your weight shifted on the backswing, start with your weight on your right or trailing leg.
—To get your weight off your right side on the forward swing, think of walking to-

### Walk Toward Your Target
*If you have a problem getting your weight shifted from your right side to your left on the forward swing, practice walking toward your target as you complete your swing. As your weight comes off your right foot on the forward swing, just pick it up and start walking.*

### Get the Left Heel Up

*To improve your leg action, widen your stance, practice getting your left heel well off the ground on the back-swing and slide your right foot forward on the follow-through.*

ward the target as you complete your swing. All your weight comes off your right foot, and you can just pick it up and start walking. This is one of my favorite drills. Gary Player practiced this way before he won the Masters in 1974 and played the same way during the tournament.

*For Hooking and Slicing*—If you are having trouble hooking or slicing the ball, solve the problem by accentuating the opposite action. To cure a slice, for example, aim to the right, flatten your swing and turn the club over quickly through impact. You probably will get a duck hook, but after a few of those you can begin to modify the swing and develop a feel that will give you just a gentle draw. If you have been hooking too much, try to slice the ball, remembering what I told you earlier about angles. Again, overdo it, then back off.

*For Better Leg Action*—To get

your legs working better, widen your stance, concentrate on getting your left heel off the ground on the back-swing and work on sliding your right foot forward on the follow-through. This also is a good drill if you are tending to come over the top.

*For Better Release*—To improve your release, practice hitting hook shots with a pitching wedge. Because of the loft on the club, you really have to get your hands and the club turning over to hook the ball.

*To Learn the High and Low Shots*—Find a tall tree and practice hitting shots over it. For example, I like to stand far enough away that I could clear the tree with a normal 9-iron shot, then try to clear it with an 8-iron simply by changing my ball position and making sure I stay behind the ball during the swing. Then try to clear the tree with a 7-iron. Then try to

**Find a Tall Tree**
To learn to hit the ball high, find a tall tree, stand where you could clear it with a 9-iron and try to hit an 8-iron, then a 7-iron over it by changing your ball position and your weight distribution. Then try hitting shots under the tree with the same clubs by setting your weight and ball position in the opposite manner.

121

**Set a Club on the Ground**
To ingrain a better alignment, set a club on the ground just outside and parallel to your target line, then practice aligning your stance parallel to that club and thus parallel to your target line. This close-in orientation will help you better relate to the target line when you get on the course.

hit a 6- or 7-iron *under* the tree from the same distance by employing the opposite angle tactics, as we discussed in Chapter 6.

*For Better Long-iron Play* —To learn to hit long irons better, practice hitting shots with the ball teed, the higher the better. This teaches you not to get your body too far in front and to strike the ball with more of a sweeping motion instead of a descending blow. It encourages swinging *through* the ball and teaches you that the long irons can get the ball in the air quite nicely without your having to give them extra help.

*For Better Alignment*—To check your alignment, put a couple of clubs on the ground, one along your target line and another along your stance line to make sure you are lining up the way you think you are or want to be. Remember that for a normal shot your stance line should be parallel to your target line.

*For a Firmer Grip*—To learn to keep your hands firmly on the club from the start to the finish of your swing, line up three or four balls on the ground and strike them consecutively without removing your hands from the club or changing your grip in any way. Doing this consciously for a while will help you do it instinctively on the course.

*To Train the Right Arm*—To learn the correct movement of the right hand and arm, practice the underhand toss as shown in the illustrations. With a ball in your right hand, position yourself as if you were addressing a shot, then simply swing the right arm back and through, tossing the ball underhanded across your body. This is the same motion of the right hand, arm and side that you want to incorporate into your golf swing.

n doing any drills or exercises, I'd suggest that you find the quietest corner of the practice range, because you're going to miss a lot of shots at first and it could be embarrassing. When I first tried to hit balls with my weighted driver, I would miss them completely. Or I'd hit a ball just 20 yards. So I wanted to be off by myself where nobody could see me.

If you continue to have problems for any length of time, one good bet is always to go back to your fundamentals, checking grip, posture, aim, alignment and ball position. Chances are you'll find the solution somewhere in your preshot preparations rather than in the swing itself.

Always spend some time practicing the short game, hitting different kinds of chips, pitches and bunker shots. Try to hit the same shot with one of two or three different clubs. Try to hit a shot two or three different ways with the same club. Practicing this way is fun, it's less tiring . . . and infinitely rewarding.

How long should you practice each time? Until you feel as if you've accomplished what you wanted to. But you should never practice when

**Hit Balls in Succession**
*Line up three or four balls and hit them in succession without removing your hands from the club. This will ingrain the habit of keeping your hands on the club firmly from the start of your swing to the finish.*

you are tired, because you're likely to fall into bad habits. Nor should you force yourself to practice, because then you make it hard work. You won't enjoy it and you probably won't benefit from it.

Finally, always differentiate between a practice session and a warm-up session. When you are warming up before playing a round of golf, then simply warm up. Don't be trying to work on your swing. All you want to do is loosen your muscles and get a feel for the swing that day.

I find it productive to base my warm-up on the golf course I happen to be playing. If I'm playing a long course like Firestone South, my warm-up will consist of a lot more full swings with the woods and long irons. If the course is short, I'll hit more short irons and pitch shots.

If you have trouble getting off to a good start, you might analyze the first few holes you're going to play. If the first hole calls for, say, a drive and a 6-iron, then hit some driver shots and some 6-irons. If the second hole demands a 3-wood and a 4-iron, then practice with those clubs. That way you'll get a feel for the shots you'll actually be playing on the course.

However you warm up, I strongly recommend that you

do it before every round. Otherwise you're going to spend the first few holes loosening up, and by the time you get warm your round may be ruined. You may think you don't have time for it, but planning those extra few minutes into your schedule will result in a lot less frustration and a lot more fun.

Im not going to get into physical conditioning and nutrition, other than to advise you of the importance of being in shape. Most people don't perceive golf to be an athletic endeavor, yet it may be the most exacting athletic endeavor there is. It requires coordination, nerve control and, yes, strength.

I swing my weighted club, I squeeze tennis balls and grip springs, I've walked with weights around my ankles. . . .all sorts of things to improve my physical strength. Most dedicated players I know do the same. I also give up coffee during a tournament and try to otherwise watch my diet, because I know the effect poor nutrition can have on my nerves and my feeling of well-being.

Talk to your doctor, a nutritionist, a therapist or any other experts about the importance of exercise and good diet. It will help you play better golf and feel a lot better.

### Toss Ball Underhanded

*Training the right hand and arm to move correctly in the golf swing is as simple as tossing a golf ball underhanded in the sequence shown. Start as if you were preparing to hit a shot, then swing the right arm back and through, tossing the ball with an underhanded motion across your body.*

# CHAPTER NINE

# START WITH THE RIGHT EQUIPMENT

**M**y first real social contact with Jack Nicklaus came in 1971 when he invited Bruce Devlin and me to his home for dinner while we were defending our World Cup title in Palm Beach Gardens. That evening I found out something that blew my mind.

I had always imagined that Jack Nicklaus, the greatest player in history and a man whose name was synonymous with MacGregor, one of the longtime great makers of classic golf clubs, would have clubs lining his house from one end to the other. Being as interested in clubs as I've always been, I asked Jack during dinner if I could look at his spare set. He said, "David, I don't have one."

I think I later apologized for my next remark, but I said, "I can't believe that you don't have a spare set of golf clubs, that you would allow yourself to be in that situation. You are traveling around the world with a golf bag that says 'Jack Nicklaus' on it. You are so vulnerable to having your clubs stolen, and I can't believe you don't have an identical set."

Jack said, "Well, I don't, because MacGregor can't make me a set that feels the same." I said, "That's ridiculous. Let me look at all the spare clubs you have here." So he took me into his little back room, and there was a whole bunch of clubs, odds and ends. At the time, Jack was playing with a Jack Nicklaus Model 271 driver, a Tommy Armour 3-wood, a George Low Wizard 600 Putter and a set of 1967 VIP irons. I rummaged around and found a set of VIPs that looked identical to the ones he was playing, and I said, "Let me take these and fiddle with them a little bit."

I started pulling the clubs apart and soon discovered what the problem was. It had to do with a change in the way MacGregor was building its grips. I said to Jack, "I think I've found why the new clubs you've been getting in the last couple of years don't feel the same. MacGregor used to glue a plastic grip cap inside the shaft, without a hole in it to let the air escape. Now they're using a rubber cap with a hole in it that fits over the shaft. So you have a completely different feel being generated through the shaft of the club." I flicked some different shafts with my finger a few times, and you could hear different sounds.

Nicklaus said, "That's unbelievable," and right then he asked me if I'd come to work for MacGregor. When my contract with Dunlop expired at

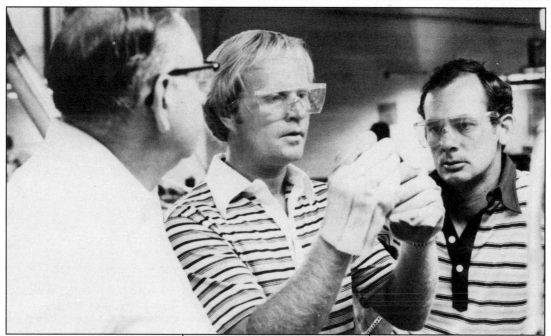

**The Bear and I**
*Jack Nicklaus and I examine a clubhead design in the MacGregor factory.*

the end of the year, I did.

I tell the story only to point out that the factors affecting the "feel" and playability of a golf club are subtle. Jack Nicklaus and most tour players have great sensitivity to that sort of thing, of course. But it's amazing how even the average amateur can tell the difference in feel between clubs. The problem is, most of them don't know what they're feeling . . . or what they should be feeling.

Almost every professional I know is meticulous about his equipment. Our clubs are the tools of our trade, and we need them to be exactly suited to the task. But I'm often asked by amateurs just how important it is for a 15- or 20-handicap player to have good equipment.

My answer is that a good, well-fitted set of golf clubs may or may not make you play any better—you still have to consider the ability of the person swinging the clubs. But you *are* eliminating one variable, and the more variables you can eliminate in golf, the more consistent you can be. It's often difficult to control your swing or your emotions or your physical condition. But you *can* control your golf equipment. It's like having a car that pings when you have cheap gas in it. You can eliminate that problem by putting in a better quality of gas. The car may or may not run any faster, but it won't knock anymore.

Similarly, if you acquire the set of golf clubs that is best suited to your physical structure and your game, you eliminate that concern and are free to work on an even more important one, your technical ability.

Golf equipment has come a long way in the 20 years or so that I've been involved with it. When I started in the business back in Australia, we used to jam lead slugs into the hosels to bring the clubs to the correct swingweight. We had to, because the shaft and grip weights were not consistent. We could make a perfect set of clubs for a Kel Nagle or Peter Thomson without putting anything but glue in the hosel, but we couldn't afford to do it for the overall production run. Today we have so much closer tolerances in shaft, grip and head weight. The clubs of today are hundreds of times better than the clubs of 20 years ago—not only better made but much more sophisticated in concept. Frequency matched shafts, for example, have been one of the great boons to all players. Frequency matching simply means matching shafts and headweights so all the clubs in a set vibrate at the correct frequency—in other words, they act and feel the same throughout the set and encourage the player to make the same swing with each club.

I think this concept has been of more benefit to the amateur player than it has to the professional. The tour player or other good player eventually will build himself a set of clubs by feel, rejecting a club here and there and putting new shafts in until every club in the set feels right to him. Bobby Jones "frequency matched" his set of hickory-shafted clubs strictly by feel. Most amateurs, however, aren't as aware of why the 5-iron hooks or why they hit the 8-iron to the right all the time. They seldom think about reshafting clubs. After all, golf is a hobby with them, not a business, and they shouldn't be expected to know that much about equipment. But this means that the opportunity to get a well-matched set of shafts and heads really means a lot more to the club player than it does the tour pro.

Because of the opportunity Jack Nicklaus gave me to work with the MacGregor people, I've been able to learn more about club design and have been able to put some of my ideas into the marketplace. I'm particularly proud of my role in designing the Jack Nicklaus Limited Edition clubs, which in my opinion are the best set of golf clubs ever made. My years of research and experimentation not only have given me a greater understanding of equipment, I think they've also given me a greater understanding of how to play golf. I've also come to have a reputation among my peers as being highly qualified in this field.

So, while I cannot fit you individually for a set of clubs, I can give you some guidelines on what to look for, making you aware of what you should have so that you can go to a qualified professional, a club-fitter or a clubmaker and get the equipment that will work best for you.

I'll warn you again that equipment alone is hardly the remedy for a bad golf swing. Unless you can bring the club in at the correct angle and get it square at the ball, the best equipment in the world isn't going to improve your score much. But at least you will have eliminated that one variable.

## BACK TO THE CLASSICS

After a decade or more of technological innovation—some of it truly helpful and some of it gimmickry—I think the equipment industry is beginning to swing back toward the conventional or classic club. That is a club that has the weight distributed fairly evenly across the back of the club, with a bit more concentrated behind the point of impact and usually a little lower on the club instead of more toward the heel or toe. I happen to feel that the classic club is not just for the better players but is for everybody. Because the club, especially in the irons, is less forgiving and demands more precision in your swing, using it eventually will make you a better player. *However,* and this is a big proviso, it only happens that way if you are willing to work on your game, take the time to practice and be patient with your rate of progress.

If you are not that devoted, or don't have the time, as is the case with most amateurs, then by all means try the so-called "improvement" clubs. There is no question that heel-and-toe weighting improves accuracy and distance on mis-hit shots. Sole weight— added weight on the sole or bottom of the club—helps those golfers who have trouble getting the ball in the air. The bigger faces on many of these clubs are a confidence-inducing factor. So this type of club can benefit you, but just remember that you are giving up the potential for even greater improvement in the long run.

A good example of the improvement club—and at the same time an exception to what I just said—is the metal wood. I think they work and are here to stay. Because they are cast out of metal, once they are designed properly you can make a million exactly the same, which is a great advantage. I don't think the metal woods let you hit the ball farther, but because they have more weight around the perimeter—equivalent to heel-and-toe weighting—your mis-hits go straighter. For that reason alone, they are valuable. Personally, I don't care for the looks of them, but that's no reason you shouldn't play with them.

I do think it's important that a golf club look good to you as it sits on the ground. I am, of course, a great traditionalist. I like a club that looks plain and easy, something that doesn't make you nauseous when you pull it out of your bag . . . or see it in someone else's bag. I'm also aware that many golfers aren't aware of—or care—what a traditional golf club should look like. I'm not trying to foist my prejudices on them. What I am saying is that you should let your intui-tion rule. If, for whatever reason, you don't like the looks of the club as you place it behind the ball, there will be a sub-conscious reaction that will work against your using that club effectively. So if it looks good, and if it fits your other needs and specifications, buy it. If it doesn't, go for some-thing else.

## THE SHAFT IS THE VITAL ELEMENT

The most important part of the golf club is the shaft. And as I said earlier, the shaft and the shaft-matching process is better than it ever was. Unfor-tunately, there are so many different weights and flexes on the market that it is dif-ficult even for the very good player to decipher them and figure out what he really needs.

Some companies are put-ting test-packs or sample clubs into the golf shop to allow the customer to try dif-ferent shaft flexes. The wise professional will encourage this and encourage his mem-bers to use them. And the wise purchaser will do so, or try any means possible to ex-periment before he buys.

As guidelines, here are some generalizations about shaft action:

The stiffer the shaft, the straighter you can hit the ball. The more flexible the shaft, usually the farther you can hit it. But there's a trade-off at both ends. A shaft that is too stiff for the amount of speed you can generate in your swing may result in a loss of distance. A shaft that is too whippy can have you hitting the ball all over the lot, par-ticularly hooking it to the left. So if you are a strong, long-hitting player who generates a lot of clubhead speed, a stif-fer shaft is better. If you have a slower, smoother swing, you probably need a little softer shaft. A further general rule of thumb is that the stiffer the shaft, the more you tend to slice the ball, because a greater amount of swing speed is required to release the clubhead and get the face back to square; the softer the shaft, the more you tend to hook, for just the opposite reason.

I've observed that most amateur players use shafts that are too stiff. My recommendation for a starting point is to find a shaft you can hit straight, say, with the 5-iron. The straight shot is ideal, as I think we would all agree. Then go from there, evaluating different stiffness for distance relative to accuracy. It will be well worth the time and effort.

You also might want to consider *where* you want the flex in your shafts. I prefer the flex point—where the shaft has its greatest amount of bend during the swing—to be as near the grip as possible. I don't want any shaft flutter or excessive vibration near the head. But I'm strong enough, golfwise, to generate plenty of clubhead speed. Players whose golf muscles are not as strong as mine might want the flex point lower in the

shaft, nearer the head, so that the shaft can give them more "kick" and help them produce more head speed. Again, you should discuss this with someone knowledgeable before you buy.

The majority of golfers probably should use clubs that have a uniform stiffness throughout the set, except that the pitching and sand wedges may have shafts that are a little softer because you have to hit so many variations of shots with them. The better player, who is more precise with his swing, may want to experiment a little. I've had the pleasure of discussing equipment on several occasions with Ben Hogan, whom I consider the most knowledgeable player-club expert the game has ever known. Hogan wanted his longer clubs stiffer, his short irons softer. The stiffest club in his bag was the driver because, as he said, "That's the club I want to hit the straightest." He feels, and I agree, that the less flex there is in the shaft, the more connected the hands are with the face of the club. Where the hands go, so goes the clubface. But his sand

wedge had a very soft shaft, because "you can't maneuver the ball with a telephone pole." He says, "When I want to hit a little flip shot over a bunker, I need a whippy shaft so I can just play with my hands and let the club do it."

Jack Nicklaus' short game improved 2,000 percent after 1980, because of improvement in his technique, of course, after lessons from Phil Rodgers, but also because he started using a sand wedge that's about as whippy as a lady's club. So if you really want to perfect your talent, try varying your shaft stiffnesses along those lines to suit individual clubs.

I also caution you to guard against the tendency to get clubs that are too heavy, which often is the result of getting shafts that are too stiff (the stiffer the shaft, the heavier it is, because the shaft walls are thicker). Within reason, lighter is better, because distance comes from clubhead speed, not the weight of the club or clubhead, and you can swing a lighter club faster. I especially like the advancement in lightweight shafts. I've always felt that

taking half an ounce of the shaft and putting it in the head, behind the ball at impact, makes sense. However, don't get so light that you lose clubhead feel and your swing gets too fast. Again, experimentation is the best course.

## MAKE SURE THE LIE IS RIGHT

One of the most critical factors in the fitting of a golf club is the *lie*, the angle at which the shaft sits to the ground when the club is properly soled. Of nearly equal importance is the length, because the two dimensions work together.

As an example, when I first became associated with Nicklaus, I kept wondering why his clubs were so short and upright. In those days I was playing with clubs that were half an inch longer than the so-called standard, but my clubs were a full *inch* longer than Jack's. And his clubs were a lot more upright than mine. I have finally come to the conclusion that Jack's clubs are the wrong length. They probably always have been, and I assume the reason

**Check the Lie**
*A club that is too upright for Player A might be too flat for Player B and just right for Player C.*

is that when Jack signed with the company back in the early '60s, the standard MacGregor club was half an inch shorter than the rest of the industry. Nicklaus, who wasn't much into equipment then, probably just told them to send him a standard set and make the clubs a couple of degrees more upright. Unbeknownst to him, the clubs undoubtedly were already a degree or so upright to accommodate the shorter length, so after they had been customized for Jack they were *really* upright. Which explains why, until he made some changes around 1980, Nicklaus always had an extremely upright swing.

That story pinpoints the problem in having clubs with incorrect lies. Everybody tries to sole the club correctly on the ground, and even a good player unconsciously will alter his posture, his setup position, to accommodate an incorrect lie. A player of Nicklaus' ability can get away with it, obviously, but why buck the odds? Get the length and lie fitted to you, instead of fitting your posture to your clubs.

As with anything else, it's best to do this with professional help. If you can't, here are some guidelines you can use on your own. When properly soled, the toe of your woods and long irons should be slightly up in the air (on the longer, more powerful swings, the shaft tends to bow *downward,* dropping the toe). A good check is to sole the club and have somebody slip a piece of paper under the toe. The paper should slide about to the center of the club before it meets resistance. As the clubs get shorter, the toe should be less in the air. With the short irons and wedges, the sole should be virtually flat on the ground. All this assumes, of course, that you are in your normal and correct setup position.

If your clubs are too upright

for your setup and swing, you will tend to hit the ball left. If they are too flat, you will tend to hit it right. The toe also will tend to dig in at impact, causing additional inconsistencies. If you are going to err, then, it's better to have your clubs a little too upright than too flat. The penalties are less drastic.

Incidentally, I'm not being critical of Nicklaus and his too-upright clubs, nor am I implying he has been any less of a player because of this. I happen to believe that, especially for a good player, the more upright your clubs and swing plane, the better. It gives you a chance to keep the club on the line longer and thus hit the ball straighter. As I've said, I gradually changed my swing from flat, or more around the body, to upright, or on a more vertical plane. I'm now at the point where, ironically, my clubs are more upright than Nicklaus'. They're also half an inch shorter than they used to be. A player who needs more distance probably is better off with a slightly flatter swing. But distance has never been a problem for Nicklaus, nor is it particularly one for me. So, within the parameters of getting the club behind you on the backswing and coming into the ball from the inside, upright is preferable for the better, stronger player.

## DON'T TAKE LOFT FOR GRANTED

One specification in a golf club that is overlooked by most amateurs—and a lot of professionals—is *loft.* It's important to be aware of the loft of your clubs for a couple of different reasons. The first is that you want to be sure the lofts are uniform from club to club, generally four degrees apart. Unfortunately, the quality control in some manufacturing plants can cause variations of up to two degrees, plus or minus, in each club. That being the case, your 4- and 5-irons, for example, both could end up being 4-1/2-irons. An unusual example? Not really. Ever wonder why you can hit your 7-iron a ton? Or can't hit your 4-iron out of your shadow? If you check the lofts, you might find that your 7-iron is really almost a 6-iron and your 4-iron is almost a 5-iron.

Loft standards also are not the same from manufacturer to manufacturer. Beyond that, some companies deliberately set their lofts stronger to make the customer think he is buying a club that hits the ball farther. As in, "Wow, I hit this 5-iron 10 yards farther than my old 5-iron!" That's probably because the club in your hand that says 5-iron actually has the loft of a 4-iron.

Secondly, you might want to tailor the loft of your clubs to fit your shot tendencies—if you hit the ball high off the tee, you might want less loft on your driver and maybe all the way through the set. If you have trouble getting the ball up, you might want more loft on your clubs.

In any event, always check with your professional or anyone who has a loft-and-lie machine to make sure that the loft of each club actually is what you want it to be.

# EXAMINE THE CLUBHEAD DESIGN

The design of the clubhead is important, especially in the iron. Without getting into all the variables of clubhead design, let me caution you to pay particular attention to the sole and leading edge of your iron clubs. For the better player, especially, it's important that the leading edge, the bottom of the face, be reasonably straight. The leading edge is what you aim at the target, and for that reason I don't like to have a leading edge that has too much radius or is too curved. It simply is easier to aim a straight line than it is a curved line.

There are some advantages to having more radius or curve in the sole of your club, mainly because it gives you more margin for error in soling your club. The reason most wood clubs are so easy to sole and are so easy to hit off the fairway is that they have a relatively great deal of sole curvature. You don't have to be as precise in placing them on the ground as you do with straight-bottomed clubs. But there is a trade-off in that irons (or woods, for that matter) with a lot of radius are harder to aim and aren't as easy to hit on target.

The "bounce" on an iron club, determined by how far the trailing or back edge of the flange falls beneath the leading edge when the club is properly soled, is important. I'll get into sand wedges later, but for the rest of your clubs the amount of bounce you need depends on what kind of a ball striker you are. If you are a "digger," one who goes at the ball with a descending blow and gouges out a pretty good divot every time, you need a club with more bounce—the trailing edge falling below the leading edge —to help the club ride through the turf and not dig so deeply. If you are a "picker," one who sweeps the ball away relatively cleanly, you don't need so much bounce.

Offset—the distance the leading edge is set behind the shaft as you look down at it—is probably a matter of personal preference. I don't buy the theory that more offset, having the clubface positioned farther behind the shaft, helps you get the ball airborne more easily. That simply puts your hands ahead of the clubface at impact, and, as I've said before, I don't think you ought to play

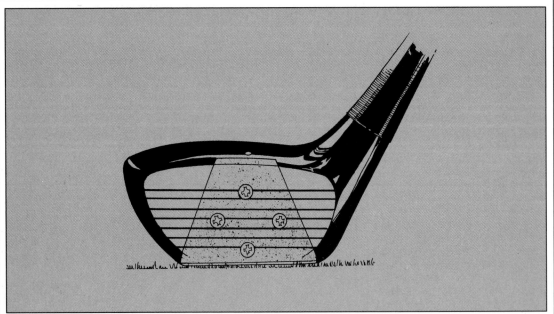

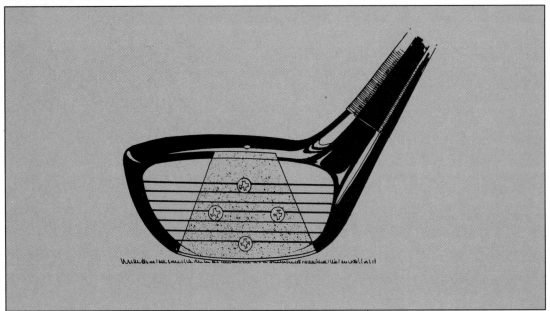

### Flat vs. Curved
*A wood whose sole is flat from front to back (top) is easier to aim, but one with a curved sole (bottom) is easier to hit off the fairway.*

golf with your hands ahead. Ideally, your hands should be even with or on top of the ball at impact. Thus, in my opinion, the best iron club would have zero offset. But that's why they make chocolate and vanilla. If a club that has some offset looks better to you and gives you comfort as you address the ball, by all means go ahead and play with it.

The consistency of the offset in a set of clubs, the relationship of the shaft to the leading edge, is important, whether you are a purist who recognizes it immediately or someone who has no idea what I'm talking about. If the clubs don't have the same "look" throughout the set, it will catch up with you eventually and you will be uncomfortable with some of the clubs without really knowing why. So make sure that, as you sole the club at address and look down at it, the leading edge always appears in the same place in relation to the shaft, whether it be a pitching wedge or a 2-iron.

Similarly, how a club is bored becomes very important, especially to the better player. This applies primarily to wood clubs and, again, affects the way the clubface sits in relation to the shaft. It determines whether the club sits open or closed and is one determining factor in how much face progression there is in a wood...in other words, how much the face of the wood protrudes in front of the shaft when it is soled. In general, without getting into the technicalities of it, the greater the face progression (the more the face protrudes in front of the shaft), the higher you will hit the ball. Again, your particular swing tendencies and what you like to look at should determine what you buy in this regard.

You'll notice that the face of a wood club is slightly curved, from heel to toe and from top to bottom. The heel-to-toe or horizontal curvature is called *bulge.* The top-to-bottom or vertical curvature is called *roll.* The reason for bulge stems from the *gear effect,* a phenomenon that occurs when you contact the ball toward either the toe or the heel of the clubface. Because the club is actually rebounding from the force of this impact, the ball momentarily moves across the face in the opposite direction. This creates the same effect as the meshing of gears, causing a shot hit on the toe to hook and a shot hit on the heel to slice. The bulge of the clubface compensates for this effect—it will start a toed shot farther to the right and a heeled shot farther to the left. Thus the curvature of the shot hopefully will bring the ball back into the center of the fairway rather than the rough.

The top-to-bottom roll acts in much the same way, sending a ball hit on the upper portion of the face higher and a ball hit low on the face lower. But since I've never for the life of me figured out why you would want this to happen anyway, I've never seen much need for roll on a clubface.

The other factor I consider is, again, the look of the club. If you like the look of a severely curved club, one with a lot of bulge, by all means buy it. If you prefer a straighter-faced club, buy that one. Your sense

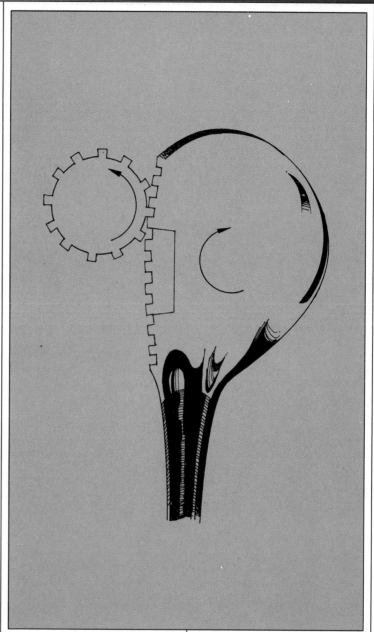

**How Gear Effect Works**
*As the club rebounds at impact, the ball momentarily moves across the face in the opposite direction, imparting hook spin on a ball struck on the toe. If the ball is struck on the heel of the club, the opposite effect takes place and the ball will slice.*

### Flat Easier to Aim

*As with the wood, the flat-soled iron has a straighter leading edge and so is easier to aim, but the sole with some radius is a bit more forgiving in riding through the turf. This characteristic is even more pronounced in irons than in woods.*

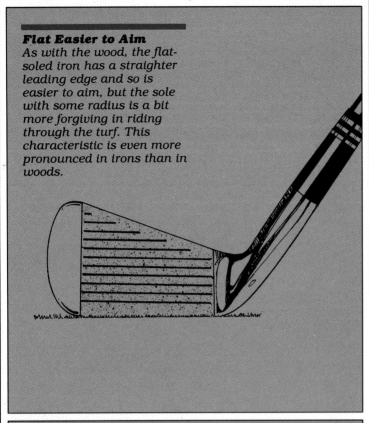

of comfort with the club will more than make up for any advantages or disadvantages that would accrue from the amount of bulge it does or doesn't have.

You should know where your clubhead's center of gravity—in effect, the spot where you want to strike the ball to get the most efficient blow—is located. In a traditional iron, one that is not heel-and-toe weighted, the center of gravity will be more toward the heel or the shaft. That's why the most effective iron is one that is "underslung," having the hosel bent toward the player in relation to the heel of the clubhead. This aims the shaft more toward the center of the club and effectively moves the sweet spot back toward the heel. This type of club is preferred by the better player who strikes the ball more precisely. A club that is overslung, with the shaft angled more toward the heel of the club and away from the sweet spot, puts the center of gravity farther away from the heel and causes a faster rotation of the toe during the swing. This would help overcome a slice, if that is your problem. As I said, I'd rather you overcome that slice by working on your swing, but if you're not going to do that, an overslung club might help.

## GRIP SIZE AFFECTS SHOTS

Another critical factor in the fitting of your golf clubs is the size of the grip. That's the only connection you have with the club. The first criterion is that the grip fill your hands. Otherwise you'll get movement of the grip in your hands that in turn gives away control of the club. Anytime that happens, you introduce more variables into your shotmaking.

In general, a grip that is too small would make you more likely to hook the ball be-

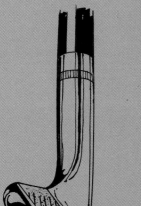

### Tailor Irons to Your Style

If you are a player who hits down markedly on your iron shots and takes a lot of turf, you might need a club with a curved or cambered sole (1) and perhaps some bounce (2). If you are a "picker" who sweeps your shots away cleanly, you can use a flat-soled iron (3) and even one with a negative bounce (4).

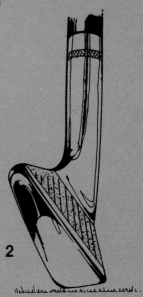

1

2

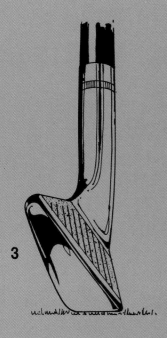

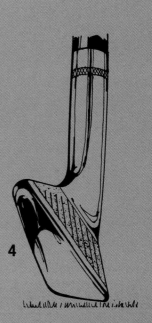

3

4

cause, as the theory goes, your muscles are less tense and you are able to release or turn the club over easier. In my opinion, the reason also could be that you don't have control in the first place as you start your downswing, so you instinctively regrip, panic a little and release the clubhead too soon.

A grip that is too large *will* cause a slice, or at least make it harder for you to hit a draw or hook, because the thick grip constricts your muscles a bit and makes it harder for you to release.

To make sure your grips are the correct size, start with your glove size. If you wear a medium glove, you probably can use a standard grip. If you wear a large or extra-large glove, your grip should be bigger by 1/64th to 1/32nd of an inch. If you wear a small glove or a medium or small cadet (that means you have short fingers), you'll want your grips smaller than standard.

A more precise guideline is to close your left hand around the club and lift the club off the ground. If, when you do this, your middle two fingers don't quite or just barely touch the thumb pad, the grip is the correct size. With the right hand, I like to be able to close the thumb and forefinger around the club and have them just barely touching.

Within those boundaries, the important thing is how the grip feels to you. If you are not comfortable with the feel, you're not off to a very good start in swinging the club the way you want to. So take the time to experiment with different grip sizes. Then buy the right size or regrip the clubs you have if they're not right. It doesn't cost that much, and the benefits will be worthwhile.

Be sure all of your grips are the same size, so you get the same feel throughout the set. Don't take this for granted. As

**Get Consistent Offset**
*Whether your irons have no offset (left) or a lot of offset (right), make sure the look of the club is consistent throughout the set.*

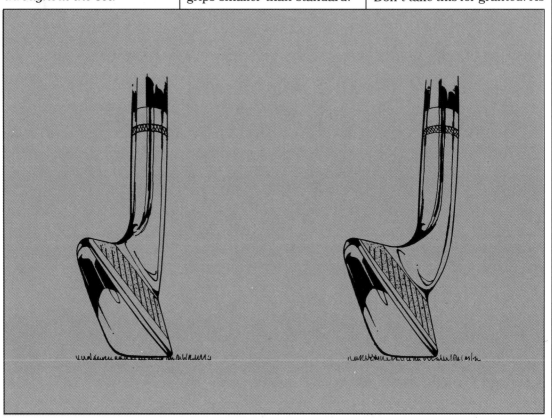

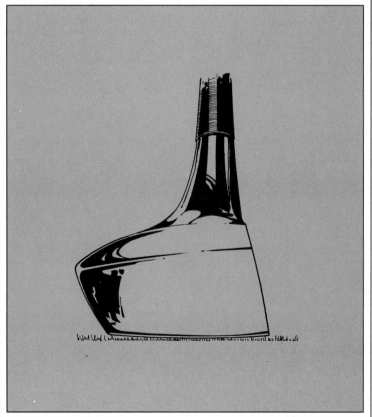

139

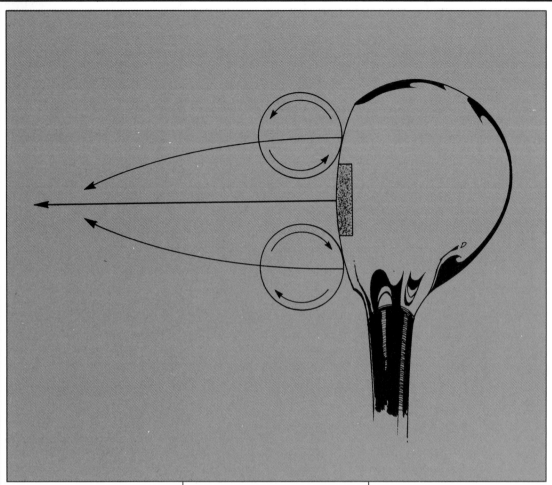

with lofts and other specifications, the manufacturers' quality control standards sometimes don't quite make it.

Another overlooked factor is the rib that runs down the back of most grips today. If your grips have this rib, and they probably do, you must make sure the grips all are on straight. You don't want one rib sitting slightly to the left and another slightly to the right. That's why most good players prefer a grip that is perfectly round, without the rib. They don't want the grip dictating where they put their hands.

The type of grip material you use—rubber, leather, cord or other variation—is a personal preference. Many good players prefer leather because it has a particularly good feel, but you may have trouble with leather if your hands perspire a lot, because leather absorbs perspiration, tends to get dirty and slick and needs a lot of care. Cord grips can be hard on tender or soft hands. The rubber grip probably is the most popular over all because it has a relatively soft feel, stays in good condition and is easy to clean. Again, try some out before you buy.

You might think that all this can't make that much difference. Perhaps so, but look at what skiers do with their skis and their clothes, how swimmers shave their bodies, all just to gain a millisecond or two. If you want to be good, you will do anything to get better. Paying attention to your grips is a small but important element. It's also inexpensive and worth your

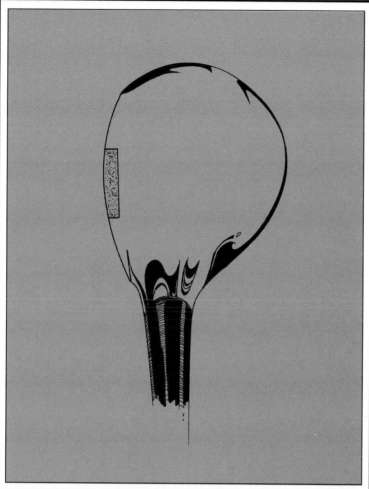

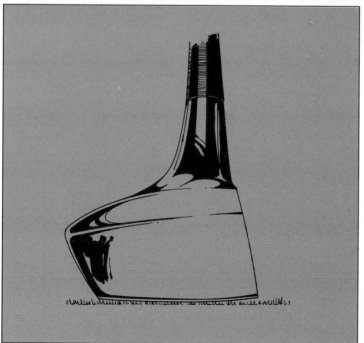

## Bulge Counteracts Gear Effect

The horizontal bulge on a wood club (top and opposite page) helps counteract the gear effect on off-center hits by starting the ball farther to the right (toe hit) or left (heel hit). The advantages of vertical roll (bottom) are minimal at best.

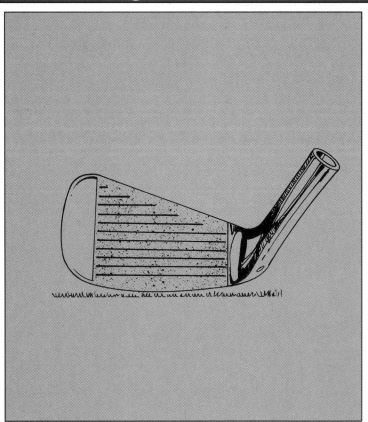

### Underslung Is Best for Good Players

*An underslung hosel (top) puts the clubhead's center of gravity or "sweet spot" more toward the heel of the club, where the better player likes to strike the ball. With a conventional hosel (bottom), the center of gravity is more toward the center or toe of the clubhead.*

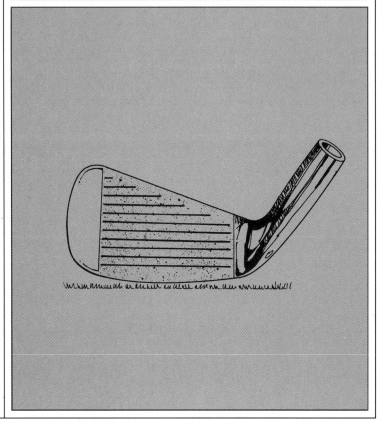

time to make sure they are correct.

# WHAT TO LOOK FOR IN THE SCORING CLUBS

The three most important clubs to any tour professional, and to most every other good player, are the driver, sand wedge and putter. And, while it's vital to drive the ball in the fairway, probably the most important clubs for most players are the sand wedge and the putter. They are the clubs that get the ball close to and in the hole.

The sand wedge can be—should be—the most versatile club in your bag, provided it is constructed properly. Unfortunately, the hardest golf club in the world to find is a sand wedge that is a good bunker club and a good pitching club at the same time. If it is great in one area, it won't necessarily be so good in the other. We can, however, keep searching.

The best bunker/pitching club is designed with enough bounce and a reasonably wide sole to help you out of the sand, yet when you lay it open or point the toe more to the right for a pitch shot, the leading edge does not come off the ground. In other words, the good wedge has the correct radius and the correct bounce, the correct grinding from toe to heel, so that when you open it up, the leading edge stays at the same height.

In playing from the bunker, having the correct bounce is much more important than having a big, wide sole. For the better player, in fact, a narrower sole is better, because it gives him more control and lets him strike closer to the ball and spin it more when he needs to. The big-headed, wide-soled clubs with a lot of bounce—I call them the "bludgeon clubs"—are fine for getting out of sand safely, but they are awful for playing a precise shot that will get the ball close. They also are terrible pitching clubs from grass.

In general, the firmer the sand, the narrower the sole and the less bounce you need on your sand wedge. If you are playing from soft, fluffy sand, the opposite is true.

I prefer a sand wedge that is not too heavy—and many of them are—because too much weight reduces my feel with the club. I also prefer a slightly softer or more flexible shaft that gives me more feel and "helps" me with the shot a bit.

In reality, most players should take a look at the three-wedge theory that has become popular in recent years. That gives a player a pitching wedge, which in reality is an extension of his set in the form of a 10-iron; it gives him a good bunker club with a loft of 57 degrees and a third pitching club with a loft of 60 or so degrees, good for the shots from 60 yards or so on in that also can be used out of the sand.

Your putter also is a very personal club. I've had more putters than I can count. There is no rhyme nor reason why one works and another doesn't, which is why it's difficult to recommend one over another. But I'll give you a few guidelines.

A putter with a longer blade, such as the Ping and other models, is easier to aim. I've always felt that the reason Nicklaus always has taken so long over his putts is that he has used a short-bladed putter that is difficult to aim. He has managed to do it brilliantly, but mortals might have more trouble. If you use a putter that points itself better, you can spend less time aiming the blade and concentrate more on the line.

There is no doubt, in my mind, that the heel-and-toe weighting in a putter has a lot of merit, especially for players who do not always strike the ball at the sweet spot. That, unfortunately, means most players. Perimeter weighting reduces the torquing or twisting that results from an off-center hit and so is more forgiving. You will strike the ball less off line than with other types.

A center-shafted putter, one in which the shaft is affixed more toward the center of the putter, probably is the most playable design. On the other hand, some great putters have used heel-shafted blades—Nicklaus and Ben Crenshaw, to name a couple.

The standard putter lengths are 34 or 35 inches, but you need not be bound by that. Raymond Floyd now putts with a 38-inch putter because bending over hurts his back. So find a length that matches your size and your putting posture. Pay attention to the loft of your putter. In general, the smoother the greens you play, the less loft you need. The rougher or longer your greens, the more loft you should have. The "standard" loft is four degrees, but you may want to adjust yours. The weight obviously is im-portant. I happen to like a lighter putter, like the Bulls-Eye, on lighter greens, a heavier putter like the Ping on slower greens. Others would disagree and tell you that a heavier putter is best on fast greens because you don't have to move it as far and can control it better. But I've won the Phoenix Open with a Ping, the U.S. Open with a Bulls-Eye, and I prefer my method.

The secret to selecting the right putter is simply to experiment and find the one you prefer, the one that works best with your stroke and on the course you play. Or select more than one, for use under different conditions. But don't stop trying to find a good one. Don't ever tell yourself you are as good a putter as you can be and you can't get any better. You can, and having the right club in your hand gives you a good start.

## ASSEMBLE THE SET YOU NEED

Manufacturers still sell "standard" sets of clubs, but you really shouldn't pay much attention to that. Choose the

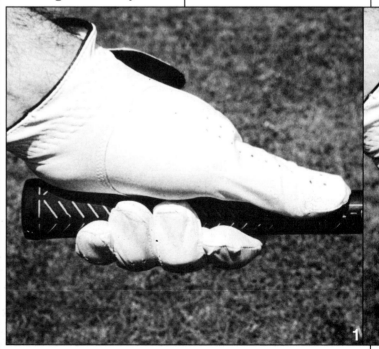

144

particular clubs you put in your bag on the basis of your abilities and, especially, the golf course you happen to be playing.

You have your choice of four or five woods, perhaps a trouble wood of the Baffler type and irons ranging from 1 to 9, plus all kinds of wedges, chippers and other utility clubs. If you are a dedicated player, you ought to carry about 18 clubs wherever you go and select the 14 allowed by the rules that best fit the course you are playing. For example, I normally carry a 1-iron except at Augusta National, where I need a 4-wood to play holes like Nos. 2 and 8 and 13 and 15.

If you don't play Augusta National very often, and if you don't really care to have all those clubs hanging around, pick the ones that work for you and are best for your home course. Of course, I don't know your specific needs, but I'd recommend that most players should do away with the long irons (only *you* know whether you can hit them well), add more woods and certainly consider

carrying three wedges. Fit the lofts and the design of the wedges to the type of course you play most, factoring in the type of sand and the kind of pitch shots you must play to the greens. If you have highly elevated greens, and especially if they are small, the 60-degree wedge will be invaluable. If your course is flat and not heavily bunkered, maybe you don't need that third wedge and can put another of the longer clubs in your bag.

I'm not in the business of telling you which particular brand or kind of clubs you should buy. Rather, I've given you some guidelines so you can seek out a competent professional for more specific assistance. Most professionals are becoming more aware of the services they must provide. Fitting and customizing clubs is one of those services. So, with my guidelines in hand, look for someone who can give you what you need. The time, effort and perhaps the little extra money it might cost will be worth it in the long run.

### Just Right, Too Big, Too Small

*If your grip is the correct size, the tip of your middle finger should barely touch the thumb pad (1). If the grip is too big (2), your fingers won't curl far enough around the club. If it is too small (3), your fingers will jam too far into the thumb pad.*

2

3

# CHAPTER TEN

# GOLF, THE MIND GAME

**W**ithout a doubt, golf is the hardest game there is. One day you have it by the throat and the next day it has you by the throat. It is never the same two days in a row. I don't know of anything more challenging.

Golf can be very depressing if you are not playing well. But on a good day it can be the most rewarding, enjoyable game you could hope to be a part of. At my level, to walk down the last hole when you are winning a U.S. Open or a PGA Championship, or any tournament, for that matter, makes worthwhile everything you have done to get to that point. I have an idea that golfers at all levels experienced the same sense of satisfaction in their moments of accomplishment.

In addition to the basic fundamentals you must adhere to, golf requires patience, hard work, perseverance, a knowledge of what propels the ball in the right direction, feel, touch, aggressiveness, conservativeness, a certain amount of strength and, contrary to what a lot of people believe, physical fitness. To be good at it requires a large, long-term commitment.

The physical factor is important, to be sure. But most important of all is the mental aspect. Above all else, golf is a mind game, at whatever level it is played.

There are two distinct aspects to that mind game. One is played from within and can be considered, simply, the control of yourself and your emotions. The other is played from without, reacting to the golf course as you find it and to the situation each shot presents. This is strategy, the ability to *think* your way around the course.

Let's look at each in turn.

## HOW TO MANAGE YOURSELF

To play golf to the level of your potential, you must have the ability to decipher what you can and can't do, to know what your limitations are as a player and contain yourself within those limitations. At the same time, you must constantly be trying to broaden those limitations. You must be able to manage your game and adapt that game to different courses and different situations.

Golf is a game in which preparation counts and physical preparedness breeds mental readiness. It intrigued everybody in Australia back in the late '60s when Jack Nicklaus, the greatest player in the world, came over and paced off the golf courses. That just wasn't done there then. Gary Player would arrive with a carry-sack full of dumbbells and weights, and he would run four miles on the golf course after he finished playing, because he believed that made him a better player. It was a way of saying to himself, "I get my strength from doing this." It impressed me. Here I was struggling and not accomplishing anything and here was millionaire Gary Player running four miles around the course.

The game is contradictory in that it requires probably the most precise physical action in all of sport, yet in a sense it is an extremely imprecise game—you have 14 different clubs, different holes on different courses, different grasses, different course conditions, different wind and weather conditions. You hit a great shot and it takes a bad bounce, so you are penalized after a wonderful effort. And you have to cope with all this with a body that cannot perform as a machine shot after shot, simply because it is a human body. It's enough to boggle the mind. Unfortunately it does boggle the minds of too many golfers, thus keeping them from playing to their potential.

The answer—at least one of them—is to accept the fact that you often won't be able to handle all the diversities of the game and never will be able to beat all of them all of the time. But you can strive to be as precise as possible within those limitations. You can't control the bounce of the ball but you can, within reason, control the way you hit it. Apply yourself to executing every shot to the best of your ability, while not getting upset over things you can't control. With that attitude, your bad shots will be fewer and not as bad, and your good shots will be better and come more often.

When I first began playing tournament golf, my mental processes were a bit suspect, to say the least. As I've indicated, there was a lot of club-throwing and other shenanigans that weren't helping me. Golf was a struggle for me, and I was hurting myself by not knowing how to cope with it.

A couple of things helped me overcome the problem. First, I began to look around at my peers in those days, and I saw that most of them who were considered very talented players were mentally inadequate on the golf course. That showed me that the mental aspect was as important as talent, if not more so. Secondly, and most important, was my association with Jack Nicklaus that began about 1969. I had always heard that Jack was the best mentally, that he prepared the best and controlled his emotions the best. When I met him and watched him in action, I saw that this was true. And I told myself that if he could control himself to that extent, then I, in my own way, could be every bit as good in that regard. So I've always used Nicklaus as my No. 1 example of the perfect mental approach to golf. And I began to work very hard on that aspect of my game.

It was relatively easy for me to accept the fact that I was going to play badly at times, because I knew that everybody was going to do the same. What irritated me more than anything else was to play well physically and not get anything out of my golf because of my mental inabilities. You can have a near-perfect ball-striking day, but if you make mental mistakes you're not going to get what you should out of the round. On the other hand, you can play badly and still get yourself around the course in decent fashion if you're in control of your mental faculties.

I always have been able to accept not winning if I hit poor golf shots. But I have trouble living with myself when mental mistakes cost me victory.

I had a special incentive to clean up my mental act. I didn't want a reputation as a hothead, as a spoiled brat... the kind of reputation I built in my earlier days in Australia. I particularly didn't want that reputation as a foreigner making a living on the U.S. tour. More to the point, I knew that with that attitude I wouldn't be able to make a living on the U.S. tour.

Part of my problem was taken care of by maturity, the simple passage of time and the circumstances that go with that. I started off in golf trying to prove to everybody else that I could be a good player, that I was a decent human being. Eventually I won a bunch of golf tournaments, got married and had two lovely children and after a while realized I didn't have to prove anything to anybody. All I had to do was satisfy my own ambitions without worrying about what anybody else thought. So I'm a lot more at peace with myself now, a lot more relaxed.

This has helped me achieve what anybody needs for mental control—*composure*. Composure is simply not being upset if you miss a three-foot putt on the first hole...or the 18th hole. It comes from knowing everybody else is going to miss one somewhere along the way. It comes from recognizing that if you hit one or two bad tee shots, chances are everybody else will do the same. Composure is accepting the fact that you don't win the golf tournament in the first nine holes on Thursday, that shooting at every flagstick on the course is not the way to win, that missing one six-foot putt does not destroy the 275 shots you have to

play, that one bad bunker shot doesn't lose a tournament, just as one good one doesn't win it.

You can apply that same philosophy to your level of competition, whether it's your friendly Sunday foursome, the club championship or the U.S. Amateur. It's a way to play better golf, for you and for me.

Everyone wants to know how to keep his nerves under control during the pressure of competition. The answer is complex—there is not a single one. I will say that it probably begins off the golf course and is perhaps as much physical as mental. Remember, physical preparation breeds mental readiness, whether it's as simple as getting a good night's sleep and cutting down on your morning coffee or as sophisticated as a strenuous daily workout program.

And certainly, no matter how good your physical condition, you're going to get nervous on the golf course. Everybody does, to varying degrees depending on the level of competition, but nervous nevertheless. That nervousness affects some more than others, but I've found that when you succumb to nerves to the point where it affects your game, it's because you add pressure to yourself. You make the situation mean more than it should, when in truth you should be doing something to take the pressure *off*, to make the situation *less* meaningful. You should focus not so much on *what* it is you are doing but *how* you are going to do it. As I indicated earlier, this is the time to concentrate on your routine. I've always talked to myself on the golf course (not out loud, because it's distracting to others and they also may think I'm crazy). I'll tell myself, "Now, David, you're playing well, so take your time, remember your system, relax and put a good swing on it." Don't think of the consequences, all the ifs, ands, buts and maybes. In particular, don't think of the negatives. If you look at the out-of-bounds on the right, you put that image in your mind, and it's amazing how often you'll end up there.

Just as I explained earlier that deep breathing is important in putting, so I feel it's important in any situation that strums the nerves and tightens the muscles. When the pressure starts to get to you, take a deep breath, hold it for a moment, then exhale it all. Do this a time or two until you feel your muscles relaxing.

You must understand that one of the prime causes of nervousness, of succumbing to pressure, is an inherent lack of confidence in your ability. As I said, we all get nervous, but the player who has ingrained a good swing and believes in it can go ahead and make that good swing no matter how great the pressure. But if you have doubts, your swing likely is going to fall apart when the heat is on. The only solution I have to that problem is the one I've mentioned a time or two thousand during the course of this book—work hard enough and long enough on your swing until you *do* trust it.

One of the keys to scoring well consistently is to stay on an even keel throughout your round and never, *never* give up. That may be a cliche, but it's a critical point. One of the best examples of this is Tom Watson. You never hear him complain. You never see him moping, hanging his head. He tees it up on the first hole, hits it, goes and finds it, hits it again . . . and does that until his caddie says, "That's it for today, you've played 18 holes." Seve Ballesteros is another example of that kind of player. He hits it and goes and finds it. Sometimes he has to go a little off line to find it, but

you would never know he's upset. That's the mark of somebody who is in control mentally. His attitude is, "OK, I'm going to hit some bad shots, drive it in the rough, hit it in the bunker and probably three-putt a time or two. But so is everybody else."

An attitude like that allows you to remain repetitive, and I want to reemphasize the value of that. I discussed earlier how important it is to have a preshot routine that you perform the same way, in the same length of time, every time. That makes the start of your swing—and the swing itself—almost automatic. A repetitive routine is easy to make happen on the practice tee. On the course, under pressure, it becomes much more difficult. The inexperienced player, one who has some doubts about his ability, usually will take different amounts of time to execute a shot relative to the importance of the shot. On the second shot to the first hole he might take 25 seconds. On the second shct to the 18th hole, where he needs a 4 to win, he might take a minute. Eventually, that tendency will do him in. So, no matter how severely you are feeling the pressure, force yourself to go through your routine the same way every time. Soon you will come to the point where you can do it without thinking about it. You actually will begin feeling the pressure less, and your shotmaking will get a lot better.

The player who wins the tournament, or the Sunday nassau, is the one who maintains his repetitive routine and swing until the final putt is holed. The player who loses is the one who lets things interfere. Usually he gets in his own way. He may be even par, but he doesn't feel like he is playing that well and can't figure out why his score is that good. Pretty soon it won't be. Or he plays beautifully for

14 or 15 holes—maybe he is six or seven over par and headed for his best round ever—and suddenly he says to himself, "Boy, I am nearly to the clubhouse. If I can just finish par, par, par, I can break 80!" The moment he starts thinking like that, he loses his repetitiveness and begins to court disaster.

The two worst things to do are worry about what happened on the last hole and think too far in advance. Which means the old "one shot at a time" theory is still the best way to play the game. It's not easy to do, for you or me or any of us. But the more you try to make that your method of play, the better and more consistently you will score.

Related to that is the need to keep your emotions on an even keel no matter how good or bad your play. You don't get dejected over a double bogey nor too elated over a birdie. If you keep letting your emotions range up and down, your nerves are going to wear thin long before the round is over.

## HOW TO MANAGE THE COURSE

Most physical aspects of ball-striking and course management are influenced by your thought processes. Repetition is a product of how much time you devote to alignment and setup, which is a mental application. One of the functions of good shotmaking and effective scoring is knowing how far you can hit the ball with each club . . . and how far you are from your target. That sounds obvious, but it's amazing how many players ignore those things.

The lie of the ball is critical. The lie is the first thing you should examine before you begin assessing a particular shot, because it determines what you can and can't do with that shot. If the ball is sitting up nicely, you can hit any kind of shot you want. The worse the lie, the fewer options you have. As a rule of thumb, the farther down in the grass (or in a divot, or on hardpan) the ball is sitting, the more of a descending blow you must make. This severely limits the types of shots you can make. Yet the lie of the ball is often ignored by handicap players. Don't you ignore it.

Be aware of the true speed of the greens and know how to find it. On the practice green, or if you get a chance to play a practice round on the course before a tournament, avoid practicing uphill putts. Instead, putt downhill to get a better feel for the real green speed. If you practice the uphill putts, the slow putts, you won't be able to relate to the speed when you face a downhiller during a round that counts. It's a lot easier to tell yourself to hit a putt a little firmer than a little softer. This also will help you putt the level putts better.

In considering your shots, club selection and the like, you must factor in the terrain, wind and weather conditions and the grass you are playing on. Obviously you need more club for an uphill shot, less for a downhill shot, more club into the wind and less with the wind. How much more or less is something you must learn through experience, through playing under different conditions. Again, *awareness* is the key.

Bent grass gives you the best opportunity to control the ball. The ball tends to fly a little farther off Bermuda grass and even farther off bluegrass, which cannot be cut as short and so tends to get caught between the clubface and the ball. If you don't know what kind of grass you are playing on, ask the course superintendent or the golf professional.

Given an understanding of those basics, course management becomes just a matter of common sense and an awareness of how to direct your mind. The basis of that, of course, is to be positive rather than negative. For example, consider the times you have yanked the ball left out-of-bounds and said, "Well, I knew I was going to do that before I hit it." Of course, you did. That's why you hit it there. Suggestion is indeed a powerful force.

Common sense also means paying attention to yourself. Think how many times you have knocked a driver through the fairway and into the woods and said, "I knew I should have hit a 3-wood." Well, why didn't you?

Is there a hole on your golf course, or any other that you play occasionally, that you really don't like, that gives you a lot of trouble? If you're like most of us, the answer is yes. It may be that the tee faces in the wrong direction, that the hole doglegs in a manner that gives you problems...or whatever. In any event, you're uncomfortable every time you play the hole. Well, don't fight it. Don't feel you have to conquer that hole every time, because if you get your hackles up, you're likely to come to grief more often than not. Instead, don't challenge the hole. Minimize your chance for error. Take a 3-wood off the tee, hit your second somewhere *around* the green instead of at the flag, *avoid* disaster rather than courting it. Take your par on your bogey and go on to play more holes, some of which you probably *can* attack.

The same philosophy should apply to a difficult pin position. For example, on the 14th hole at Harbour Town, a difficult par 3 over water, there is one pin position during each Heritage Classic that is short and right, not eight yards from the water. If you hit the ball in the water, you have to walk to the drop area at the front of the tee and have an even more difficult shot to the flag. The solution, of course, is simply to hit the ball 20 or 30 feet to the left of and past the hole, give yourself a chance to hole a long putt for a birdie and at least insure your par. Not only is this strategically sound, it eliminates a lot of apprehension as you begin your downswing and gives you a lot better chance of making a successful shot.

The point of all this is that you don't force things, don't exceed your limitations, don't buck the odds and try to do what you probably can't. I've always admired Jack Nicklaus for having the discipline, when he's in contention and especially in a major championship, to hit 3-woods into the middle of the fairway, hit his second shots to the middle of the greens and play for pars. More often than not, it pays off.

I lost the French Open in 1971, when I was defending champion, because I was unable to control my emotions. I was a shot behind playing the par-4 15th. The pin was back, and there was out-of-bounds behind the green. I chose a 6-iron, which I thought at the time was too much club, but I wanted to get the ball back to the flag and have a chance at a birdie. I hit the ball solidly and hard, because I was a little pumped up. It hit the back of the green, bounced out-of-bounds and I made 7. As it turned out, the leader went bogey, bogey, and I got beat by one shot. That was one of my first and most critical lessons—let somebody else make the mistakes.

Now I consider it my obligation just to do the best I can and not ask more of myself than my ability can handle. Hale Irwin is a wonderful example of that kind of player. He may be outdriven on every hole, but he just keeps playing his game. He knows what his limitations are and he never tries to exceed them. He never tries to hit a 2-iron when he knows it's a 4-wood shot. And he'll beat you almost every time.

Play the odds. If it's going to take your best 3-wood ever to clear the water and get to the par-5 green in two, you're a lot better off laying up and trying to make birdie from the safe side. If you knock the ball into the woods and could get to the green by rifling your next shot through a six-inch opening, don't start looking for a small miracle. Chip the ball out sideways so you can knock your next shot on the green and maybe hole a putt for par. If you can't, bogey is a lot better than triple bogey.

Once you have accepted that philosophy and have the discipline to stick to it, course management becomes nothing more than good planning. Don't just step up and whale away. Think about where you want to put the ball so your next shot will be as easy as possible. Think about where you want to *miss* the ball. If the pin is cut to the right side and there is only 12 feet of green between the hole and the rough, don't aim the ball into the rough and try to hook it. If it doesn't hook, you have a real problem. Instead aim the ball at the center or left-center of the green. If you hook it, you're on the left edge of the green. If you put a nice little fade on it, you might be close to the flag.

Similarly, if you have a 20 or 30 foot putt on a slick green, the last thing you want is to have a four-foot downhiller coming back. Almost everybody is going to two-putt from that distance, anyway, so cozy the ball up under the hole, take your two putts and go to the next tee.

Of course, there are times you will want to gamble, when you *must* gamble. If you're one down going to the 18th and need a birdie to tie, go ahead and fire it at the flag no matter what is in your way. But those occasions are rare. In the long run, the conservative approach will pay off. You'll make just as many pars and birdies . . . and a lot fewer of the big numbers that ruin your score and your disposition.

We all play golf for different reasons. When I first started to play golf, I approached it as something that could give me what I wanted out of life—success, security, recognition, that sort of thing. I didn't have much of an alternative. Once I made my decision, if I hadn't become successful at golf, I don't know what would have become of me. So my option was to do as Gary Player once told me—if I were going to be successful, I had to work harder at my game than the next guy. So I decided to become the hardest-working player in Australia.

I suspect that your goals in golf fall somewhat short of mine, as well they should unless you are making your living out of it as I am. I'm certainly not advocating that anybody work as hard at golf as I have. What I am saying is that you should ascertain just why you *do* play golf and what you want out of the game. That probably will determine how hard you want to work at it. And be honest with yourself. Almost all golf is competitive, whether it's in the U.S. Open, the club championship or the Friday Mixed Twilight League . . . don't they call those Divorce Opens? Don't be kidding yourself that you don't care how well you play when really you want pretty badly to win that $2 bet or that fifth flight trophy.

Once you have determined how well you *really* want to play, you must come to grips with the fact that to play better you are going to have to put some amount of work into the game. You must have an understanding of the functions of your golf swing, plus an understanding of how to *play* the game, the subject we have been discussing in this chapter. How much time you can or are willing to spend is a personal thing, but your improvement will be directly related to that amount. There are no quick fixes in golf.

The prospect actually is not grim at all. The more you challenge this great game—and yourself—the more fun you will have. The satisfactions are great. I don't regret one minute of the effort I have put in at learning to play better. I have been richly rewarded with far more than money. I hope that this book will provide you some information and some incentive that will help you share in those rewards through a lifetime of better golf.

# SECTION TWO

# CHAPTER ELEVEN

# THE EARLY TRIALS AND THE AWFUL CHANGE

**M**uch has been written—most of it exaggeration—about my humble beginnings and the so-called school of hard knocks from which I emerged. Well, I wasn't exactly from the country club set, but I always had three meals a day and nice clothes to wear. My father, Albert George, was a naval clerk in Melbourne and always provided for us. As it turned out, though, he didn't think much of golf, and that's when things started to get tough.

My first exposure to the game came around 1958, when I was 12 years old. I rode my bike to and from the Box Hill Grammar School and would take a shortcut through the Burwood Cricket Field, which doubled as a football field. When it wasn't being used for cricket or football, people would be out there hitting golf balls. Those were the first golfers I saw. One day I found some old clubs in the garage—they belonged to my mother, who used to bash the ball around Wattle Park a bit—and I thought I would go out and give this game a try. Unfortunately, the clubs were left-handed.

So, even though I was a natural right-hander, I began hitting balls left-handed at Burwood. As I eventually found, that was a mistake, although I actually became pretty successful as a left-hander. By the time I was 13 and had been playing for a year, I carried a legitimate 1-handicap and won the Wattle Park Junior Championship as a lefty. Wattle Park was not a Merion, but it was the first championship I ever won and I was proud of it. I still am.

Those early days were a great learning period for me, but they also were incredibly frustrating. I hit a lot of balls, and often, at Wattle Park, the nine-hole muny course in Melbourne. I would go there after school and hit balls until dark. Then I would start leaving school to hit balls. I'm not trying to justify it, but golf is nonexistent in the Australian high schools and not much stronger in the college system. I've been very vocal in my criticism of the system, which has, to some extent, hurt my name and reputation in my native country. But I believe strongly that it's the main reason Australia hasn't produced more world-class players. Conversely, the school and college system is the reason the United States does produce so many of the world's best players. A player has a chance to learn and be competitive virtually from the time he becomes a teenager. I'm not saying that this kind of emphasis on any sport is good or bad within the school structure. I'm just saying that it's one of the big reasons for American success in world golf.

At any rate, when you become as avid as I did about the game at a young age, quitting school to pursue golf started to become very attractive. I knew it was a gamble, because I would lose a formal education, but it was a gamble I was certainly starting to consider.

The Wattle Park professional, a wonderful individual named John Green, eventually took a liking to me and asked me to start working in his shop after school and on weekends. It was a pretty easy duty, really—making coffee and cleaning the floor and fixing the buggies, and occasionally I got to work on the starting times for the players. I worked 14 or 15 hours a day at the shop on Saturdays and Sundays, and it was a great education. Most of the golf shops in Australia did all their own club repair work—still do, in fact—buying the equipment in components and assembling the clubs themselves. That's where I first learned to whip a club, do reshafting, change the soleplate and regrip, and that first sparked my interest in equipment and club design.

But my most significant remembrance of that period is the time I came home and told my mother, Patricia, that I needed a new golf bag. She and I got on a bus and went to the Wattle Park shop, and she bought me a new bag, one of those little carry bags. Coming back on the bus I clutched

that new bag, the greatest thing I had ever seen. It's a memory I'll always have.

For almost a year I did little except go to school and work in the golf shop, and one day, when I was still 13, I came home and told my mother I wanted to quit school and become a professional golfer. My mother, bless her heart, stood behind me, but she warned

**The Early Righty**
*Here is David Graham at about 15, shortly after the transformation from left-hander to right-hander. Any resemblance between then and now is strictly coincidental.*

me that my father would have none of it, and she was right. It was a closed subject the minute I tried to discuss it with him. He said, "I'm against it. If you quit school, hit the road."

In retrospect, you can't really blame him for that attitude. At that time, golf in Australia didn't offer a very lucrative future. There was no tour to speak of, and the club professionals were not highly paid. In all my wisdom, however, that didn't deter me at all.

Across from our house on Lillian Street lived a successful shoe company executive named Graham Smith, and through him my mother met George Naismith, head professional at Riversdale, one of the nice private clubs in Melbourne. I don't know what my mother told Naismith in their first meeting, but it must have been something like, "I have this youngster who wants to be a golf pro and would you do one of two things—either give him a job or try to talk some sense into him."

Mother arranged for me to have a meeting with Naismith, and I'll never forget it. I had to wear a shirt and tie and long pants, and I was as shaky as a newborn calf. But the minute I met Naismith, I liked him. He asked me how badly I wanted to become a golf pro and I answered, "Real bad."

"How hard are you prepared to work?" he asked.

"Work doesn't bother me," I said. "I will work." So I got the job, and the day I turned 14, the legal age for quitting school in my state of Victoria at the time, I left school and never went back. The next day, May 23, 1960, I became the junior apprentice at Riversdale. I didn't even have a vacation day in between.

My first day on the job I was told to paint a whole lot of buggies, pull carts, that were rusty and in terrible shape. I put on a pair of overalls, took the carts into the caddie room, sanded them down and painted them. I worked 16 hours a day for about three days before I got them finished. Much later, I learned I had impressed Naismith greatly by the way I went at the task, and when the senior apprentice left after two months, I took his job.

My father didn't actually kick me out when I left school, but our house became split. My parents had not got along for years—I can still remember them battling—and I guess my decision just triggered the break. My mother and I lived in the back half of the house. My father and my sister, Jennifer, who is two years older than I, lived in the front half. We never had any communication. The only time I ever went into the front of the house was after he had gone to work in the mornings. He used to leave his change in a big glass, and I'd occasionally pinch a couple of bucks so I had some money in my pocket. I'm sure he knew I was doing it.

For the next three and a half years I did all the things at Riversdale that apprentices do. I worked in the shop, cleaned clubs, ran the caddie shed, washed my boss's car, cleaned his office and repaired clubs. We had a pretty good club repair and club-making operation going, and I ran the whole thing. We assembled all our clubs, because finished clubs were so expensive. We had bins of shafts and heads and grips and just fiddled around with the lengths until we felt they were right. In the early '60s in Australia, nobody had heard of swingweight. We also took in a lot of outside work from a couple of municipal clubs. I was the only apprentice in the shop, working seven days one week and six days the next, and many a day I worked from sunup to 10 or 11 at night trying to keep up. I started out making 12 pounds a week, went to 15 pounds a week the second year, 18 the next and finally to 25 a week in my fourth year. That was big money for me, and I never spent any of it. I never went out, never did anything but work. Every red cent went into the bank.

**R**ight away I had started to bug George Naismith to come watch me hit balls, and one day, not too long after I took the job, he said, "Son, get your 2-wood and we'll go down and hit some balls." Then he said, "And bring a right-handed 5-iron." I asked him why and he said, "I just want to see you hit some balls."

The driving range at Riversdale was probably 225 yards long, although it seemed like 350 then. I hit two shots with my left-handed 2-wood. They went as straight as I could hit them and finished about 10 feet apart. Naismith said, "That's pretty good. Now let me see you hit two balls with this 5-iron."

I said, "Mr. Naismith, I have never hit a ball right-handed." He said, "Go ahead and try it."

So I made two ungodly swings with that right-handed club. I think I connected with one and hit it about 10 yards. I took three or four swings at the other one and finally hit it, tearing up a divot about eight inches long and four inches deep.

With his golf shoe, Naismith scraped some lines in the turf and said, "This is straight back, this is inside, here is the ball and this is straight through. You can take an hour off and hit some balls. I don't care if you hit the ball or not. All I want you to learn to do with that 5-iron is to take the club straight back on line, bring it down on the inside and swing it straight through the ball."

I protested. "Mr. Naismith, I just hit two perfect shots left-handed."

He said, "I don't ever want you to pick up a left-handed club again. You should play right-handed."

As you can imagine, that was quite a shock to me. Looking back, it took an incredible act of faith to make the change. But here was a man who had won the Australia Open back in the late '30s and had played in England on the Australian team. He was a close friend of Norman Von Nida and Eric Cremin and Ossie Pickworth. Peter Thomson was his most famous protege. I worshipped the ground George Naismith walked on and I trusted him, so when he told me to change to playing right-handed, I did it without a question. I made myself a set of right-handed clubs and went to work.

About 18 months or so after I started working at Riversdale, my mother and I left home and went to live in a boardinghouse, and Mother eventually got a divorce. She opened a pet store with a friend in a shopping arcade in the little suburb of Burwood. It did not do well, unfortunately, but it provided us with some income for a while. I've only seen my dad once since then, at the U.S. Open at Hazeltine in 1970. I haven't seen my sister since the day I left the house.

Working on my golf game, this awful change I was making, became an obsession. I worked on it in the wee hours before work and in the dusk after work, on my days off, just any time I could squeeze in between the long hours I was working in the shop. Even then, while my immediate intention was to become a club professional, my aspirations were to be a professional golfer. I used to get in a lot of trouble with the members because I spent so much time on the golf course and the practice range. I'd be the first one there hitting balls in the morning and sometimes the last one to leave at night. I'd be on the putting green on Saturdays, and that would upset the members. Remember, in those days an apprentice wasn't even allowed in the clubhouse. The only part I ever saw was the kitchen, where I could go and eat with the staff. But George was behind me 100 percent and always bailed me out with the members.

For a while after I switched sides, I still putted left-handed. But I was on the putting green a few months later and Naismith walked by and said, "What are you doing, putting that way?" I said, "I can get it lined up better this way, Mr. Naismith." He said, "If you are going to play golf right-handed, do it all right-handed."

So I threw away my left-handed putter, and the biggest adjustment I had to make was to learn to putt right-handed. I'm convinced that even today that's why I putt with my hands slightly behind the ball. Everybody has a dominant eye, and my right eye is so dominant that when I line up my hands, the clubface and the ball, the angle that looks straight to me actually has my hands behind. When I played left-handed, with my right eye over the ball, I could always get my hands in the correct position and the shaft straight up and down. But when I switched to the right side, the hands automatically drifted a couple of inches behind the ball.

It actually had taken me only a couple of days after I switched to be able to make contact consistently and get the ball airborne. Remember, I was a natural right-hander, and I did have youth on my side. But I spent many miserable, frustrating months before I began to make the progress I wanted. The major problem was that visual change, in the full swing as well as in putting, created by being on the opposite side of the ball. The angles were different. It's as if you were shooting a gun, aiming first with your left eye closed and then with your right eye closed. In looking at the clubface and ball through my dominant right eye, there was about a two-inch difference in angle with, say, a 39-inch 2-iron in my hands. So I've always had a tendency to position my hands too far back of the ball at address. It's an adjustment I've never been able to make completely, because I can't change my vision tendencies.

In any event, it took me two years, hitting balls every daylight minute I wasn't working, to get back to the level I had reached as a left-hander. I hardly ever went on the golf course. I had played in assistants' tournaments every Monday when I started working at Riversdale, and I quit playing in them for those two years. I virtually disappeared. When I finally learned to play, I showed up at an assistants' tournament as a right-hander and nobody could believe it.

I've been asked on occasion what might have happened had I never changed, and I can answer that quite easily. I don't think I ever would have accomplished anything as a left-handed professional for several reasons, the major one being that I never would have been strong enough physically. When he told me to change, Naismith gave me his theory of the stronger hand being on the bottom. He realized at the time that I never would have that 60 percent of my (then) 128-pound body in the right place to hit the golf ball. Had I been a strong

200-pounder I might have been able to get by somehow. But at my size I never would have had the strength to play as well as I wanted, and I certainly couldn't have become as technically capable as I wanted to be.

I'll be forever grateful to George Naismith for insisting that I change.

# CHAPTER TWELVE

# FROM TASMANIA TO PORTLAND

**D**uring my life, there have been certain people in certain periods who have been very influential, who more or less replaced my father. George Naismith was one. So were Eric Cremin and Alex Mercer. So was Tom McKay, who came into my life when I was 17.

Naismith had retired from Riversdale, at the age of 54, in 1964. Out of my love for him, I elected to leave rather than stay on under another professional. I went to work for his brother, Ted, at a course in Melbourne named Mt. Waverly, and a few months later I was offered the job as head professional at Seabrook Golf Club, a private club in Tasmania. Now, we're not talking Preston Trail or Bent Tree Country Club in Dallas. We're talking about a little golf club in a small community on the northwestern tip of a very small island. But it was uptown for me. I was a head professional. When I arrived, however, it turned out that my golf shop was a little construction shed on bricks, not even as nice as a mobile home, that they dumped 50 yards from the clubhouse.

So I was a big-time professional, but without very good facilities and knowing nothing about the business. I'm sure the reason I got the job in the first place was that I was young (only 17 at the time) and cheap. The members were getting a service for very little money. One of the flaws of the Australian PGA at the time was that assistants could become professionals without having any qualifications, passing any business tests or playing tests or anything else. In my case, I could barely add 2 and 2, let alone know anything about buying and selling, inventory and profit and loss.

But I ordered a whole bunch of golf equipment, being extended more credit than I should have been by the sporting goods companies, and stuffed that damned shed with it. I let the president of the club, who had the local General Motors dealership, talk me into buying a new car that I couldn't afford.

My mother hadn't come to Tasmania with me. She followed me there later, although we didn't live together. I boarded with a lady down the road from the club, so my living expenses were not high. Nevertheless, I began slowly going broke.

Tom McKay was a Seabrook member. He owned a big lumberyard and in my eyes was very wealthy. He was my salvation during the time I spent there. If I needed a couple of hundred bucks, he would come up with it. If I wanted to play in a tournament, he would pay my expenses. He helped me with the bank when I got into financial trouble. I still communicate with him, but I'll never be able to repay him for the help he gave me.

A lot of my financial problems at Seabrook were self-inflicted, of course. I spent too much of my time on the practice range, not giving enough lessons and having the shop closed too often. But I've often wondered why some of my members didn't realize that I was young and inexperienced and that there was really no way to make any money out of the job even if I had been paying attention. I eventually suspected they were even going to send me on my merry way while I was up to my eyeballs in debt. Even though I was not blameless, I've never really forgiven those people for allowing me to get into that situation and then turning their backs on me. Tom McKay was about the only one who didn't turn his back.

About that time, slightly less than three years after I had come to Seabrook, I got possibly the biggest break of my life.

There was a new company in Australia called Precision Golf Forgings. It had become a major manufacturer of golf clubs and was making some fabulous equipment. On the PGF staff were players like Kel Nagle, Billy Dunk, a great player who just didn't like to leave home, Alan Murray and Frank Phillips, who played on the U.S. tour for a while. Eric Cremin, the 1949 Australian Open winner and a famous teacher, a Bob Toski-type, was the company's national public relations director. He would travel the country promoting the company, doing exhibitions, and clinics.

Cremin came to my club for an exhibition in 1965. Unbelievably, as far as I was concerned, I now had to play golf with him. I remember that I had been watching American golf on television, and the big thing then was those alpaca sweaters with the puffy sleeves. I had a lamb's wool cardigan that had the puffy sleeves, but the wristbands weren't tight enough. So Tom McKay's wife, who thought I was crazy, I'm sure, spent two days weaving elastic into the bands so I could wear the sweater during the exhibition.

A couple of hundred members came out to watch. I wanted to play only nine holes, but everybody else wanted to make it 18, so that's what we did. I didn't play all that well, but when we were finished Cremin asked me what I was doing there.

"I'm trying to make a living," I replied.

Cremin said, "I think you could be a pretty good player." He was the first person of that stature who had ever said that to me.

"I think you should come to Sydney," he said. "If I can get you a job at Precision Golf Forgings, you can work in the factory and you can play in some pro-ams and tournaments around Sydney. That's the hub of golf in Australia, and if you're going to be a good player, that's where you need to be."

It took me about three days to sell everything I had and leave. I still had $5,000 or $6,000 worth of debts. But Cremin arranged for me to meet with the founder and chairman of Precision, Clare Higson, who called up the sporting goods company to which I owed money and figured out a way to take money out of my paycheck (I was making $42 a week). With the help of a little bit of prize money coming in from pro-ams, and later from tournament winnings, I eventually paid back all the money.

Now I was 20 years old. My main job at PGF was to work in the showroom and fit people for custom clubs, which was the company's main stock in trade. That also got me back in the factory and the research and development area, where I learned an awful lot more about golf equipment.

At the same time, I was becoming frustrated because I wasn't getting to play much golf. I would play in pro-ams on Mondays and occasionally would play at Moore Park, a course that was super for a municipal layout. They didn't have any practice facilities there, so the rest of the time I practiced at a cricket field. I used to get run off for digging up the turf and hitting balls out into an adjacent road. I often go back to Sydney now and stay in an expensive hotel suite, and I make a point of taking my American friends past that cricket field. I just shake my head when I recall the hundreds and hundreds of hours I spent there, in rain or hail or whatever, hitting balls off a dirt area about the size of the hotel rooms I now stay in.

I t wasn't the happiest of times. I was a young kid in a strange town, boarding with a family in one room of their house. I didn't have a car, so everywhere I went had to be by bus or train. The only people I knew were a few golf professionals and the people who worked at the factory. And I wasn't very popular, because all I did in my spare time was hit golf balls. I was searching for the gold ring, and the only way I knew to find it was through golf.

Cremin was giving me a lot of help with his coaching at the time. And not too long after I arrived in Sydney in late 1965 I met Alex Mercer, the head professional at Royal Sydney Golf Club and a very respected guy. He was *the* teacher in Sydney and also one of the staff members at PGF. He was working with Bob Stanton, who in those days looked like he would be one of the best players in the world. Although I was known as a hard worker, I didn't have a reputation, at least not then, as one of the new young lions on the Australian tour like Stanton, Bob Shaw and Bob Mensil. But Mercer took a liking to me and I got to spend a lot of time with him. In those days a professional was not allowed to teach anybody who wasn't a member of his club, and I remember having to get permission from the secretary at Royal Sydney before I was allowed to take a lesson and hit balls on the driving range there.

Mercer had, without a doubt, the best golf swing I had ever seen to that time, a fluid, straight-up-and-down swing. He had a beautiful grip, and that was the biggest change he made with me. He told me my grip was too strong, turned too far to the right. I must have spent six months working on it, and I made some improvement but not enough. He also wanted me to shorten my swing, because he said I took the club back too far and lost control. But like a lot of things I did in those days, I went from one extreme to the other. I worked so hard on the change that I went from too long to too short, and I've spent a lot of the rest of my career trying to rectify that.

Mercer also taught me a lot about leg action, about where the power comes from in golf.

He stressed getting the left knee behind the ball on the backswing and getting the left shoulder fully turned. That's where I got the good turn away from the ball that I still have today.

And I started playing better. In December, 1967, I won my first big professional tournament, the Queensland PGA in Yerongpilly, shooting a course record 67 in the first round and finishing at 282, 10 under par. I began to get recognition as one of those "young lions" to watch in Australia.

But I was in a hurry, maybe too big a hurry. I once was quoted that I was going to have to hit 1,500 balls a day in practice instead of 1,000, and I meant it. I didn't have many friends. I spent my time hitting balls instead of playing snooker with the boys, and some of them resented that. But I had worked since I was 13 years of age, and I didn't know what it was to go out and have a good time. I was often vocal in my criticism of the Australian golf system and of the people who ran it, and a lot of them resented that. I thought I was just being honest, but others saw it rather as shooting off my mouth. Looking back, I think I did it when I wasn't a very good player, because I wanted some attention. It was my way of saying, "Hey, guys, I'm alive. Somebody care about me." I went through a period where I was very frustrated and really had a chip on my shoulder.

I also had a hair-trigger temper, and my course demeanor wasn't always what it should have been. I drew more than one reprimand from tournament officials in those days. I think it stems from the fact that I felt, rightly or wrongly, that I was an underdog. My hot temper came from the fact that I was so desperate. It meant so much to me to play well, and

I'd get so disgusted when I didn't that I couldn't contain myself. I've always felt that I played my best golf when I needed $200 or $300 and had to play like hell to win it. Lee Trevino has said that pressure is playing a $10 nassau with $5 in your pocket. Well, I didn't gamble, but I was putting out a lot of money for expenses, and in those days if you didn't finish in the top two or three, you lost money. I remember playing in a pro-am in Sydney that paid about $90 to the winner and 12th place was worth $4. Four of us tied for 12th and each of us got a $1 bill. I should have framed it . . . probably would have if I hadn't needed it.

One of the strongest driving forces in my career was trying to prove my dad wrong, along with trying to crack that elite group of coming stars. For a long time none of the writers or anybody else included me in that group. It was sheer damned stubborness that

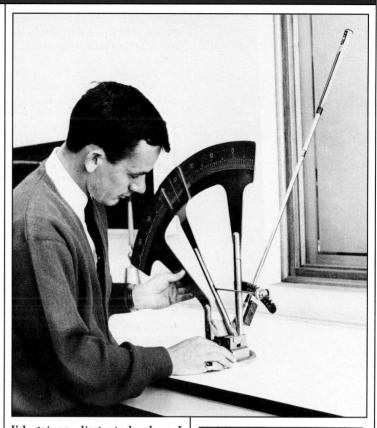

**Learning the Business**
*Here working with a loft-and-lie machine, I learned about equipment at Precision Golf Forgings.*

made me work to become recognized. I knew that without a formal education I had to be a success in golf or else a failure in life. Gary Player once told me, ''The word 'can't' is not in my vocabulary,'' and I lived by that for many years.

I let my determination to succeed get in the way of a lot of things, social graces and etiquette—both on and off the course—among them. Once I was fined $25 by the Australian PGA for ordering breakfast in a northern Australian motel coffee shop while still in my pajamas. At the time, I just didn't know any better. I had never taken the time to learn.

Occasionally I would be criticized by my fellow players and warned by officials for playing slowly. I've always been a deliberate player and certainly am not the fastest player in the world today, but back then my slow pace mainly was dictated by my inexperience, by not being sure of my swing and my abilities. I felt that every time I hit the golf ball, if I didn't do it right, it was going to cost me money that I couldn't afford to lose.

I wasn't a very personable performer on the course, either—Lee Trevino never would have considered me a rival for the affection of the galleries. In my early tournaments—and actually for quite a while thereafter—I was silent and withdrawn during competition. I wasn't out there to be personable. I was out there to score. I was only trying to concentrate as best I could, but my outward appearance often was misunderstood.

I really was very shy and withdrawn, because I didn't know how to act. I had never had the parental guidance in these things. I was always afraid of making a mistake and making an ass of myself, so I just never said anything. I also was scared and desperate, and I knew that if I wanted to play better golf that I had to have my emotions under control. Climbing within myself and shutting myself off from the rest of the world was my way of doing that.

But already there were some who appreciated where I was coming from, what was driving me. Alex Mercer was one who did, and he encouraged me often. He took a lot of time to get to know me, the individual. As time went on, there were others who began to understand. More important, I slowly began to understand myself, to bring my emotions under control and to polish my relations with others, something I was beginning to realize I had to do if I were going to be successful in my profession. At one point I read Dr. Norman Vincent Peale's book, *The Power of Positive Thinking*, and it was a big help to me.

I still have a temper today, but not many know it. And I still have a tendency to voice my honest opinion, wisely or otherwise. But it stays beneath the surface most of the time. It's called maturing, I guess. It's a process everybody must go through, and it's especially critical for a golfer. And it was especially difficult for a young man who didn't have much of an education, was living in a fishbowl and was trying to become the greatest golfer in the world a lot quicker than he knew how.

The 1967-68 season was both gratifying and frustrating. I played the Australian tour as a PGF staff member and played very well—as I recall, I finished in the top six in a dozen or so straight tournaments. But I didn't win, often because I had trouble holding my game together in the last round. That's not uncommon for a youngster in his first real competitive season, but it grated on me. That was the year, in the Australian PGA in November, that I cried. I had just shot a six-under-par 68 the day before and had just made birdie to go one under through five holes for the current round and was in contention. I stroked a 25-foot putt for a birdie on the sixth hole. It went in, but Billy Dunk's caddie, who was holding the flagstick, failed to pull it. The ball struck the stick as it toppled in the hole, so my birdie 4 became a bogey 6. I wouldn't think of crying today at such outrageous misfortune, having seen much of it in the years hence, but I cried on that day. Fortunately for me in the long run, my antidote for such frustrations was just to work harder, hit more balls, learn more about my swing so I could come to trust it under pressure.

Less than a month after my "tragedy" in the PGA, I had what turned out to be the biggest stroke of luck in my life. I got married.

I had met Maureen Burdett in 1967. One of the Australian tour stops was in Cairns, the Black Marlin Capital of the World, situated in the subtropics on the northeastern tip of the country. During the tournament several of us went out for dinner one night and, on the way back to the motel, stopped at a cabaret. There were a lot of girls in there celebrating somebody's birthday. Maureen was one of them. I asked her to dance, then asked her out for dinner the next night. I took her out another time during the tournament, but she never came to the golf course, and when the tournament was over, I left.

A year went by, and I didn't call or write her once. When I returned for the tournament

in 1968, I called and invited her out to dinner. She had a date but agreed to go out with me on Friday. I took her to dinner Friday night, took her to dinner Saturday and proposed. She said, "Well, I'll have to think about this." I said, "I need to know by tomorrow, because it's the last round of the tournament and I'm leaving Monday morning."

Maureen's dad was very strict, and I'm sure he didn't approve of me. He thought that professional golfers were like sailors—in and out of town, a girl in every port, that sort of thing. But I took her to dinner on Sunday night and she accepted.

Now I didn't know what to do. Maureen had a very good job in a bank and I had six months of tournament play left that year. I told her I'd go back to Sydney, buy her a ring and mail it to her. I paid $125 for the ring, an awful lot of money for me, and told her to set a wedding date after the tour was finished. She picked November 30.

I didn't even own a car. Dan Cooper, a good friend of mine in Sydney who treated me very well, loaned me his big Valiant station wagon and I drove the 2,000 miles to Cairns. It took me five days and I finally arrived on Thursday, two days before the wedding. I stayed with an ex-tour player named John Hadley, the pro at the local club, and asked him to be my best man because I couldn't afford to fly anybody up. I went out and hit balls that Thursday afternoon, John and I played the next day and on Saturday I got married.

We spent our wedding night in a Cairns hotel called the Tradewinds...it was about 110 degrees with no air-conditioning. The next morning we piled all Maureen's stuff and all the wedding presents in the station wagon and started the drive back to

Sydney. When we got back to the one room with one single bed in the house where I was boarding, we stuffed all the presents under the bed and in the corners, and our great adventure was on.

We both were too incredibly young and too incredibly poor to get married, and I think we both knew we were taking a huge gamble. Everybody we knew, including our parents, told us we were crazy. Maureen's home situation was not that pleasant, and I think she married me, at least in part, to get out of it. Because of my deportment, I was kind of the black sheep of the tour and was very lonely, and I needed a companion.

None of that is much of a basis for marriage, especially when a young girl from a remote town is marrying a professional golfer who travels all over the world, often without her. It took a lot of adjusting, but it turned out to be the best thing for both of us. She was independent and I was independent, and suddenly we had to start thinking about each other.

We were partners, although it didn't always work out. For a while after we got back to Sydney we would walk down to a park that was not far from our house and she would shag balls for me. It wasn't long before she said, "There's no way I'm doing this again. This is for the birds." She couldn't figure out why the balls were coming so close to her. Finally she realized I was aiming at her. She's never done that since. But she did clean my shoes, keep my bag sparkling and even clean my practice balls every night.

The only time Maureen ever got angry with me was after we had rented another little apartment in Sydney. It had a guest bedroom with white carpeting in it that I used for a storage room and a workshop. In those days, before the invention of two-way tape, we used to regrip our clubs with a black glue that came in a big can. I can't begin to describe the color of that carpet by the time we left the apartment.

Even though she doesn't chase balls or clean shoes for me anymore, Maureen is responsible for everything I am and have today. She made me knuckle down and work even harder. She made me change my personality, asking me why I was so different on the golf course than off it. I really had a Jekyll and Hyde personality in those days. Maureen considered me a pretty easygoing, thoughtful person off the course, and she couldn't understand what she was seeing on the course. For instance, I used to throw my share of clubs, and one day she told me she thought that was disgraceful and if I ever threw a club again she wouldn't come out and watch me anymore. I did and she didn't, for quite a while. Eventually she got her point across.

I think that when two people start with nothing and begin working at a relationship, they learn to understand each other better. And we've had a wonderful relationship that has just grown and grown. The more I worked the better I played . . . and the more fun we had. Today, 17 years and two children later, we're still having fun.

For a while, though, I'm not sure she thought it was going to turn out so well. I had won $4,500 on the Australian circuit in 1968, a lot of money for a kid living on fish and chips and baked beans. And there was a bigger reward in store. Precision Golf Forgings had an incentive program for staff members who played well enough that provided an air ticket to play the Asian

Tour. I qualified for that ticket as a result of my play in 1968. Dan Cooper loaned me some money for expenses. Without a friend like him, life would have been a lot tougher. And off I went in January of 1969 on my first overseas venture...without Maureen, of course, because I didn't have enough money to take her along. I was to be gone three months, and she couldn't understand what was going on.

I didn't play well in the first tournament, at the Wack Wack Golf Club in Manila. But in the second tournament, in Singapore, I shot a 62 in the second round and tied for first, then lost in a playoff. I won $2,200, which seemed like a million, and I called Maureen and told her to get on a plane and meet me in Hong Kong. She traveled the rest of the Asian Tour with me that year.

It must have helped, because I played very well. I didn't win a tournament, but I finished second in the Malaysian Open and scored low enough in the designated events to qualify as the Asian representative in the Alcan Golfer-of-the-Year tournament to be played in September in Portland, Ore. The papers back home were full of stories about me taking the Asian Tour by storm. In 12 weeks I had gone from nobody to a little bit of somebody. Although I didn't fully appreciate it at the time, I was on my way.

I didn't win during the rest of 1969, either, although there may have been some reasons for it. I was so dedicated to playing well in the Alcan that for four months prior to the tournament I played with the American ball, 1.68 inches in diameter compared with the 1.62-inch British ball I was used to and that everybody else played in Australia and around the world at the time.

This gave an advantage to my fellow competitors, because in the wind and on the links courses on which we generally played in Australia, the small ball goes farther, is easier to control and putts better. But it was an advantage I was gladly willing to yield. The Alcan represented the biggest opportunity of my career, and I didn't want to waste it.

Maureen went with me to the Alcan, and it was the biggest trip either of us had ever made. I was the first player to arrive at the Portland Golf Club. I played practice rounds with Kel Nagle, the Australian representative, and was suitably overwhelmed by the whole scene. The tournament, carrying a first prize of $55,000, was the richest—by a whole lot—of any I had ever played in. In the first round I was paired with Billy Casper, and that finished me off. I was a skinny young kid who didn't know much, I considered it a small miracle that I was there in the first place, and I just couldn't handle it. I played terribly, finished about 22nd in a field of 24 and thought I had blown my big opportunity.

Before we left I bought about 15 pairs of Foot-Joy golf shoes in every conceivable color—in Australia, that was like wearing Guccis—and all the other American clothing and equipment that I could find and afford. I figured if I didn't get it then, I'd never get it. I told Maureen that I'd really like to play on the U.S. tour, but when we got on that airplane to fly back to Australia, I honestly believed I'd never get back to America.

# CHAPTER THIRTEEN

# BREAK-THROUGH AND BREAKDOWN

**From West to East**
*My physical game and my competitiveness were sharpened by playing golf all over the world, from Britain (above) to Japan (right), where here I'm driving at the 17th on the way to winning the Yomiuri International in 1970.*

Somebody once figured out that in 1970 David Graham won more golf tournaments than anybody in the world. None of them, unfortunately, was in the United States, but at the moment that didn't matter to me.

Early in February on the Australian circuit, I won the Tasmanian Open and Victorian Open back to back. Both victories were especially pleasing to me, for obvious reasons, particularly the Victorian, which was played at Riversdale in Melbourne and where my 19-under-par 273 beat the tournament record by two shots. I felt the championships were somehow vindication for all the hours I had practiced in those places in the face of all those who doubted me.

I narrowly missed an unprecedented triple the next week when I tied for first in the New South Wales Open but lost in a playoff to Frank Phillips.

On the Asian Tour, I won the Thailand Open and the Yomiuri International Open in Tokyo, finishing second in the Asian point standings and earning a berth in the British Open at St. Andrews. Although hampered by four stitches in a cut on the index finger of my right hand, incurred while I was regripping clubs, I played reasonably well there but putted poorly and finished tied for 32nd. Shortly after that, however, I shot a final-round 64 to win the French Open. It was my fifth individual championship of the year.

I was riding high. I had been named the New South Wales Rookie of the Year and Most Improved Player for 1969 and now was being hailed as Australia's newest star. My friend Peter Thomson, who gave me much good advice on my approach to the game at this time, called me "the best we have in Australia." Coming from such a great player and great person, that meant a lot.

My golf game had improved, of course. I exercised regularly and was gaining weight and getting stronger. My short game always had been good and I had become significantly longer off the tee. More important, I'm sure, is that the experience I was getting was sharpening my competitive instincts, helping me keep my nerves under control so I could function better under pressure. Once a kid who couldn't hang on in the final round, I now was getting a reputation as a final-round charger, a player who not only could hold onto a lead but

**A Winner in Japan**
*Exultation is the mood as the final-hole putt goes in at Yomiuri for my fourth victory of 1970.*

Woy, the American manager from Akron, Ohio. One of his growing stable of clients at the time was Lee Trevino, and he had accompanied Lee to the Dunlop International at Yarra Yarra in Melbourne. He announced he wanted to sign "the best young Australian golfer," and he was impressed with the way I played. Tom Ramsey, the noted Australian golf writer, told him, "The best young guy in Australia is David Graham. He has more determination than anybody." So Woy came to me and said he wanted to sign me. He essentially would pay my expenses in return for a percentage of my earnings. I didn't have $50 in the bank, so I signed the contract without reading it. Buoyed by this "financial independence," I was free to concentrate on my golf, and there is no doubt it helped me for a while.

Maureen and I also had signed a six-month lease on a furnished apartment in Sydney, paying $24 a week. That made her happy and made me very nervous, because I had never signed anything like that before. As it turned out, it was a lot better than the contract I signed with Woy.

Despite my misgivings a few months before, I had quickly got back to America and qualified for the U.S. Open at Hazeltine in Chaska, Minn. I missed the cut, but the experience again was invaluable.

It was at Hazeltine that I met my father for the first and only time since my mother and I had left home those many years before. I was practicing on the range when a marshal came over and told me there was a man who wanted to say hello. I went over to him and he said, "Hello, David, I'm your father." He was working for the Australian government in the United States at the time.

could storm from behind to win. It didn't always happen that way, and I had my share of collapses, but I guess I played well on the last day often enough to get some attention. One writer, about this time, compared me with Arnold Palmer—but you don't always want to believe what you read in the papers.

I also had some peace of mind...at least for the moment. Late in 1969 I had signed a contract with Bucky

We had lunch together and chatted awhile. I felt very uncomfortable and it was a very difficult conversation. He tried to give me all the reasons for what happened and how much he regretted it. I was still either too young or too bitter to want to listen. I was too busy trying to do my own thing, achieve my own goals. I also was in shock that he was there in the first place. Maybe it was unfair of me to tune him out, but finally I said, "If this is all you have to say, then I have to go play a practice round. I don't have time during a U.S. Open to talk about all this when I haven't seen you for eight or nine years. My obligation is to go play a practice round and try to play well this week."

I haven't seen him since. He lives in Melbourne and has remarried. My mother lives there, too, and I see her when I go back, but I don't see my dad. Many of my friends have suggested that I contact my father when I get back to Australia. Paul Harvey once said on his syndicated radio show that it would be nice if my father and I could get back together. I've given it much thought, and I'm sure we both may live to regret our stubborness. I have learned to live without him. I have blocked him out. It may come back to haunt me, but that's something I have to face when the time comes. I no longer have any bitterness. I guess I don't have any feelings one way or the other. I would like nothing more than to share my success with my entire family, but I don't know that that will ever be.

I also played in the Cleveland Open and the Western Open while in the United States, missing the cut in the former and finishing tied for 35th in the latter to win $522. That didn't excite the world, but it added a couple of blocks to my foundation of experience.

My deal with Woy made it definite that I would try to get my U.S. tour card at the qualifying school that fall. While in the U.S. I had stayed with him in Akron and had tied for the lead in the district qualifying at Silver Lake, Ohio, with a 54-hole total of 214, two under par. So I was all set for the main qualifier at Tucson, Ariz., in September.

In the meantime, I was selected to play with Bruce Devlin in the World Cup in Argentina, mainly because Guy Wolstenholme was ruled ineligible because he had not been an Australian resident for five years and also thanks to Peter Thomson's intervention. Fred Corcoran, head of the World Cup organization, had asked that Bob Stanton be named to replace Wolstenholme, but Thomson, Australian PGA president at the time, insisted that I partner Devlin or Australia would not send a team. I had met Devlin in 1969, when he came back to play in the Dunlop International in Canberra, and Alex Mercer arranged for me to have lunch at Devlin's house. But I really didn't get to know him well until we played together in the World Cup. It turned out to be probably the finest and most rewarding relationship of my life.

On my way to the World Cup I breezed into Tucson to tee it up at Tucson National and take the rookie school by storm . . . and I missed qualifying by a stroke. It was partly a case of overconfidence, underestimating everybody else's ability and overestimating mine. I also was not that familiar with the big ball. It's hard to realize today how different that adjustment used to be. Foreign golfers like Greg Norman, Seve Ballesteros and Bernhard Langer seldom played with the small ball. But the Cramptons, Devlins, Players and Grahams, when we came to the United States, had to spend about a year learning to play with a difficult golf ball.

In any event, as I look back on it, missing the qualifying school in 1970 may have been a blessing in disguise. It forced me to play another year of international golf and prepare myself better for the U.S. tour.

The pain was eased considerably the next week at the Jockey Club in Buenos Aires. Devlin and I simply blew away the field, totaling 544 to win by 10 strokes. I shot 65-67-65 the first three rounds, including a drive out-of-bounds the third day, and had the International Trophy that goes to the individual winner in my grasp. Then I shot 73 the final round to lose by a stroke to Roberto De Vicenzo under crowd conditions that were so bad it was hilarious. Roberto is a national hero in Argentina, of course, and his fans did everything they could to help. There was no gallery control, and Bruce's ball and mine kept mysteriously ending up in the rough. Roberto's kept mysteriously ending up in advantageous positions. On one hole he nailed a shot that carried over the bleachers behind the green. By the time we got there, the ball was on the green 20 feet from the pin.

Roberto, one of the fine gentlemen in the game, was distressed about it, and I was privately steaming for a while after the round. But we had won the World Cup for Australia, I had made more of a name for myself and my second-place finish earned me an invitation to The Masters the next April. I had earned more than $40,000 so far that year, and, even with the disappointments, things were a lot more right with my world than they ever had been.

Devlin and I flew back to Miami—where Bruce was living at the time—in first class, the first time I'd ever sat in first class in my life. It was just one more reminder that playing well has its rewards. And on the long trip Bruce and I cemented the friendship that had begun that week. I think we had an instant respect for each other. I respected him for what he had done in golf, and he respected me for what I was trying to do. His life growing up hadn't been that easy, either. His dad was a plumber, and Bruce was in the plumbing business for a time. He jumped that hurdle, and he recognized that I was a kid who was trying to do the same.

Our friendship has been a consistent one ever since. He has just been great to me, and I've come to love and admire him very much. His house always has been open to Maureen and me. He has got me sponsor's exemptions in tournaments, introduced me to the right people, picked me up at the airport when I needed a ride, given me a car when I needed a car, given me a place to sleep when I needed a place to sleep. And eventually he made me the player I am today. I can say without reservation that I would not be where I am if it were not for Bruce Devlin.

Storm clouds were gathering on my horizon by this time, but it was a while before I saw them coming. There were to be two problems, one with Bucky Woy and one with David Graham, that were to make the next few years a lot more tribulation than triumph.

The problem with David Graham was that his golf game, good as it had been for the last year, wasn't as sound as he thought it was. Having played most of my career with the small ball, mostly on links-type courses under windy conditions, I—like a lot of overseas players—had developed the old British style of swing. I swung with my arms on too flat a plane and hit the ball with my hands. I had a very restricted backswing, not enough turn and not a very good leg action. I never moved my left foot on the backswing, never got my left knee behind the ball. The shorter your backswing, the better it was under windy conditions, because you had more control and didn't chance losing your balance. I basically would just beat on the ball with my hands. Consequently I had learned to play with a strong grip. That and the flat swing made me hit the ball low with a hook. That was ideal for most of the courses I played, under the conditions I played them. But it wasn't going to work in the United States, where the lusher, heavily bunkered courses demanded that you get the ball in the air. I'd see all these players in the U.S. with big turns and a lot of leg movement, and I soon learned why they were swinging that way.

I ignored my impending crisis for some time. I had been offered substantial expense money to play on the Caribbean Tour early in 1971, and I accepted. It was a move that drew some criticism back home, because I would miss most of the Australian summer circuit, but it was a chance not only to cash in on my new "fame" but also to get more experience playing under different conditions. I won the Caracas Open, the second stop on the four-event tour, scoring an eight-under-par 272 to beat a tough field that included Tommy Bolt, De Vicenzo, Wilf Homeniuk, Florentino Molina, Ramon Munoz, Dow Finsterwald and several other U.S. tour players.

I then flew back to the United States to be honored by the Metropolitan Golf Writers Association at its annual Gold Tee dinner in New York, another great thrill. Baked beans are not on the menu at functions like that.

In addition to my Masters invitation, I had received U.S. sponsors' exemptions into the Greater Greensboro Open, the Westchester Classic and the American Golf Classic. The rest of the year was to be spent mainly on airplanes, shuttling between the United States and the rest of the world. Incidentally, I missed the cut in the first two of those tournaments and tied for 42nd in the AGC.

Playing in The Masters at Augusta National was the biggest thing that had happened to me in the U.S. to that point. It also provided me with my biggest shock. I shot 297 and tied for 36th, which was disappointing enough. More important was the realization, after watching players like Jack Nicklaus, Arnold Palmer, Lee Trevino and Tom Weiskopf, that I wasn't half as good as I thought I was.

I remember coming back to our room at the old Richmond Hotel in Augusta and telling Maureen, "Either I am going to learn to play golf properly or I am going to quit. If I continue to play the game the way I am playing it, I might as well forget about it. It is going to be back to Australia, back on the international tour and hope to hell I can make a living. I don't like the thought of that. Either I am going to play golf full time in the U.S. or we will go back to Australia and I'll do something else."

I never really intended to quit, of course, and in truth I didn't really do much about my golf game for a couple of years, although I probably should have.

Just a month later I won the Japan Air Lines Open in Tokyo, beating Masashi (Jumbo) Ozaki in a six-hole playoff after we tied at

**Not a Swing for the U.S.**
My flat, handsy swing was better suited to the links-style courses in Britain and Australia than to the United States, where the lusher, more heavily bunkered courses require higher shots.

**The Burdens of Victory**
*The trophy for winning the 1971 Japan Air Lines Open was almost more than I could handle.*

11-under-par 277. That was to be my last victory of the year, although some good things were to happen. So was something bad, which was to keep me preoccupied for the next four years.

In June of 1971 I told Bucky Woy I wanted out of my contract, the contract I had never read. When I finally did examine it, I found that it called for Woy to receive, as my manager, 20 percent of my gross earnings. As my sponsor he was to get 50 percent of my net earnings. He was both my manager and my sponsor, and in the latter role he was giving me $200 a week in expense money to play golf around the world. I later got that raised to $300, but that

still didn't cut it on the international tour . . . or anywhere else. Out of the approximately $45,000 I made during my first year with him, I didn't have much left to put in the bank.

Shortly after I joined Woy, I was befriended by a gentleman named Bill Richards, who was chairman of the board of a company called Bellows Valvair and at one time a stockholder in Woy's company. He signed me to a $10,000 contract to represent Bellows and gave me a couple of credit cards. One was an international air-travel card, and without those cards I really would have had problems.

Woy and his company, Consulting Services, Inc., already had lost Trevino and Orville Moody. And I didn't feel he was doing a thing for me. I didn't think he was trying to promote my name overseas, on the international tour, where I had gained my reputation and could have been expected to cash in on my success.

Woy, of course, refused to let me out of my contract, which ran through 1974. So I stopped sending in money, breaching the agreement, and Woy promptly sued. The case eventually was heard in federal court in Cleveland. I wanted to go to trial, but my attorney advised against it and the judge advised me to try to settle out of court. Woy opened the discussions by asking for a $250,000 settlement. Well, I hadn't earned $250,000 since the day I was born and told him I couldn't possibly pay that.

The lawsuit dragged on for more than a year before it was finally settled, but there were some bright spots during that time. Although I wasn't playing particularly well, I did qualify for the U.S. tour in the fall of 1971 with a six-round score of 440, tied for 10th, at PGA National in Palm Beach Gardens, Fla.

Woy finally agreed to let me out of the contract for $110,000, payable over three years...at 6 percent interest, incidentally. I couldn't afford that either, but by that time I had become good friends with Mike Marinelli, a wealthy Hollywood, Fla., businessman, and David Aucamp, the president of a bank in Hollywood. They both advised me to agree to the settlement. "If you can't pay for it, they can't get blood out of a stone," they told me. "If you're playing well and can pay, go ahead and do it and get it over with."

It was good advice, of course, but the debt weighed on my mind, not to mention my bank balance, for the next three years. It wasn't until 1976 that I finally got the monkey off my back, and there's no doubt in my mind that this contributed to the relatively slow start of my U.S. career.

**D**evlin and I defended in the World Cup in October of 1971, also over the PGA National course. Nicklaus and Trevino won it, and the highlight of the week was being invited with Bruce to Jack's house for dinner one evening. That opened my eyes. Here was the greatest player in the world taking time to invite a young Australian kid to his home, and that impressed me. That night Nicklaus started talking to me about golf clubs. It was the beginning of a long-standing friendship and business relationship.

It wasn't long afterward that I formed another relationship and got the first home for Maureen and myself in the United States. Devlin and Bob Von Hagge had just finished building a golf course in Hollywood, Fla., for a private club and real estate development called Emerald Hills. Bruce—bless him—arranged for the club to sign me as its touring professional, a deal that carried with it a free condominium in the development. It was beautiful, three times nicer than anything we could have afforded previously.

The people at Emerald Hills turned out to be wonderful to Maureen and me, and the best part of it all was that I met Mike Marinelli. A member there, Mike has turned out to be one of my dearest friends, a man who would do anything for you and has done almost everything for me. He has advised me on many financial matters. He guaranteed the loan on my house. He is the godfather of both my children and was present at their births when I was not, hurting his already bad back in lifting Maureen into the car when she was ready to deliver. You get much help from friends in life, if you're lucky, and Mike and his wife, Marion, have given us more than anyone could ask.

These were friendships that were to help us get through the next few hard years.

# CHAPTER FOURTEEN

# THE REBUILDING

**The Climax**
*Winning the 1981 U.S. Open trophy has been the highlight of my career, but there were a lot of aches of all sorts that led up to it.*

The start to my career on the U.S. PGA Tour was inauspicious, to say the least. To say the most, it was lousy for somebody who was supposed to be "an international golf star." I had my moments, including a second-round 63 in the Citrus Open at Rio Pinar. But through almost the first six months of the 1972 season my best finish was 18th, and I missed the cut about as often as I made it. Through the U.S. Open in mid-June, I had not made enough money to crack the top 100 on the list.

I was not playing as well as I would have liked, of course, but my problem also was the same that anyone faces playing on this tour. In international tournaments, there were perhaps a dozen players I had to beat in any given tournament. In the U.S., at that time, there were 50 or 60 capable of winning. Today there are even more.

It wasn't long before I was getting desperate, and midway through the spring I asked Bruce Devlin for help. We were at the Colonial National Invitational in Forth Worth. I was out of contention and Bruce was at or near the lead, as I recall. He came out with me about 4 o'clock one afternoon to the 10th fairway, which they used as a practice range in those days after everybody had made the turn. "I am open to any suggestions," I told him.

In order, he told me that my clubs were too flat, which was why I stood too far away from the golf ball, which was why the plane of my swing was too flat and the arc was coming too much from the inside, which was why I hit the ball too low, sometimes hit it fat and always hit it to the left. He said my left hand was too strong on the club, which made the problem even worse. At the top of the backswing my wrists would bow, causing me to lay off the club or point it left of the target. Oh yes, he also told me my stance was too wide and my weight was in the wrong position.

After he had finished, I looked at him and said, "Well, now that you've told me I have no chance to play worth a damn, what do I do now?"

The first thing he told me to do was make my clubs more upright, which would force me to be more erect at address and eventually make me swing on a more upright plane. The flat lie of my clubs was simply accentuating all the other faults in my swing. I had always believed that upright clubs cause you to hook the ball, and that's true if they don't fit your address position and swing plane. My address and swing plane, as it turned out, left a lot to be desired.

So I bent my clubs one degree more upright, and I felt like I was standing right on top of the ball. I have since moved them an additional three degrees more upright. Moving your clubs from two degrees flat to two degrees upright is a big change, believe me. And the results weren't very encouraging at first. I went from using flat clubs and hitting the ball low with a big hook to more upright clubs...and hooking it even worse. But I persevered, working on the plane of my swing to get it more upright and working on the grip with my left hand to get it in a better relationship with the face of the club. Eventually it helped, but it took a lot longer than I'd had in mind. But then, I never have done anything the easy way. Come to think of it, I'm not sure anyone ever does in golf, at least anyone who accomplishes anything.

While my swing improvement was gradual—and changing the swing probably cost me money while I was doing it—there were some surprising results just a short way down the road. It might even have been equipment that accounted for them. I continued to struggle through mid-June, but at the U.S. Open at Pebble Beach, Arnold Palmer expressed a liking for the putter I was using and wondered if he could have it. I told him I'd trade the putter for a matched set of clubs. He thought that a bit stiff, but he opened the trunk of his car, where it looked like he was keeping 500 golf clubs, and came out with a set of matched irons. They were swingweighted at D-6, much heavier than the D-2 clubs I had been playing with, but I took them and used them the next week to finish sixth in

the Western Open, my best showing of the year by far. I played with those clubs for more than a year, until I signed with MacGregor, and I still have them, for sentimental value.

The next week, in the Cleveland Open at Tanglewood Country Club, I shot 68-73-68 in the first three rounds, added a 69 on the final day and found myself tied with, of all people, Bruce Devlin. On the first extra hole, Bruce missed a three-foot par putt to let me stay alive. On the second hole I made an eight-footer for par and Bruce missed from just short of that. Suddenly I had won my first American tour tournament and was $30,000 richer.

I had a twinge of regret. If there was anybody I would not have wanted to beat in a playoff, it would have been Bruce Devlin. There also were some whispers that Devlin deliberately had missed the short putt on the first hole to let me win. Both he and I

***A First in the U.S.***
*Maureen and I hold the check for my first United States victory, the 1972 Cleveland Open.*

## Happy Times...
## Off-Course
*The birth of Andrew, our first son, in late 1974 brightened a rather dismal period in my career for Maureen and me.*

know that's not true, because if he had it would have been the end of our friendship.

The victory was a nice birthday present for Maureen (I hadn't even had time to buy her a card), but deep down I couldn't fool myself. The tournament had been played under rainy, muddy conditions with preferred lies. The conditions helped both Bruce and me, who probably were more used to that sort of thing. The field was not very strong. And I putted all week like I had never putted before. That made up for a lot of ball-striking deficiencies.

I was a winner, yes, but I think the victory was more fate than good golf. I think the golf gods were saying to me, "We are going to give you a little taste of victory, and if you want to badly enough, you can have more. Yes, you have enough talent to do it, but you haven't got it all. We'll let you have just a little nibble to get your interest, but don't think you've arrived."

I really didn't play badly for the remainder of 1972. I tied for first in the Liggett & Myers Open before losing in a four-man playoff and finished 38th on the U.S. money list with $57,827. Most of that, of course, came from my lone win and runner-up finish. I added about $60,000 overseas, $32,500 of it when I lost to Gay Brewer in a playoff for the Taiheiyo Club Masters championship in Japan. I also lost to Peter Thomson in a playoff for the Australian Open title.

But I was by no means happy with the way I played over all. I was working on my "new" swing, which tended to let me down at crucial times. It's a problem that occurs any time you make a change, but it's hard to deal with when you're out there trying to make a living. And things were to get worse before they got better.

The next three years were the worst I've had on the U.S. tour, or anywhere else, relatively speaking. They weren't disastrous. I did make progress, but it wasn't the kind of progress I had anticipated. I failed to win a tournament anywhere in 1973 and 1974. On the U.S. tour, I made $43,062 in 1973, finished 71st on the money list and lost my exemption. I was trying a new putter about every other day and was experimenting with different clubs. My eyes were bothering me, and I tried wearing glasses— several different pair, of course, plus contact lenses. As it turned out, I was becoming a little near-sighted, and I've worn contact lenses on the course most of the time since. It's not a big deal, but thank God for the yardage books.

I also was penalized that year for slow play in the Byron Nelson Classic, mainly because I had so little confidence in my swing that I couldn't bring myself to pull the trigger. I even developed a nervous twitch in my face. I was a nut case.

Maureen gave premature birth to identical twin boys in September of 1973. One lived 24 hours, the other about 72 hours, and that was a mentally shattering experience for both of us. I have become very family-conscious, undoubtedly as a result of my own family situation, and losing those two boys was, momentarily at least, like the end of the world for me.

The Bucky Woy judgment continued to prey on my mind during this period. And there was always the work on my confounded swing, trying to make it better and better. Sometimes I wonder now how I ever got through all that, but I guess at the time there was never any question that I was going to.

I did make $61,625 in 1974 and finished 41st on the money list to regain my exemption, winning $30,000 in my last six tournaments to do

**Rewards of Victory**
Maureen and I pose with the Chunichi Crowns trophy in 1976 while sitting on an extra prize for winning, A Datsun 240Z. Unfortunately, the hood collapsed, which I guess proves it's a better car than chair.

**On the Way to a Win**
*This putt missed, but more of them went in on the way to victory in the 1976 American Golf Classic.*

it. Our son Andrew was born in November of that year, and things were starting to look up. It didn't look up a lot in the U.S., where my winnings dropped to $51,642 in 1975, but that was good for 44th and let me keep my exemption. Again I played well late, tying for 10th in the PGA Championship and tying for second in the B.C. Open in August, but I kept doing things like shooting 65-81 in the Western Open, among other clever performances. I did finally win a tournament somewhere, returning to Australia to capture the Wills Masters in October. It was my first victory in my home country since the Victorian Open in 1970.

It was typical of my frame of mind at the time that I almost blew that one. I overslept on the morning of the final 36 holes and got to the course just 25 minutes before my tee time. I had time only to gulp down a meat pie before I was off. Also, I was almost penalized two strokes—or disqualified—because my American caddie, Steve Hulka, had been on the course, just finishing getting the pin positions, when play had started. But all that got settled and I shot 69-72 to win, my stomach growling all the way.

The victory put me in a good frame of mind for the 1976 season, and I got the idea it might be a good year when I tied for fifth in the Bing Crosby, the third tournament of the year. It was, in more ways than one. In April I sent my check for $40,000 to Bucky Woy to wipe that slate clean. The next week I won the Chunichi Crowns tournament in Japan and with it a check for, ironically enough, $40,000. Back in the U.S., I had three more top-10 finishes before heading to New York for the Westchester Classic in mid-July. There it all came together. I opened with an eight-under-par 63

and added 68-70-71 for a four-stroke victory. The winner's check was $60,000, the largest purse of my life and more than I had won on the whole U.S. tour the previous year.

A month later I tied for fourth in the PGA Championship at Congressional, and two weeks after that the magic appeared again. At the Firestone North Course in Akron I shot 69-67-69-69—274 to win the American Golf Classic by four strokes and pocket another $40,000.

That qualified me for the World Series of Golf the following week on Firestone's monstrous South Course, and I shot one over par there to finish fourth and earn another $15,000.

In October, at the Piccadilly World Match Play tournament in England, I came from behind with some fantastic putting to beat Hale Irwin for the title, keeping him from his third consecutive championship and earning another $42,500 for the Graham bank account.

My prize total for the year was about $289,194, including $176,174 for eighth place on the U.S. money list. That ranked me second only to Jack Nicklaus' $316,086 on the worldwide money list. I had flown back to Sydney to be honored as New South Wales Sports Star of the Year. My debts were paid, I was getting more confidence in my swing and for the first time since I had come to the United States I felt I could play at a high level. I was ready for bigger and better things.

■ soon found out that nothing is automatic and that in golf, as in any other sport, I guess, what you did yesterday has nothing to do with your success today. With the Woy monkey off my

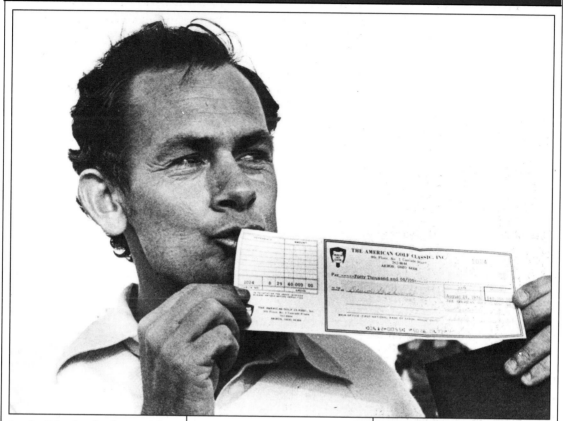

back, I had a letdown. I had become quite involved in club designing with Jack Nicklaus and the MacGregor Company and got interested in a few other business situations. I also had ended my connection with Emerald Hills and had purchased a new home at The Hamlet in Delray Beach, Fla., at the same time agreeing to represent the place on tour. All that had occupied quite a bit of my time. Frankly, I became a little complacent, strange as that may sound for someone who was always as driven as I was. I guess it was the first time in my career that I could afford to be complacent. It wasn't that I had a lot of money. It's just that my mental reaction was, "Hey, the heat is off."

I've always had to give golf 100 percent, preparing well, practicing well and employing good course management to feel totally positive and be effective. I've never been able to go out and play half-

heartedly and expect to do well, and I think I did some of that in 1977.

The U.S. year wasn't a total loss, even though I only entered 18 events. I earned $72,086 with only four top-10 finishes. Not long before, that would have been a wonderful sum for me, but it wasn't very good after 1976.

Two occurrences rescued the year in very satisfying fashion. Our second son, Michael, was born in October, and six weeks later I won the Australian Open after all the years of trying and several near-misses. It was the best field the championship had ever had, including Jack Nicklaus, U.S. Open winner Hubert Green, several other top American players and all of the home stars. At the Australian Golf Club, a difficult Sydney course redesigned by Nicklaus, I shot 284, four under par, and beat Don January, John Lister and Bruce Lietzke by three strokes.

***No. 2 in '76***
*My second U.S. victory of 1976, and this check for $40,000, came in the American Golf Classic at Firestone North.*

**Finally, My Home Open**
*You can imagine the joy behind this gesture as I sink the final putt to finally win the Australian Open in 1977.*

There wasn't much carry-over value in 1978. I finished second in the Citrus Open and tied for ninth in the Masters, but I had only three other top-10 finishes (all 10th-place ties) and won just $66,909 to finish 43rd on the money list. The only thing I won anywhere else was a little tournament called the Mexico Cup. I was trying to spend more time with my family and my outside interests were distracting me a bit. I was still experimenting with club design, which didn't help my golf game very much. But I also was continuing to work hard on my swing, trying to get it more upright, trying to get physically stronger. All that was soon to pay off.

Actually, it took a woeful performance in the 1979 Masters to wake me up. I shot 79 and withdrew—legally—during a rain delay. Then I got disgusted and decided I had to spend more time swinging golf clubs than making them. I began practicing more and concentrating better, and I started to develop a more positive attitude.

Beginning in early June, I tied for third in the Atlanta Classic, finished seventh in the U.S. Open at Inverness and tied for fifth in the Canadian Open in consecutive weeks. In late July, a week before the PGA Championship, I tied for sixth in the IVB-Philadelphia Classic, opening with a 65 and missing the playoff by just two strokes.

Oakland Hills, the "Monster" in Birmingham, Mich., had been softened by rain the week of the PGA, but to shoot 272, eight under par, still was a great thrill. To shoot 272 and just *tie* for the championship was not so great a thrill, considering the circumstances.

Capitalizing on my new-found confidence, I shot 69-68-70 in the first three rounds. But I still found myself trailing Rex Caldwell by four shots and Ben Crenshaw by two at the start of Sunday's final round, and I was tied with a couple of rather dangerous fellows named Jerry Pate and Tom Watson.

For 17 holes, then, I proceeded to play the purest round of golf I had ever played. I made four birdies and no bogeys to turn in 31. At that point, Crenshaw was the leader and Caldwell and I were tied, a stroke back.

I birdied the 10th with a 30-foot putt and the 11th with an eight-footer. On the 15th, a 388-yard dogleg, I thought I had won the championship when I drove with a 1-iron and hit a 4-iron eight inches from the hole to put me 10 under and two strokes ahead of Crenshaw.

I still had that two-stroke lead when I fought through the crowd to the 18th tee. I was facing a 459-yard par 4, the hardest hole on the course, but I thought I had everything under control. Then, almost at the start of my backswing, the magnitude of the whole thing hit me. "David," I thought to myself, "you are about to win a major championship." And my drive sailed about a million miles to the right.

Even so, my second shot was not that difficult. I had a near-perfect lie in the rough and a relatively clear shot to the green. But, because I was so far off the beaten track, I had no idea how far away I was. I momentarily lost my composure, and, instead of waiting for the marshals to clear away the crowd so I could determine my actual yardage, I decided that it had to be either a 6- or 7-iron. As it turns out, both Watson and Pate had been in almost the same spot earlier in the week and each had hit a 7-iron. But I didn't know that. I selected a 6-iron that I must have hit 200 yards, over the green and into the rough beyond, above

**An Honor from Home**
*Here I'm accepting the award in Sydney, Australia, as the 1976 New South Wales Sports Star of the Year.*

the flag. When I saw the ball in the air, I thought it was going to land in the clubhouse.

I left my first chip shot short, still in the rough, then played the next one perfectly, leaving myself a five-foot uphill putt with a slight right-to-left break. Then I hit it too hard and watched the ball spin off the edge of the cup. The 20-incher I had left wasn't so easy, either, but I got it down. Walking off the green, I felt about six inches high. In my mind, at that moment, I had blown my major.

Still shaken when Crenshaw and I walked to the first tee, I hit my drive into the left rough and had no chance to get to the green. I knocked the ball out short, then hit a good pitch that landed on a down-

slope and ran 25 feet past the hole. After Ben had putted up for a sure par, I thought, "David, you are in a playoff and it's not over. You haven't lost the golf tournament yet." My putt was a tricky down-hiller, but it was the same putt I had seen Jerry Pate have earlier, and I had watched as he putted it. It broke about two inches to the left. Call it brilliant concentration or a stroke of luck, but I blocked out any thought of misreading the putt and just tried to hit it two inches outside the hole. And it went in for a half. Suddenly I thought, "Maybe it is meant to be." On the par-5 second, Crenshaw hit his second shot to within 15 feet of the hole and I hit mine just over the green. I chipped to 10 feet away, he missed and I made. Then I began to be sure destiny was on my side.

The third hole is a 202-yard par 3, and Crenshaw blocked his tee shot into the right bunker. I nailed a 4-iron to within eight feet. Crenshaw failed to get up and down, which made my birdie putt academic. But I made it anyway.

The one thing that stands out in my mind about that moment is the grace and class with which Ben Crenshaw handled himself. Victory would have been just as meaningful to him as it was to me. He didn't say anything special...just the normal congratulations. But his demeanor said more than words. In the face of what to him was a crushing defeat, he reacted like a true gentleman and champion. It's why he's one of the most popular players on tour and why our friendship has flourished over the years.

After the huzzahs and the presentations, after the interviews and the champagne in the press tent, I began to think about what it all meant. I thought back to something

**A Winning Huddle**

*Embraced by my caddie, I'm congratulated by Ben Crenshaw, always a gentleman, at the end of our three-hole playoff in the PGA Championship.*

Jack Nicklaus had told me some years before, that I was a very good player and might win a major, but that my long-range future was in designing golf clubs. I guess Jack was right on both counts, although perhaps not in the way he meant.

As much as I cherish the U.S. Open title I won two years later, the PGA Championship has had the biggest impact on my life. As an Australian living in the United States, even as a permanent resident, I was always aware of my exempt status on tour and the need to maintain it. I'd been through Monday qualifying, and it didn't appeal to me. Nor did I find the thought of returning to Australia and again playing the international tour full time particularly attractive. Maureen and I enjoyed living in the United States, my sons were U.S. citizens and I was involved in several ventures in this country.

With the PGA title, I suddenly had stability, a 10-year exemption from qualifying that meant I could stay here and play golf for the next decade. We could start making some long-term plans, start putting down some roots and foster some friendships that would last.

The victory itself had a significant impact on my career. It made me realize that I *can* play this game, that maybe I was a little better than I had thought I was, that all my dedication in the early years was worth it. You have to go back to your priorities. I had known all along that I wasn't going to win a whole lot of major championships, as Jack Nicklaus had. But it was in the back of my mind that if I played well at the right time, I could win one or two. Winning the PGA proved that I was of major caliber.

I almost won the Westchester Classic two weeks later, holding the lead going into the final round

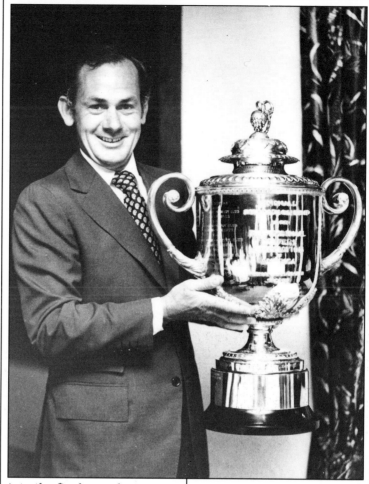

ing by a shot and tying for second. That was worth $35,000 to go with the $60,000 I had won at the PGA, and the mortgage payments were safe for another little while. I finished the U.S. season with $177,683, my best-ever total and good for 16th on the money list.

Late in the year I won the West Lakes Classic in Adelaide, Australia, and the Air New Zealand-Shell Open. In January, I was named the Australian Broadcasting Commission's Sportsman of the Year for 1979.

On my trip back to Australia, I looked up George Naismith and gave him the gold money clip presented to each PGA Champion. I had, it seemed, finally arrived, but I hadn't forgotten where it all started.

**The First Major**
*In more dignified attire, I display the PGA Championship trophy won in 1979.*

# THE REWARDS

**There's Hope . . .**
*Another reward for moving toward the top in golf is the opportunity to mingle and play with real stars and great human beings, in this case Bob Hope.*

The rewards for success come in many forms. First and foremost, you instantly begin to play better. At least I did. We all know that confidence breeds better play, whether it's at your home club or on the professional circuit, and my confidence level had never been higher. In addition, winning the PGA Championship immediately let me become more relaxed. I became more financially secure, and I no longer had the worry in the back of my mind that I had to qualify for next year's tour. If I'm to be honest, I think that before I won the PGA I was playing, at least subconsciously, to make sure I got into the top 60 money winners. Afterward, I could play to win golf tournaments.

Something that I wanted most—undoubtedly as a result of my earlier "black sheep" reputation—was to have friends, to be liked and to be respected. Just winning a golf tournament doesn't get you all those things, but the stability that the PGA Championship brought to my life gave me a chance to cultivate them. Earning close friendships, as I have, greatly improves your attitude toward life, and that carries over to the golf course.

So the victories seemed to come more easily, and even a little more plentifully, after 1979. In 1980 I won the Memorial Tournament at Jack Nicklaus' Muirfield Village course, defeating Tom Watson with a 30-foot birdie putt on the final hole. It was a win that was especially satisfying because of the course it was played on and because of whose tournament it was. That was my only U.S. victory during a year in which I won $137,819 in this country, but I also won the Heublin Classic in Brazil, the Mexican Open and the Rolex World Mixed Team Championship with Jan Stephenson.

In 1981 I won the Phoenix Open early in the year and, of course, the U.S. Open at Merion, winding up 13th on the U.S. money list with $188,286, my best total to that time. Later I won the Lancome Trophy in Paris.

I repeated in the Lancome in 1982, my only victory in what was something of an off year, for reasons I'll explain in a moment. But in 1983, although I won only at Houston, I made $244,924 and finished 11th on the tour money list. It was my first time over $200,000 domestically and it moved me past Bruce Crampton and become the leading Australian career money-winner in the U.S.

Another of the rewards is the financial gain, of course, for a professional golfer. I finally was in a position to command good money for exhibitions, outings and overseas tournament appearances. And I was lucky enough to have competent people around me who could help me take advantage of opportunities and advise me wisely on financial matters. I had signed with Mark McCormack's International Management Group in 1972, and those people are able to help you make all the extra money you want. I also moved to Dallas in mid-1980 and have met men like Mac Rankin and Bill Saxon, who not only have been good friends but have given me astute counsel on business dealings.

I've worked very hard at making money since I won the PGA, and I'm not ashamed to say that. This is the way I provide for my future and my family's future. Any professional who doesn't tell you the same thing is not being honest. We're all in this game because we love it, but it also is our living.

Sometimes I've worked too hard, perhaps to the detriment of my golf game. I tried to capitalize on my U.S. Open victory in 1981 by scheduling a 13-week tour that took me nearly around the world. That wasn't wise. In the first place, I was still in a bit of a letdown after winning the Open, and I was having trouble coping with the pressure of being the man who shot perhaps "the most perfect round of golf ever played on the last day to win a U.S. Open." I started thinking people were expecting me to play like that every time, and I couldn't handle that. Nobody could. Also, I got so tired during my tour that I could hardly take the club back. As a result, I didn't play very well. It also took me about half of the next season to recover, and I'll never do

anything like that again. Making money is one thing, but ruining your golf game doesn't fit into the formula.

I drew a lot of criticism, especially in Australia, for my poor performance that year. I was paid an astronomical amount of money to play in two tournaments there, and I missed the cut both times. I went from hero, a guy they were calling perhaps the best Australian player ever, to bum in a hurry. It was insinuated in the newspapers that I took all that money and deliberately played badly. The Australian professionals were resentful of the money I was being paid to play in their tournaments. I suppose if I had been in their shoes, I would have felt the same. But I haven't been the only top player from the United States getting good appearance money to play in Australia, and I haven't deliberately hit a bad shot in my life.

The criticism upset me so much that I didn't return to Australia the following year—that was the reason, not a dispute over appearance money, as was reported in the papers there. I have returned

**. . . And There's Ford**
*Telling ex-President Gerald Ford how the putt breaks is undoubtedly the most important piece of advice I'd be allowed to give somebody at his level.*

### ...And By Air

*Whatever is the best way to get to the first tee on time, the professional golfer will find it.*

since, and I will again, but it saddened me that I would be judged like that in my native country, one that also has honored me.

I've been severely criticized at times for not supporting golf in Australia as well as they think I should have. Perhaps the critics are right, but they forget—or don't realize—that my first obligation as a golfer is to the United States and the American tour. I have won, or been a part of winning, 29 golf tournaments around the world, but the United States has given me almost everything I have today. I have won almost a million and a half dollars on the PGA Tour. More important than that, my kids were born and are being raised here, my wife loves it here, all of our close personal friends live here. I am a member of Preston Trail, one of the most prestigious clubs in the world, and I like to think it's not just

because I can afford it but because I'm accepted as a person. A golf star doesn't impress anybody at Preston Trail, most of whose members could buy and sell me with their pocket change.

One of the problems with my image in Australia, I suspect, is that I've refused to be a hypocrite by telling them, "Look, I miss Australia and I'm playing in America under sufference, but I'm making a lot of money. Be patient until I've made enough, and then I'm going to come home again." I won't say that because it's not true. I'm in America to stay.

That's not to say anything against my native country. In 1982, sitting alongside George Naismith, who was to die later that year, I was made an honorary member of Riversdale. That honors me deeply. It's not that I love Australia less. It's that I love America more.